Environment and citizenship

Integrating justice, responsibility and civic engagement

Environment and citizenship

Integrating justice, responsibility and civic engagement

Mark J. Smith and Piya Pangsapa

Z

Zed Books

LONDON | NEW YORK

Environment and citizenship: integrating justice, responsibility and civic engagement was first published in 2008 by Zed Books Ltd, 7 Cynthia Street, London N1 9JF, UK and Room 400, 175 Fifth Avenue, New York, NY 10010, USA

www.zedbooks.co.uk

Set in OurType Arnhem by Ewan Smith, London
Cover designed by Andrew Corbett
Printed and bound in Great Britain by CPI Antony Rowe, Chippenham, Wiltshire

Distributed in the USA exclusively by Palgrave Macmillan, 175 Fifth Avenue, New York, NY 10010, USA

A catalogue record for this book is available from the British Library
Library of Congress Cataloging in Publication Data available

ISBN 978-1-84277-902-6 hb
ISBN 978-1-84277-903-3 pb

For Harry, George, Tate and Skye, who
caused none of these problems but will
end up bearing all the responsibilities

Contents

Figures, tables and boxes

Acknowledgements

A book covering the range of environmental issues considered here in so many different places in the world incurs many intellectual debts from colleagues and friends. The fieldwork underpinning this work was funded by the Baldy Center for Law and Social Policy, the Gender Institute (University at Buffalo, SUNY) and the Open University. The greatest thanks must be directed to the many activists, NGO members and politicians who have helped us build a picture of the complex relations and processes involved in contemporary environmental problems, civic engagement, and linking social and environmental justice more explicitly, in particular, Ing K and Manit Sriwanichpoom, Jaime Netto and Janet Howitt. Most of all it is the activists concerned with the environment, labour standards and human rights that have inspired our work.

We also thank the *Environments* journal for the use of materials for Chapter Three of the book and the University at Buffalo Special Archives for advice and support in revisiting the Love Canal case as well as UB Faculty members Ted Steegman and Mike Farrell. At the Open University we would also like to thank Dave Humphreys (for challenging the logjam and prompting the idea of doing this book), Engin Isin (for his clarity on citizenship theory), Andy Dobson (for his work on ecological citizenship at the OU and beyond) and Grahame Thompson (for his illuminating thoughts on corporate citizenship). In addition, we learned a great deal from the anonymous reviewers of the book and we drew upon the ideas of William Outhwaite, Bob Jessop, Steve Yearley, Jim Petras, James Fahn, Pasuk Phongpaichit, Chris Baker and Michael Burawoy for inspiration in ways that have helped frame this project.

Special thanks are due to the commissioning editors at Zed Books, Susannah Trefgarne, Ellen McKinlay and Tamsine O'Riordan, who saw the potential for a book on this topic and helped guide us to the completion of this project, as well as the excellent and understanding professional staff at Zed, in particular, Ewan Smith, Ian Paten and Daniele Och.

Finally, we would like to thank our families for their love and support throughout this project. We hope that in some small measure this contribution helps to pave the way for the citizens of this one planet to address more effectively environmental and social injustice and promote greater environmental responsibility in the future. This book is dedicated to Harry, George, Tate and Skye, who like all future generations will face the task of finding solutions for the problematic environmental legacies of the twentieth century.

Box 3.1 is an edited version of an article published in *Society Matters*, the annual publication of the Faculty of Social Sciences, the Open University, and is used with kind permission. Box 4.2 is an edited version of a webpage of the Food and Agriculture Organization of the United Nations and is also used with kind permission.

Introduction: environment, obligation and citizenship

The purpose of this book is to offer a series of new challenges on how we think through our relationship with the environment. At this time in both human and environmental history we have reached a tipping point in terms of anthropogenic impacts on environmental stability from the broad-based effects of climate change to the accumulated local toxic effects of industrial waste that have been piled up in the neighbourhoods of communities that have been least active in challenging the activities and decisions of politicians and companies for generations. For four decades, we have witnessed the growing awareness of environmental injustices, initially singly and isolated but gradually combining with other environmental problems so that they now impact on most human communities with varying degrees of harm, depending on where you live and who you are. Initially, this led to a turnaround in civic engagement in the most affected communities, by environmental justice movements in North America, community livelihood movements in Latin America, Asia and Africa, and citizens' initiatives and environmental safety groups in Europe. Recently, however, this increased awareness and willingness to mobilize of localized movements has generated a broader groundswell that acknowledges the trans-boundary impacts of many issues, from acid rain to marine conservation and the global impacts of climate change.

Right from the start we want to emphasize the importance of recognizing that environmental issues cannot be separated from questions of social justice – that there is no contradiction between addressing environmental issues and social inequalities. These are necessarily complementary issues, not contradictory ones. Even the preservation of wilderness areas and the conservation of transformed and managed landscapes have social implications both in terms of the access to environmental goods of people traditionally excluded from these benefits and the social justice concerns that directly pertain to rural folk and traditional livelihoods that can often be relegated to insignificance by environmental campaigns that some NGOs have initiated without consultation or forethought. Much environmental thought and ethics, as well as specific academic fields such as green political theory, has fixated on the environment as a ring-fenced and isolated issue. Even discussions of sustainable development tend to focus on its oxymoronic status rather than establishing the connections between environmental and social justice. This is often combined with a corresponding assertion that most Western citizens need to engage in considerable *material* sacrifices in order to achieve a lighter ecological footprint. On the opposing side, environmental sceptics challenge environmentalism by focusing exclusively on the ways in which eco-improvement expenditures could be redeployed in order to promote poverty alleviation, health provision and education services. The battle lines drawn here tend to emphasize the differences between a materialistic conception of development and economic growth as a means to reduce human suffering and a post-materialist conception of a steady-state economy and, in some cases, a transformation to low-impact lifestyles with an improved quality of life.

The first problem with such a stark and in part ideologically driven contrast is simply that both sides of the equation have merit. We should be concerned with social injustices on a global as well as national scale and with the asymmetrical power relations between globalizers and globalized that feed both environmental degradation and increased differences between rich and poor. We should also recognize that the remaining pristine wilderness and biodiversity hubs are under threat, as well as acknowledging the need to push for lower human impact. While the environmental message has often been subsumed into established discourses of citizen rights and national energy security, increasingly it has recalibrated these discourses by making civil rights discourse and energy security a means of avoiding environmental harms and securing sustainable outcomes. Witness the events in the climate-change slow-coach, the USA, during 2007/08. The focus on alternative energy by the Bush administration in order to aid national security in a world where many oil-producing societies are seen as hostile to US interests has been rearticulated across the political spectrum in the primaries for the 2008 presidential election. Leaving aside a few sceptics at the Conservative Political Action Conference (CPAC), who regard Arnold Schwarzenegger as an 'eco-extremist', security concerns have now been subsumed by a recognition that sustainable energy should also be a source of green-collar employment, technological innovation, lower manufacturing costs and an improved quality of life for all citizens.

The second problem is that this academically and politically driven distinction between environmental and social issues ignores a fundamental change in the environmental debate. In the 1980s and 1990s the concern for environmental justice was often couched in terms of how academic and legal experts could act as the voice of groups that had no other means of addressing their grievances – with environmental activists, NGOs and researchers placing themselves in the shoes of the most affected groups and speaking on behalf of the powerless. Much the same was seen in the work of development NGOs' charity campaigns on famine, poverty and health, and the official announcements on international aid programmes made by both Western and rapidly developing states such as China – acts based purely on compassion and altruism (perhaps sometimes a little guilt as well) rather than justice. This does not mean that humanitarian efforts are misguided; in fact the opposite is the case, for the *ties that bond*, which recognize the existence of a commonwealth of humanity, are just as important in resolving global environmental problems as the *ties that bind* based on justice. The fundamental change addressed in this book is the growing importance of citizenship and all its associated civic engagement practices – we note in particular that the distinction between public and private spheres hinders a better understanding of how to make policy and action more effective. Moreover, this points to a fundamental analytical shift marked by what has been described as the redefinition of 'the political' (Mouffe 2000) or the 'sociality of politics' (Smith 2000a, 2000b) – the way we comprehend the state, politics, national governments and even intergovernmental institutions is fundamentally shaped by the ways we understand civil society rather than being institutionally distinct.

The final problem is the role of ethics in current debates on these questions and issues. In the past we have been locked into an ethical stand-off between two dominant ethical traditions – utilitarianism, with its long-standing manifestations in both conservationist and state policy concerns with human welfare, and Kantian contractarian assumptions that underpin liberal politics through the principle that what applies to one must apply to all (including variations that include non-human animals as subjects of life in what counts as 'all'). Here, we also draw on an older tradition that has resurfaced in the late twentieth century, virtue ethics. Whereas the dominant traditions pose universal ethical solutions in terms of outcomes and rules respectively, virtue ethics focuses on how individual citizens engage in self-improving activities that benefit the community. In this way, it provides an alternative framework for linking the decisions of all actors, including citizens, NGOs and companies, to broader objectives established through political institutions.

Gone are the days when environmental activists were treated as marginal, irrelevant and slightly deranged. Gone are the days when a corporate CEO could announce at a general meeting of shareholders that a woman in the audience offering an environmental challenge to the company's waste policy should go home and look after her children.

3

Gone are the days when the concerns of marginalized groups on grounds of race, gender and class were also marginalized in debate on environmental harm in Western societies. After all, the activist impulses of these movements have routinely been based on the combined experiences of ethnic minorities, lower socio-economic status groups and gender. Environmental concern is now a rubric through which other policies are increasingly viewed, and with that the ground rules inevitably change. So, on the one hand, it has evolved from an oppositional movement to one embracing active involvement in policy-making. On the other hand, effective policy depends on changes at all levels of society, including personal behaviour and community organization, in ways that cannot be directed or achieved purely by financial (dis-)incentives. The debate on environment and citizenship brings these concerns together by addressing the ways in which civic engagement practices inform policy-making and how citizens understand the reasons for, and ethical assumptions underpinning, being environmentally responsible.

In developing these points, Chapter 1 explores the important questions of why, how, where and when the debate on environment and citizenship matters. This is followed by case studies on the Love Canal incident and the combined environmental and social effects of migration on the Thai–Burmese border. The first, in a developed society, is a classic worst-case incident in the history of environmental movements. Here we focus on the essential facts of the case, but as part of updating what has happened since (the issue is still ongoing) we address the central questions on environment and citizenship. The second focuses briefly on cross-border migrant labour and environmental issues in South-East Asia to consider how the role of NGOs is changing from one of advocacy to being agents of civil engagement as well as integrating environmental and social concerns.

Chapter 2 provides a summary of some recent relevant debates in citizenship studies and considers how the proliferating accounts of citizenship indicate its essentially contested character. In particular, it charts the shift from citizenship as bound to national political communities, how relations between entitlements and obligations should not always be seen as reciprocal, and the important contributions on cultural difference (especially the debate on group rights) and gender identity. It concludes with a heuristic model of circuits of justice and how these can inform the discussion of citizenship when considering environmental ethics. This chapter adds a new concept of citizenization to highlight how conceptions of citizenship are always provisional and in process.

Chapter 3 focuses on the recent discussions of environmental and ecological citizenship, explains their differences and considers their strengths and weaknesses. As advocates of ecological citizenship we use this part of the book to conceptually clarify the meaning of rights, entitlements, duties and obligations, as well as to explore the benefits of using virtue ethics to prepare the way for new research in the field. We also develop the argument for a strategic focus in research that moves from concrete conditions to academic theory rather than the other way round. In this way, this chapter addresses how new research needs to address how theory and practice can be integrated more effectively while also linking acts in everyday life to ethics and policy. Both of these chapters start from the premise that the personal is political and challenge how 'the political' has been understood.

In the remainder of the book we concentrate on practical politics. By building and elaborating on the concrete case studies in earlier chapters, we address the political institutions that operate on local, regional, national and intergovernmental levels as well as addressing how personal actions feed into environmental movements and, in turn, affect policy-making. Chapter 4 addresses the intergovernmental context of environmental policy, action and ethics and the considerable obstacles to developing effective global agreements on issues as diverse as deforestation and climate change. In addition, it considers the governance experiment developed by the EU in linking social and environmental justice, the role of social movements and green parties and how environmental movements mobilize resources, before considering what aspects of this institutional framework have applicability in Asia.

Chapter 5 explores the potential and perils of corporate environmental responsibility, the increased role of self-regulation, and how codes of responsible conduct can be made more effective. The key issues covered are ecological modernization, ecopreneurialism, intangible assets and, crucially, the emergence of corporate citizenship. Chapter 6 focuses on the different ways in which borders can affect environmental responsibility, transnational activism and civic engagement through case studies from the Great Lakes region in North America, southern Europe and South-East Asia. Chapter 7 builds on these case studies by exploring environmental mobilizations in the South-East Asian mainland, taking account of development policy, cultural and religious beliefs, the rural–urban divide and social class differences to better understand conflicts over water and land use as well as energy projects and pollution. This chapter concludes with a discussion of participatory research and how it has informed civic engagement in this context.

The concluding chapter explores the issues raised throughout the

5

book, in particular how to integrate ethics, policy and action in the context of the new vocabulary of ecological citizenship, drawing upon aspects of virtue ethics. It also draws attention to the increased importance of urban sustainability. Central to the case developed here and throughout the book is the growing importance of qualitative research methods that enable us to gain a better understanding of how the relations between entitlements and obligations (as well as rights and duties) are context dependent. The story developed in this book is that an awareness of social and environmental injustices is not enough in itself. Not only do we need to identify how they exist side by side, in some cases making the effects of each worse, we also need to recognize that the promotion of environmental responsibility depends on broad-focus civic engagement strategies that translate the affected constituencies into stakeholders in the decisions that affect their lives.

PART ONE

Theory informed by practice

1 | From environmental justice to environmental citizenship

Citizens, exclusion and the politics of obligation

Contemporary political rhetoric in Western societies often refers to rights and responsibilities in terms of issues as diverse as crime, education, healthcare and the environment. For the most part, it attempts to establish contractual relations between state and citizens but also increasingly between citizens, supposedly to promote respect for others: respect of migrants for the host culture, of students for teachers, of the young for the old, and, as an act of remorse and rehabilitation, of former criminals for their victims, and so on. Key to this development is a greater awareness of the importance of obligations within the terms of citizenship, an understanding that the enjoyment of rights carries corresponding duties to act in a manner that contributes to one's community or at least to restrain behaviour that could inflict harm on others, including distant strangers. For over two centuries, citizenship has been fixated upon rights and entitlements, glossing over duties and obligations. While being a citizen has always involved working on the boundary between state and civil society, the distinction between public and private spheres has been an unquestionable assumption, thus neglecting the power relations that operate through each. With the limited capacities of states to make a difference, and with most problems, especially environmental problems, demanding clear transnational responses, personal decisions need to be linked to environmental responsibility in ways that are more effective than intergovernmental policies and treaties. This is not a justification for states to privatize environmental responsibility – shifting the burden on to citizens and away from political authorities. The emergent new forms of citizenship, from sexual citizenship through to ecological citizenship, over the last two decades are an explicit attempt to address these issues, and the objective of this book is to highlight how debates on environment and citizenship can not only create spaces for partnerships between institutions and citizens but also point to the more dynamic and varied conceptions of citizenship that are yet to come into being. Ecological citizenship is part of a new generation of kinds of citizenship that take the politics of obligation seriously.

The 'why' question

Why environment and citizenship, and why now? Environmental problems are certainly viewed as key issues in contemporary politics. Even environmental sceptics acknowledge their importance, if only to renounce obligations of the human species towards ecological systems, habitats, non-human animal species and strangers both in global and intergenerational terms. Citizenship, however, has often been tied to membership of a given political community, often conceived in very narrow terms of national territory and the entitlements and obligations that follow from holding a particular passport and identity card. Since the 1990s, citizenship has been fundamentally redefined as a site of contestation between competing projects on what we are entitled to, what obligations we owe and to whom and the relationship between them, especially when these have legal force in terms of rights and duties. Citizenship is now articulated with culture, technology, identity (particularly gender), science, transnationalization and cosmopolitanism, but here we remain focused on the environment.

Citizenship has a more complex history, of course, and we are obliged to remember the debates over civil, political and social citizenship – debates that assumed the entitlements and obligations (as well as the associated rights and duties) as reciprocal. Civil citizenship is a concrete expression of the idea of a bargain whereby some of the liberties of owners are sacrificed in exchange for legal protections for private property. Political citizenship involves the entitlements to vote, association and free speech combined with reciprocal obligations to comply with the legislation produced by representative democratic institutions. Social citizenship provides for a wider range of entitlements, such as social welfare provision, healthcare and educational opportunity, combined with obligations to pay taxes within the context of a progressive taxation scheme alongside mandatory national insurance in order to fund pensions as well as sickness and unemployment benefits. In each of these cases, the assumption was that rights and duties were intimately connected. Emergent conceptions of citizenship have, however, challenged certain assumptions about what citizenship means. In all of the above two characteristics are present: 1. a clear distinction between state and civil society (and their associated conceptions of public and private spheres); 2. the fact that citizens have reciprocal entitlements and obligations (with a special emphasis on rights and entitlements that often leave duties and obligations as residual categories). Discussions of environmental and ecological citizenship challenge both these assumptions. For environmentalists, change is required in both the public and private spheres based on an integrated strategy. In some ways, this is attributable to the feminist influence on green politics, demonstrating that the personal is political. In addition, while environmental movements have made significant headway using the discourse of rights (including the propositions that animals, trees and nature have rights), there has been a shift towards recognizing the obligations to future generations (especially since the Brundtland Report of 1987), habitats (conservation and preservation movements), the biotic community (Leopold 1949) and even certain mystical conceptions of the planet as a self-regulating organism (Lovelock 2000). The politics of obligation also raised the possibility of human obligations towards natural things without assuming the relationship was reciprocal, with Smith (1998a, 2005b) and Dobson (2003a), among others, highlighting how the ties that bind can be diverse and complicated, even when just considering the asymmetrical power relations of living generations.

The reinvention of 'citizenship' in so many forms over such a brief time (explored in more detail in Chapter 2) has opened up the concept to many interventions that seek to develop ways of challenging its association with membership of national political communities. Following the 'principle of proliferation', an array of different kinds of *sites* of citizenship have come into being, including 'citizen science' (Irwin 1995) and cultural citizenship (Kymlicka and Norman 2000; Stevenson 2001, 2003a, 2003b; Couldry 2006), technological citizenship (Couldry 2006) and ecological citizenship (Dobson 2003a; Smith 1998a, 2005b), which, according to Engin Isin (forthcoming; see also Isin and Nielsen 2008), have different *scales* (street, locality, city, nation-state, transnational arenas and the globe) and involve a wide range of *acts* beyond voting and political party membership (such as volunteering, participating in community initiatives, exchanging knowledge, blogging, protesting in innovative ways by using cultural performance as a vehicle for dissent, activist networking and organizing). The range and diversity of forms of citizenship and the kinds of civic engagement strategies that span both public and private spheres demand a different methodological approach. By drawing on both quantitative and qualitative evidence, we are better able to see the intersubjective character of citizen construction, recognizing that we need to understand as well as explain environmental ethics, policy and activism.

Challenging environmental common sense through science: the 'how' question

Understanding and explaining environmental problems have often been characterized as the task of the detached scientist generating knowledge that can be verified by other scientists through replication or identifying similar processes in other contexts. Theories and hypotheses that generate accurate predictions are regarded as having explanatory value. Sometimes this is relatively uncontested, as with the causal relationship between chloroflourocarbons (CFCs) and ozone depletion, but few environmental issues have generated a clear consensus on cause and effect. Unlike in the case of the localized effects of traditional factory pollution, as Ulrich Beck (1992, 1995) argued, causal attribution of the effects of such pollution as nuclear waste has become more difficult. One aspect of the problem can be seen with recent disputes over the anthropogenic causes of global warming and climate change – the range of variables and their interaction is so complex that scientific accounts can identify only patterns, tendencies and ranges of change (from the best to the worst scenario). There are also difficulties in measurement, for global warming has to be distinguished from urban warming while changes in hurricane intensity and glacial ice cover have been subject to variation. Nevertheless, through the auspices of the Intergovernmental Panel on Climate Change, a general scientific consensus has arisen on the role of greenhouse gases (carbon dioxide, methane, nitrous oxide, CFCs and HCFCs). The rhetorical character of the debate on climate change on both sides of the environmentalist/sceptic spectrum often involves references to science as the authoritative basis of each standpoint, while at the same time dismissing the opposing view as politically motivated or ideological expressions of interests. For the proponents of anthropogenically induced climate change, the sceptics are conservative defenders of national and transnational business interests; for the critics of global warming theories, the scientific consensus suppresses scientific dissent in the interests of maintaining a research funding bonanza. It should be added that environmental scepticism and neoliberal critiques of global warming theories are often informed by a view of environmentalism as a distraction from developing strategies to tackle poverty and social injustice or as a stalking horse for state regulation that impedes free market solutions. The debate has been fought out over the identification of relevant empirical regularities, for example between carbon dioxide levels and average temperature change or between sunspot activity and atmospheric change. This debate has many of the same characteristics as the debate between the Club of Rome on the 'limits to growth' in the 1970s and the advocates of technofix solutions to the problem of finite resources (that human ingenuity would find new ways of identifying carbon-based resources or new alternatives). The main difference, however, is that the focus has shifted from the depletion of 'natural resources' to the capacity of the environment to absorb the side effects of human activity (even resource depletion, such as deforestation, is often primarily assessed in terms of a loss of an important carbon sink).

Nevertheless, this still focuses on the role of natural science, including climatology, oceanography, botany and conservation science, which (unlike the experimental method) study open rather than closed systems (Smith 1998b). Sciences such as meteorology and seismology always faced problems in developing predictive accuracy in much the same way as social science. As the debate on climate change illustrates, a practically adequate understanding of contemporary environmental problems also has to take account of the social dimension. The way we see environmental problems, like all social representations, is also subject to the mechanisms of social construction. Pollution has been characterized as 'matter out of place' (Smith 1998a), as a natural symbol, and all environmental issues are articulated through media representations. It is arguable that the speed of the formation of the international regime on CFCs in the Montreal Protocol (1987, in force from 1989) was culturally facilitated by media coverage of the dangers of skin cancer and the use of dramatic representations such as the imaging of the ozone hole over Antarctica. The relationship between the recorded rise in average temperature and climate change is much harder to represent in such a direct way, for the visual representations of storm activity, flooding, oceanic dead zones and extreme drought are often viewed as more context dependent. Anecdotal accounts of severe weather conditions or sudden unseasonal cold spells are easily capitalized on in the context of political debates. During the cross-examination of Al Gore by the Senate Environment and Public Works Committee (2007), Republican senator James Inhofe, reflecting on unusual snowfalls in the USA, commented, 'where is global warming when we need it'.

Rather than treating science as an authoritative basis for action or an unquestionable 'resource', it needs to be supplemented with authentic knowledge that accurately represents the lives of those affected by environmental problems, and scientific knowledge should be seen as much as a 'topic' of research and open to deconstruction and problematization as a resource. Science is not immune from the politics of knowledge production (such as the willingness of political bodies and research councils to address certain research questions and methodologies rather than others). Also, the internal dynamics of scientific communities make it difficult to justify research projects that are contrary to the received wisdom of an established scientific consensus. One of the purposes of this book is to open up a dialogic space for environmental activists and

13

sceptics to treat each other less as enemies (for example, in the labelling of sceptics as 'deniers', which carries the connotation of 'holocaust
denial') and more as adversaries who respect each other's standpoints.
This is especially important in creating the ground for bridging the divide
between social and natural science.

Integrating social and natural science: the 'where' and 'when' questions

The key question, however, is how to integrate social and natural
scientific accounts of environmental issues. While cultural and media
interpretation plays a part, other social dimensions also need to be
addressed. The institutional dimension is especially important. The
characterizations of environmental movements as new social movements,
post-materialist responses to the growth mania of the Western state-
industrial complex, bottom-up responses to conventional party politics
or cultural lifestyle laboratories tend to reinforce the liberal distinction
between state and civil society. Similarly, in North America during the
1980s and 1990s, environmental movements and NGOs became increasingly concerned with environmental injustice, the fact that certain groups
of people have experienced a disproportionate impact of environmental
'bads' while others enjoyed a surplus of environmental 'goods', such as
access to green spaces.

As the debate on environmental racism and injustice has developed,
the connections between environmental and social justice have become
more apparent, with outsider groups moving into the inside track, especially in the context of urban sustainability. Nevertheless, the experience
of being outsiders has generated a new legacy in seeking ways to develop
broad-focus civic approaches that encourage the involvement of a wide
range of stakeholders. In addition, there has been increased concern
with how bottom-up and top-down environmental policy formation has
become increasingly interconnected with environmental NGOs becoming
more incorporated in policy formation and decision-making processes. In
some contexts, such as the EU, this has developed into eco-corporatism
(explored further in Chapter 4).

The institutional opportunities for effective intervention and political
responsiveness to resource mobilization by environmental campaigns
vary according to issue, context and the political articulation of interests.
This last factor may refer to how some interests may arise on the agenda
and not others, why a particular issue is couched in a particular way (the
interests of a polluter may be persuasively expressed as in the public interest while those of the affected community are presented as sectional), how

some interests are seen as requiring special concessions (demonstrated at the intergovernmental level by the concessions acquired by China on phasing out CFCs), or how some interests are regarded as key security matters (such as in the case of the US federal government's refusal to ratify the Kyoto Protocol). To explore how all the questions considered above are relevant to a particular situation, the next section considers one environmental event that has come to epitomize the struggles of the environmental movement in both a symbolic and practical way.

How not to deal with 21,000 tons of toxics: revisiting Love Canal

To illustrate how these questions matter, it is useful to explore a long-standing environmental hazard incident that provided a landmark case in environmental activism, Love Canal. The problem was a legacy of the Hooker Chemicals and Plastics Corporation (a subsidiary of Occidental Petroleum, whose interests in coal ironically were represented by Albert Gore Senior), which stored hazardous waste on the site previously used for petrochemical and military waste storage. Between 1942 and 1952 the unfinished canal, which had originally been designed to provide a trade route around Niagara Falls, became a waste disposal landfill for an estimated 21,000 tons of toxics, including PCBs and dioxins. When the site was full, Hooker Chemicals sealed it in impermeable clay. The site was subject to compulsory purchase by the Niagara School Board against the wishes of Hooker Chemicals and the legal advice of both sides (who were well aware of the possible future litigation), so the company set the notional price of US$1 for the deal and secured a clause in the contract that absolved them of legal liability (although after sixteen years of litigation about the relationship between ownership and negligence, in 1995 Occidental Petroleum agreed to pay the Environmental Protection Agency – EPA – US$129 million to cover the costs of the clean-up of the site with interest within the terms of the 1980 'Superfund Law', CERCLA – the Comprehensive Environmental Response, Compensation and Liability Act that resulted from the Love Canal incident). Over the next two decades, as part of the effects of the baby boom, an elementary school and, following sub-development contracts, housing projects were built on and around the site with the construction of building foundations resulting in damage to the clay seal on the toxic dump.

The first environmental assessment, in 1976 by the Calspan Corporation, resulted in the EPA conducting its own investigation in 1978. With toxics detected in the homes in 'Ring 1', New York State declared a health emergency and evacuated residents whose properties were located immediately above the dump. This alarmed residents outside the immediate evacuation area of 'Ring 1', who initiated a campaign through the Love Canal Homeowners Association (LCHA), led by the unrelenting Lois Gibbs. The LCHA highlighted the potential effects of various toxins produced by the plant as a result of the complementary feedstocks for both pesticides (such as DDT, Mirex and Lindane, all listed in the 'Dirty Dozen' covered by the Stockholm Convention on Persistent Organic Pollutants, which came into force in 2004) and plastics production. The resulting disposal of toxic materials included dioxins and PCBs (also listed under the Stockholm Convention) as well as benzene and chemicals with solvent properties or uses in the extraction of oils from plants, such as chloroform, trichloroethane and tetrachloroethane. These and other toxins had detrimental health effects on residents and the children who attended an elementary school on 99th Street that was in close proximity to the storage facilities. The contamination in this case was not a result of poor storage but of subsequent building, drainage and sewer construction. This incident also raises interesting questions about who is responsible and for what.

At the heart of the difficulties was contradictory scientific evidence: the New York State Department of Health did not find convincing evidence while ad hoc community research conducted by campaigners in conjunction with health experts at the University at Buffalo (SUNY) highlighted a range of symptoms among residents which contradicted conventional public health evidence. While individual professors such as Adeline Levine (sociologist and founder of the Love Canal archive at SUNY), Vincent Ebert (geographer), Wayne Hadley (biologist and brother-in-law of Lois Gibbs), Stephen Barron (neurologist) and Ted Steegman (anthropologist), as well as Beverly Paigen (Roswell Park Cancer Institute), were directly involved in collating the evidence from residents, this was not conducted in terms of established epidemiological procedures, while SUNY sought to avoid official involvement for fear of being sued. Observed effects in the community included higher-than-average birth defects and miscarriages, a range of illnesses, short stature in the children on the site and some indications of borderline nerve exposure effects (Steegman 2001). As Ted Steegman indicated, 'science here was a long way from the clinic or the laboratory. It was rough, fast fieldwork at a low level toxic exposure site – a situation designed to promote borderline results and disagreements' (ibid.: 181).

The contents of Love Canal included:

1 *dioxin*, the most toxic chemical known to man and cause of cancer, birth defects, mutations, fetal death in laboratory animals.

2   *tetrachloroethylene*, a carcinogen which also exhibits adverse effects on the central nervous system and the liver.

3   *chloroform*, a carcinogen which also causes narcosis of the central nervous system, destruction of liver cells, kidney damage, cardiac problems.

4   *dichloroethane*, a carcinogen whose toxic effects include central nervous system disorders, depression, anorexia, kidney and liver dysfunction.

5   *lindane*, a carcinogen which also attacks the liver, the central nervous system and causes adverse reproductive effects. (Love Canal Archives, USA)

The evidence produced by local activists was challenged for being based on an overly difficult questionnaire, unsystematic blood tests (some of which were lost), the fact that data collectors were not trained and the absence of a control group. There were also difficulties in acquiring the medical records of residents, inhibiting medical condition verification. In response to questions about the miscarriage and birth defect rates outside 'Ring 1', Gibbs also developed the 'swale hypothesis' – suggesting that the health effects of the dump appeared to be concentrated along filled-in stream beds and wet areas (swales and ponds) – but this was initially questioned in the context of residents who knew of the swale hypothesis and thus could have over-reported (contrary to the double-blind methodology of epidemiology). It later emerged that voles, a potential indicator of the toxic effects, were largely absent from the area in the vicinity of the dump and those present had lindane in their tissues (Christian 1983).

Nevertheless, the swale hypothesis was recognized by the Department of Health in 1979, resulting in a partial evacuation of children and pregnant women. In 1980, the EPA highlighted the possibility of chromosomal damage (a study that itself remains uncorroborated but generated a greater sense of urgency for political actors), alarming the community, which took two EPA investigators hostage, so by October the homes in the outer ring were bought out by New York State. The subsequent Lewis Thomas Panel, appointed by the state governor to establish a basis for reconciling scientific disagreement on Love Canal, announced that the EPA chromosome study was 'a paradigm of administrative ineptitude' and challenged the basis of activist research for using small samples, using anecdotal evidence and assuming that health problems were present without clear proof, and claimed that causal attribution had not been demonstrated. Questions have since been raised about the qualifications of the panel for assessing field research in a community environment – suggesting that the conditions of a closed system cannot be assumed in complex conditions (Smith 1998b) and, given the potential vulnerabilities of residents, the pressures for policy-relevant information and explanation make the lengthy full peer review processes inapplicable.

The Love Canal incident also provides a clear indication of how citizen movements form and mobilize resources to have an impact on political decisions, as well as highlighting the reasons for civic engagement. The LCHA was not alone in mobilizing the resources of the community and drawing in concerned citizens in the area. While the residents were not unified in their views (older residents without dependants were much less concerned about the health consequences and were critical of Lois Gibbs), a broad local alliance emerged combining residents, academic scientists from SUNY and religious leaders such as Sister Margaret Hoffman, executive director of the key activist group, the Ecumenical Task Force (ETF) of the Niagara Frontier. For the ETF, this was a 'moral and ethical problem' which demanded that rather than standing by, citizens had to stand up for affected individuals and families to assert the responsibility of polluters, state agencies, legal professionals and other civil society organizations. The leaders of the ETF saw their role as both pastoral and prophetic (attending to the needs of the community whether in terms of health or psychological damage but also having an explicit advocacy linking recognition of environmental injustice to the need for responsible stewardship). The religious basis of the values of this organization was apparent in the rhetoric, for example when citing Proverbs 29:18: 'The major task is to have the respect and the foresight of how to respond. "Where there is no *vision*, the people perish"' (ETF 1998: 9).

Addressing the question of who is responsible, all actors involved discovered they were, even if for many actors it was an unwelcome revelation. The company that placed the waste in storage did not want the site to be subject to redevelopment and in its land sale negotiations with the school board attempted to limit its liabilities as part of the contract for sale. The legal advisers for both parties indicated that the development project should not go ahead given the risks involved for residents and the possibilities of future litigation. The political authorities in New York State and at the federal level procrastinated on the need for action on the grounds that the evidence of contamination was insufficient or fell short of epidemiological procedures. Ultimately, the full evacuation ordered by President Carter was initiated not on the grounds of a comprehensive public health analysis but as a result of media reports of the possibility of chromosomal damage among residents. Subsequent medical studies also cast doubt on the reasons for the evacuation, suggesting, for example, that the cancer rates of Love Canal residents matched those of other New York State residents outside New York City. As a result of the dispersal of the residents following the evacuation, the generation of conclusive scientific evidence was no longer feasible, and by the 1990s the Love Canal Revitalization Agency (LCARA) was able to initiate the sale of housing projects in the outer ring of the evacuation area.

This raises two issues about scientific uncertainty in relation to environmental problems. First, the complexities of conducting epidemiological studies within the context of the presence of various environmental hazards ensure that, even if correlations can be identified, the plausibility of a particular explanation depends on the strength of the association, the presence of consistent empirical findings in different situations, specificity (i.e. that a specific source is the likely cause of a particular health effect), a temporal relationship being evident (i.e. that the cause is followed by the effect) and a biological gradient or dose-response curve being apparent (i.e. where there is greater exposure to an identifiable cause this generates a greater effect on the health of those affected). Second, since the causal attribution for pollution is difficult to establish, then environmental responsibility and legal liability are also problematic. Even if there are clear indicators in terms of the first issue, the second depends on the plausibility of existing scientific knowledge, its coherence with existing explanations of the pathogenic causes of illness and the requirement that these are supported by experimental and/or analogous evidence. Even here, as the benchmark article for testing epidemiological effects by Austin Bradford Hill (1965) states:

> indisputable evidence for or against the cause-and-effect hypothesis and none can be required as a *sine qua non*. What they can do, with greater or less strength, is to help us to make up our minds on the fundamental question – is there any other way of explaining the set of facts before us, is there any other answer equally, or more, likely than cause and effect?

Beyond Love Canal: environmentalism gets serious about who, what, where and when!

The long-term effect of the Love Canal case cannot be overestimated. As the publicity spread about Love Canal, Lois Gibbs received calls from individuals throughout the USA engaged with similar health hazards, leading her to found the Citizens Clearing House for Hazardous Waste, which in 1981 became the Center for Health, Environment and Justice

(CHEJ). This NGO has provided organizational support and technical expertise for over ten thousand local community campaigns, initiating campaigns against everyday environmental hazards (such as PVC products) as well as organizing events to share knowledge and coordinate strategies on a wider scale. The character of the Love Canal movement has thus become a prototype for subsequent mobilizations against local environmental hazards as explicitly involving civic engagement (as both a political and legal challenge to the effects of industrial contamination).

> We already know that it is legal to pollute and poison people, so obviously that's not enough. We can get some compensation but how do you compensate for a lost baby, how do you compensate for a dead parent, how do you compensate for a dead child – there is no compensation for that ... so the legal system does not work, so what we need to do is move into the political system, we need to organize. ... We were blue collar, we only made US$10,000 a year, we had a limited formal education and we brought the President of the United States to our stage, to give us relocation. We the community of 900 families, raised enough stink, raised our voices, united together, stood together and demanded that the government make right and they came to Love Canal. (Gibbs 2006)

While Gibbs has often emphasized the priority of politics over the law in the USA, the prominence of civil rights discourse in law, politics and the media has also created opportunities for change within the legal system. Bob Bullard has often highlighted the importance of using civil rights discourse as a lever through which the environmental rights of the socio-economic groups that are often overlooked can be protected. The transportation, storage and disposal of waste has often taken place along the 'path of least resistance', in communities that are marginalized and relatively powerless – in Bullard's terminology, on the 'wrong side of the tracks'. So, with Love Canal as a largely white, blue-collar movement, a key dimension of the US experience is overlooked – the racial factor. The structures of social inequality and the history of political representation of different groups in a particular location often play a key role in the siting of environmental hazards. Since the Commission for Racial Justice study of *Toxic Waste and Race in the United States* (1987), a study of demographic patterns initiated by the United Church of Christ, there has been a perceived connection between hazardous waste processing and storage and non-white households.

This was confirmed to be the case in the follow-up CRJ study in 1994, and subsequent work has consistently demonstrated that environmental hazards are disproportionately distributed in predominantly African-American and Latino neighbourhoods. It is even possible that race matters more than social class in this context. According to Vicki Been (1994a, 1994b), there was a negative correlation between neighbourhoods with high poverty measures and waste facility locations, which were more likely to be located in working-class and lower-middle-income localities. In addition, she noted the capacity of higher-income residents to move away from landfill and incinerator sites, leaving lower-income residents stranded in an area where property prices were adversely affected. These housing market effects then draw in minority populations with lower socio-economic status, with the result that environmental policies may reinforce racial segregation and unequal environmental quality (even though a correlation may be empirically established between minority populations and hazardous plants, economic factors may be the underlying independent variable). Jonathan Adler (1995) presents the issue more starkly by suggesting that one of the defining characteristics of the environmental movement has been its 'whiteness', that the social composition of the movement has led to a situation where institutional racism is also a problem. In many cases, environmental regulation has had a detrimental social and economic effect on ethnic minorities in terms of economic opportunities and employment. The most established environmental groups rarely consulted with minority groups such as Native American Indians and, like the leadership, the membership of these organizations has remained homogeneous (despite attempts by groups such as the Sierra Club to diversify the social composition of its representatives and membership base). The dissolution of the National Toxics Campaign Fund (NTCF) in the USA has been attributed to a lack of representativeness by campaigners concerned with the differential racial location of toxins, while Winona LaDuke has stated that 'environmental groups make decisions that affect other communities without the input of those communities' (1993, cited in Adler 1995: 131). The problem then has two dimensions – the leadership that engages in environmental advocacy does not reflect and does not always engage in consultation with the affected groups. We should add another underlying issue. Since the areas that are selected for such facilities often suffer from social and economic deprivation (and may well have a history of environmental degradation), then initial proposals for the location of a waste processing plant or landfill scheme are often couched in terms of enhancing the economic opportunities of the local population (although this may not be the result).

For environmental justice campaigners, it was not just a matter of the income levels or the racial characteristics of the communities that experienced 'Locally Unwanted Land Uses' (LULUs) but how the political authorities have responded to immediate hazard situations. More recently, much has also been made of the selective responsiveness of federal government and emergency services in the USA since Hurricane Katrina impacted on New Orleans (a case of a natural disaster complemented by human-caused hazards). Ironically, it has been argued that the victims of the hurricane could be in a better situation economically after the disaster – that it takes a disaster for the federal authorities to address extreme social inequality and respond to long-standing toxic hazards.

Beyond the NGO revolution: negotiating the social and environmental justice conundrum

It should be emphasized that concern about the environment and social justice do not always dovetail neatly, since much depends on the context. In terms of existing theories of citizenship there are two pathways. One is to extend human rights to situations where groups with the same structural location in aggregate have their common individual rights ignored or transgressed. The other is to think in terms of citizens having group rights where certain entitlements have been neglected within the existing legal system because it fails to recognize the sovereignty of that group or cultural minority in terms of governing its own affairs. In a world characterized by transnational relationships the problem is a particularly thorny one and increasing in frequency. In one example, considered later in this book, the migrant workers in Mae Sot on the borderlands between Burma (Myanmar) and Thailand have experienced extreme labour exploitation within the sweatshops of the Special Economic Zones of north-west Thailand. These migrants cannot return for political reasons or because their livelihoods have been severely compromised.

Plainly, their position as stateless migrant workers excludes them from the rights established in Thailand for workers who happen to be citizens by reasons of birth. In addition, they hold dear their cultural identity as, for example, members of the Karen or the Mon tribal cultures. As documented later, these peoples have experienced forced displacement as a result of the military actions in another country (causing them to be political and/or economic refugees), and they have found that their per capita income is higher in exile than it was in their country of origin (although this takes no account of their losses in terms of subsistence income as well as cultural autonomy). Presently, the international system endorses labour standards but not labour rights with the same standard as human rights. Standards simply do not have the same moral and political force as rights without vigilance and the capacity to act.

This is where it becomes really interesting, especially bearing in mind that within the existing international state system any proposed solution would require application on both sides of the Thai–Burmese border – that while some results are achievable in Thailand (subject to the return of the 'rule of law' and democracy following the coup of 19 September 2006) few will probably be realized without the demise of the military government in Myanmar. In terms of addressing environmental degradation, group rights for the indigenous peoples of Burma across these national boundaries would be more likely to secure a more sustainable and less exploitative outcome on both sides of the border. In the absence of this rosy scenario, however, the extension of human rights to cover labour relations for non-Thai citizens would clearly prevent the worst excesses of sweatshop production processes for displaced peoples in the Thai economy. Later, we will explore the close relationship between environmental degradation and labour standard violation on both sides of this border but, for now, it is sufficient to state that what is feasible is more important than what is necessary.

In addressing the relationship between social and environmental justice, one new area of citizenship studies has made considerable headway, i.e. those that focus on what have been traditionally described as civil society actors and movements rather than exclusively on the generation of citizenship legislation in the national context. Most important here is the increased awareness of transnational civil society. For example, when addressing human rights Claude Welch (2000, 2001) highlights the quantitative proliferation of NGOs operating in this context but also having a qualitative effect, for they perform an integral role in monitoring and resolving human rights issues in particular cases (through gathering information, influencing public opinion, the provision of assistance for individual victims of abuses, setting standards and lobbying governments and international agencies to act). Of particular importance is the growing role of NGOs in setting standards that have become international norms since their involvement in the drafting of the Universal Declaration of Human Rights (UDHR, 1947) and the establishment of standards on torture and the rights of children in the 1970s and 1980s. In addition, NGOs have become the primary mechanism for monitoring violations of the UDHR. More critically, he adds that 'if NGOs lack political space with which to operate, or resources necessary for fact-finding and publicity, it stands to reason that human rights abuses will continue' (2000: 3).

Welch, like other researchers in this area, is concerned not only with the abuse of individual rights but also collective or group rights (an issue considered in more detail in the next chapter). Concerned with the situation of Africa, he argues that the *aura of pessimism* in this context has emerged owing to the failure to address rights abuses. NGOs can make a difference, however, and, in the absence of citizenship legislation in specific countries, they have become a major avenue for political change – 'society more than state has become the watchword for analysis' (ibid.: 42). This illustrates how when institution-led change fails then citizen-led movements (in this case often linked to kinship groups) have filled the gap and acted in partnership with political authorities, which are increasingly proving to be more effective at the transnational rather than the national level. NGOs occupy a special place for Welch – they are advocacy groups organizing public opinion around pertinent issues and interacting with governments, so much so that he suggests there has been an 'NGO revolution' because they are less concerned with relief and aid and more concerned with development and political mobilization (ibid.: 45). Their capacity to engage in transnational campaigning is also crucial, as demonstrated by the Ottawa Convention (on the Prohibition, Stockpiling, Production and Transfer of Anti-Personnel Mines and on Their Destruction), when along with government support over 1,200 NGOs added weight to the case developed by the International Campaign to Ban Landmines.

Similarly, environmental NGOs are playing a major part in intergovernmental negotiations and treaty formation, although some researchers perceive environmental networks, despite the importance of ethics in this field, as 'not as clearly principled' as those concerned with human rights (Keck and Sikkink 1998: 121). This perception stems from the assumption that environmental movements are preoccupied with broader conceptions of guardianship or stewardship of natural things rather than immediate human impacts (sometimes described as the cult of the wilderness). In addition, environmental issues, when they impact upon society, are often conveyed as road traffic issues, waste management, urban renewal within industrial societies and in terms of corporate social responsibility, the management of development or the protection of indigenous cultures in the global South – i.e. what makes these issues 'environmental' is subsumed within a broader field of concern. It is only in the last fifteen years that the perception of these concerns as genuinely 'environmental' has really hit home. This is where the tale of environment and citizenship in the global imagination starts, and it is seen increasingly in personal actions, community campaigns, pressure group activity, party politics and various new innovative techniques of civic imagination, which are now seen as a 'green thread' running through all policy communities.

There has, of course, been substantial NGO activity, but the range of environmental issues has diffused the activism – they have lacked the focus of issues such as human rights and labour standards. It is often said that the vision of the earth as a fragile planet spurred the environmental movements into existence and the emergence of environmental groups as new social movements. The Club of Rome report on *The Limits to Growth* (1972), the 1972 UN Conference on the Human Environment, the Montreal Protocol, which addressed ozone depletion, as a result of anthropogenic causes such as CFCs – all provided a platform for generating environmental awareness. The emergence of the debate on 'sustainable development' was an initial step in opening up a debate on linking social and environmental justice, although it was primarily focused on the difference between developed and developing societies, between globalizers and the globalized.

Following the Earth Summit in 1992, NGOs have participated on the Council on Sustainable Development with equal status to governments, further challenging the distinction between advocacy and civic engagement. Alongside this, institution-building in conjunction with NGOs with an environmental focus has remained issue-based (and often with specific geographical orientations), for example organized around the International Tropical Timber Organization or the International Whaling Commission. Nevertheless, the idea of a simultaneously multi-level and multi-issue response to environmental change in the political mainstream and as part of citizenship practices in everyday life is fairly new.

Welch retains the conception of NGOs as advocacy groups and, drawing on Ann Marie Clark's (2001) research on Amnesty International, stresses how the maintenance of political impartiality and factual accuracy are crucial in securing political access, operating as an organization in authoritarian countries, and in legitimizing the 'principled norms' that become part of treaty drafts. As Welch recognizes, however, NGOs have moved from just providing technical expertise to a more explicit political role, what we describe here as being agents of civic engagement. Since achieving objectives in human rights, labour standards and environmental sustainability demands private actors to contribute to and implement policies (partly through external regulation but also through self-regulation), like other non-state actors such as private corporations, NGOs are no longer simply external advocates but integral to policy and treaty formation, monitoring and enforcement. This does present some

25

From environmental justice to citizenship

difficulties for NGOs (whether they are concerned with environmental problems and/or human rights or labour standards violations) operating in authoritarian contexts. If it is perceived that their fact-finding is based on a client relationship with another state or intergovernmental bodies viewed as hostile to the political regime, then this is not only likely to create problems of access but also personal security concerns for NGO representatives at work in the field. One of the most important recent developments is a reorientation from environmental advocacy (the conversion strategy) to deliberative and dialogic processes (the engagement strategy) that mobilize affected constituencies. This demands a rethinking of well-established conceptions of networks as 'political spaces' to include civic engagement as well as communication and the production of meaning. It also goes beyond campaigning for norm implementation and monitoring, for the participants would also be involved as stakeholders in the decisions that affect the constituencies that NGOs and other groups and movements represent. This does not mean that the capacity of NGOs to collect and communicate evidence and information is less important (in fact the very opposite for transnational networks); what is needed is a clearer understanding of how rapid reactivity has been married to civic engagement.

In addition, so far the emphasis has been largely on rights (or the conflicting rights claims of different groups) rather than securing an appropriate balance between entitlements and obligations. Once we take the cultural identity of those concerned into account and acknowledge the different obligations and duties of actors in a specific situation, then the situation alters dramatically. This book explores how responsibility, obligations and duties are just as crucial to addressing environmental issues as entitlements and rights, as well as how environmental problems link to human rights and labour standards. Subsequent chapters will highlight how discussion of every environmental issue involves questions such as who is responsible, to whom are obligations owed, what obligations are appropriate and justifiable, and whether such obligations should be established in a more legal-formal way as duties.

2 | Citizens, citizenship and citizenization

The new terrain of citizenship

Citizenship is no longer fixated on membership of a particular nation-state legally defining the rights and duties of individuals, but acts as a contested space for a variety of identity construction projects that shift the focus from a fixation with rights to a concern with some combination of entitlements and obligations. It was with this in mind that Smith (1998a) highlighted how ecological citizenship presents us with a 'politics of obligation'. Adding complexity, the agents that are seen as acceptable in political processes should no longer be seen as only living humans but should reach further forward to future generations and, through some form of stewardship, include aspects of the support systems that make human life possible. To qualify this further, the relationship between entitlements and obligations (or more formally between rights and duties) is no longer seen as one characterized by reciprocity. In addition, obligations are seen as flowing from living people in a specific time and place to a variety of actors, including distant peoples or strangers, strangers in the future and even strangers in terms of species, so that these 'strangers' can be seen as friends and even as citizens.

As a result, the ways in which the meaning of citizenship (itself a contested discursive space) has been articulated redefine whose interests should be considered. Excluded groups of people (such as many indigenous peoples) are now more likely to inhabit this space; also, categories such as non-human animals, forests, ecosystems or even the 'biotic community' (Leopold 1949) are now seen as legitimate constituencies that require stakeholder status in decision-making processes. The key question, then, is how can the interests of constituencies be realistically translated into the expressed views of stakeholders or stakeholder guardians and contribute to deliberative processes that inform decisions and policies?

The research literature on citizenship has often been fixated upon entitlements and rights, a by-product of the Western liberal democratic preoccupation with market-based claims to ownership. What we own and what we have a right to have been central not only to advocates of private property relations and more recently neoliberal ideological movements but also to leftist currents concerned with entitlement to social welfare and environmental quality, such as social democratic and identity recognition movements. As Engin Isin and Bryan Turner state, 'what is new is the economic, social and cultural conditions that make possible the articulation of new claims and the content and form of these claims as citizenship rights' (Isin and Turner 2002: 1).

Beyond civil, political and social citizenship

One of the effects in academic research has been to separate the discussion on recognition of rights and identities from the awareness of economic distribution, as if identity politics and the associated conceptions of inclusion and exclusion were somehow disconnected from matters such as socio-economic difference, social class and structural inequality. While the causes of this process have often been attributed to globalization or the proliferating discourses loosely associated with postmodernism, this is more often an indication of the effects – a symptom of the feeling that traditional structures have been challenged – rather than a cause. A central demographic reason highlights one of the enduring features of the human species, its capacity to migrate. While the restrictions created by national identity stymied (although did not prevent) population movements during the twentieth century, the response from capital has been to move production elsewhere in search of resources and cheap labour as well as fewer regulatory costs from the state. Western societies that have been more willing to accept migrant populations (even on a temporary basis) have, however, often demonstrated the strongest and most sustained economic growth, such as in the UK.

Where social rights have been entrenched in order to aid the cohesion and functioning of society, such as in corporatist political systems (like those of France and Germany), then the presence of entrenched reciprocal relations between citizens and between the state and citizens are more clearly established through the emphasis on community membership and the goal of social cohesion. Interestingly, the focus on individual rights in liberal political systems – or when both individual and group rights are emphasized in political systems prevalent in Scandinavian social democracies grounded in republican citizenship – provides a better basis for expanding entitlements. When taking account of a wider range of constituencies, and where the conflict over the construction and expansion of such rights is central to political contestation, then the obligations of relevant actors and the causal attribution for environmental problems (implying responsibility) can be established. Isin and Turner provide a useful summary of the connections between political systems and citizenship traditions, as presented in Table 2.1 below. As with all typologies, some societies combine elements of different political systems and citizenship traditions (for example, the UK and Canada combine

TABLE 2.1 Political systems and citizenship traditions

Types of political system	Liberal	Corporatist	Social democratic
Relationship between civil, political and social rights	Emphasis on civil and political rights with social rights allocated via the market	Emphasis on social rights but these are not universal	Strong emphasis on universal social rights
Citizenship traditions	Liberalism – individual rights or liberties that apply to all citizens	Communitarianism – priority placed on just functioning and cohesion of the community or society	Republicanism – both individual and group rights recognized; highlights the conflict in the expansion and construction of rights
Societies	United States, Australia, Switzerland	Austria, Italy, Germany, France	Sweden, Norway, Denmark, Finland, Netherlands

Source: Adapted from Isin and Turner (2002)

elements of liberal and social democratic systems). The implications of liberal, communitarian and republican traditions of citizenship for environmental issues will be assessed in the next chapter.

The literature on civil, political and social citizenship is fairly well developed. By way of a brief summary, civil citizenship concerns property rights and respect for the ownership of property by others. The kudos of ownership (particularly of land) was reinforced because it was a qualification for political citizenship. Civil rights are still relevant as the rights established via same-sex civil unions or even marriages testify – i.e. same-sex partners should have the same entitlements as heterosexual relations. In terms of political citizenship, the development of universal male suffrage followed by female political emancipation and the rights to free speech, association and mobility were counterbalanced by duties to avoid slander, libel, sedition and public disorder. Again, contemporary relevance should not be overlooked in situations where political participation is circumscribed. In these two cases, bearing in mind that citizenship rights and responsibilities (a mix of duties and obligations) are the result of legislation, the distinction between the public sphere and private life were rigorously maintained and the boundary remained for the most part stationary.

The emergence of social citizenship, where rights to welfare, education and housing are linked to corresponding duties to pay taxation on a progressive scale, had a more seismic effect on the positioning of the public–private boundary. Within social citizenship relations, situations regarded previously as personal difficulties (unemployment, housing squalor, educational failure) were now regarded as social problems that required policies and governance regimes that addressed these problems. The emergence of neoliberal governance (for example, Thatcherism in the UK) in the 1980s and 1990s in many Western societies was an attempt to shift the boundary back in the opposite direction by depoliticizing social and economic problems and by shifting responsibility back on to citizens. Nevertheless, citizenship continues to evolve and the relations between civil, political and social citizenship have moved on as well. Staying with the UK example, rather than simply embracing neoliberal ideology wholeheartedly, the New Labour government (1997–) oversaw the emergence of neo-social citizenship, emphasizing responsibilities rather than rights and showing willingness to recognize that the state has to act in some circumstances but in return demanding citizen compliance with obligations to society (such as with Job Seekers Allowance, which is conditional on the behaviour of the claimant in the UK).

In neo-social citizenship, state intervention is restrained in a manner akin to the neoliberal preference for facilitating change rather than reacting to problems, but the state is more willing to engage in micromanagement strategies to solve social problems (such as the introduction of academy schools in areas with problems of educational failure or Anti-Social Behaviour Orders – ASBOs – to regulate youth and neighbourly behaviour). In terms of civil relations, the creation of rights that ensure that citizens have medical and sexual control over their own bodies (such as the decriminalization of homosexuality or the protection of people with mental health problems) and recently the emergence of same-sex civil unions that facilitate civil contracts between gay partners indicate that civil citizenship is also evolving. In terms of political citizenship, the rights of people with disabilities that have been established through legal statute (some thirty years later than similar measures on equal opportunities regarding sexual and racial discrimination) are also indications of the expansion of political rights to minority groups and the increased protection of those rights.

While the kinds of citizenship and associated rights and duties so far addressed have universal application, participation rights are often much more focused where there is a demonstrable relationship between contending parties, such as in industrial or labour market relations, where one actor has considerably greater power than the other. Such rights include not simply anti-discrimination measures and rights to retraining, occupational placement and security, but also go beyond the individual rights to social justice such as those associated with pensions. Participatory citizenship recognizes the role of groups in collective negotiation and co-determination in the decision-making processes that affect the lives of group members, such as work councils having an impact on the investment strategy decisions of private corporations as part of mechanisms for economic democracy. This also applies to community representation in policy-making when that community, for example, experiences environmental health impacts (although this is distinct from the legal right to retrospective compensation for members of the group adversely affected by previous decisions or actions). A great deal depends on the configuration of entitlements and obligations. For example, in liberal democratic societies, individualism is more likely to dominate as an embedded assumption, meaning that citizenship is characterized as being primarily about negative liberty, i.e. the right to act without harming others. When obligations are elaborated in more detail, however, a variety of group rights can be recognized, deliberative institutions can be constructed to accommodate the different interests involved, and responsible actions that work towards just outcomes can be generated.

Citizenship and agonistic democracy: adversaries rather than enemies

It has often been stated that the tensions between the logic of democratic self-government and the logic of liberalism (with its emphasis on individual rights) can be resolved in a rational way. For Chantal Mouffe, both are constitutive of liberal democracy and it is a futile act of self-deception to insulate politics from our inescapable experience of value pluralism. Although the tension is ineradicable, it can still be negotiated in various ways. Attempts to impose a rational solution, however (whether this is means-ends rationality of aggregative models, deliberative or communicative), place inappropriate demands on the process of political debate. Mouffe argues that the real problem posed by allegiance is that it is secured through ensembles of practices that make the constitution of 'the democratic citizen' possible – thus emphasizing the need to focus on the types of practices, not the forms of argumentation. Rather than seeing individuals as prior to society, it is only through power relations, languages and cultures that agents come into existence.

In this account, rules and procedures exist only as ensembles of practices (with rules as abridgements of practices). How we bind ourselves to others as well as the bondedness we feel to a particular political space are inscribed in the *forms of life* and the agreements that are forged to put rules and procedures into effect. When we recognize that citizenship is expressed through lived experience, then we are acknowledging a whole range of human feelings, sensibilities and perceptions based on different social positions. After all, there is a world of difference between the experience of scraping a living on the refuse dumps in Guatemala City and that of bringing up a family in downtown Toronto in Canada or suburban Hampstead Heath in London. In addition, much depends on our identities: our gender, race or ethnicity, religious beliefs, political affiliations and so on, as well as our advantages or disadvantages in being globalizing or globalized citizens. For example, the experience of being a woman in an advanced industrial society with extensive civil, political and social rights differs considerably from the experience of being a woman in a sweatshop factory in Mexico or China, not least in terms of perceptions of what constitutes (in-) justice. Alternatively, 'hi-so' (i.e. high-society) members of the urban elite in a rapidly developing Asian mega-city can draw upon the entitlements of citizenship much more effectively than both the peasants and workers of their own countries or the marginalized social groups in industrial societies with established liberal democratic systems. Taking account of 'social position' in a hierarchical and unequal global context prompts us to think again about the complexity of citizenship and the precise balance of entitlements and obligations in each social location. Whether the disenfranchised and de-citizenized can mobilize and secure recognition has and will depend on the opportunities for and obstacles against the formation of movements in each location, although it must be emphasized that success also depends on capturing the imagination of communities (and how they imagine the environments they defend) as well as their capacity for generating support in transnational activist networks (see Box 2.1).

Box 2.1 Transnational networking and the environment

Environmental advocacy networks that bring activists and NGOs together originated in response to the 1972 UN Conference on the Human Environment in Stockholm and subsequent formation of the United Nations Environment Programme (UNEP), but as a result of their focus on the limits to growth, these networks lacked the capacity to galvanize support in the developing societies that often saw economic growth as the route to alleviating poverty. In much the same way as contemporary critics of the global warming hypothesis, both governments in the global South and NGOs concerned with development saw 'environmentalism' as a smokescreen for defending the interests of developed societies. As a result, the networks remained focused on particular issues, such as conservation strategies. Two significant developments emerged from these events. First, groups such as the International Union for the Conservation of Nature (IUCN) and the World Wildlife Fund (WWF) found that there was strength through coordination, realizing that concerted action often ensured influence. Second, they discovered that environmental advocacy was more effective when scientists and NGO activists work in tandem. They recognized the need to link up strategies for conservation and the alleviation of poverty, and the end result was the emergence of the concept of 'sustainable development' to try to reconcile the demands of current generations with those of future generations. The urgent need for conserving resources for futurity was featured in the Brundtland Report (1987) and influenced a significant number of intergovernmental negotiations regarding issues such as deforestation (in this case, through the International Tropical Timber Organization).

The form of networking that surfaces depends not only on the focus of each group but also on their organizational form. NGOs such as Friends of the Earth and Greenpeace have offices and members in many different countries, allowing for concerted transnational action as well as national and local campaign work, although the focus is usually on countries in a specific region (such as the Greenpeace South-East Asia campaign on urban toxins in Bangkok, Jakarta and Manila). In addition, new network linkages have emerged, bringing together urban and rural movements and NGOs in the global South with those in the global North, as well as bringing together issues often seen as separate in the past, such as the campaigns against environmental degradation, political corruption and human rights and labour standards violations.

First, urban–rural linkages developed as conservation NGOs have responded to urban sprawl and the expanding ecological footprints of (mega-) cities. For example, the supply chains for cities such as Rio de Janeiro, São Paulo and Guatemala City transformed land uses and the established practices of communities that the land previously sustained (such as those experienced by the rubber-tappers in Brazil highlighted on p. 43). The concern here has become how to make the impacts of cities lighter on the land while also addressing both social and environmental justice.

Second, NGO activities in the global South have used rapid-reaction techniques with NGOs in Western societies to highlight the inadequacies and sometimes the misinformation of transnational brands and outsourced manufacturing companies when addressing the codes of conduct that have been promoted under the auspices of corporate social responsibility. Similarly, the World Conservation Union (IUCN) created a context for knowledge sharing and coordinated lobbying that led some NGOs to achieve consultative status with United Nations agencies and establish more formal coordination with organizations such as the Pesticides Action Network and the World Rainforest Movement. While the latter emerged as a result of obstacles faced in the former, these developments increased awareness of the need to move beyond advocacy strategies and recognize the importance of civic engagement in intergovernmental institutions.

Third, the most recent development, in part the result of the adoption of the UN Global Compact as the baseline for corporate responsibility, has created opportunities for human rights groups, labour unions and federations and environmental groups to recognize that conflict zones and authoritarian regimes are often associated with the worst examples of environmental degradation and the suppression of independent union activity. These multi-issue activist networks may face huge obstacles and are prone to instability owing to potentially divergent interests, but this does not diminish the importance of the task. For example, rapid industrialization in developing countries usually depends on preventing union mobilization, weak regulation of the use of natural resources, ignoring or condoning human rights violations of indigenous peoples, violating land rights, and taking paramilitary action against any movement that seeks to articulate grievances. Put more directly, the people working in sweatshops at the end of the global supply chain are often members of families who used to make their livelihood in a more sustainable way from resources that are now devoted to factory and commercial production, and, in the worst cases, they have been forcibly displaced through murder, arson, torture and rape.

The road to the slums and shanty towns of rapidly growing cities and Special Economic Zones in the global South is paved with the violation of all ten principles of the UN Global Compact. Effective solutions therefore have to link these different but connected processes of dispossession, despoliation and exploitation – to highlight *who* is responsible and *how* these acts can be redressed. Rather than adopting the often 'righteous' discourses of many NGOs, however, effective change depends on treating the institutions that facilitate these impacts (from the World Bank and nations to private corporations and local administrations) as adversaries rather than as enemies, for these institutions will not be dissuaded from current activities and encouraged to adopt new ones unless there is a direct engagement with the rationale of modernization, development and poverty alleviation. While environmental justice without social justice is ecotopian, social justice without environmental justice is barren and self-defeating.

By concentrating on 'forms of life', passions and emotions in political activity can be recognized and new political subjectivities can be invented to avoid these passions being articulated within anti-democratic and fundamentalist political projects. If we are to take pluralism seriously,

Mouffe argues, we need to move from the slippery ice of total grasp and return to the rough ground of concrete circumstances. In place of a public sphere in which power can be supposedly eliminated, even if notions such as the ideal discourse and the search for consensus are merely treated as regulative ideals, we must start from the assumption that power is constitutive of social relations and that any appeals to objectivity (social, political or ethical) are acts of power. In short, what is regarded as legitimate is simply the result of successful power. To this end, Mouffe proposes a distinction between 'politics' and 'the political'. If we start from the assumption that political spaces contain antagonisms, i.e. struggles between social forces (with antagonism as inherent in the social and with conflict always present), then 'politics' involves the ensembles of practices, discourse and institutions that attempt to create a sense of order and organization, manage potential conflicts and domesticate hostilities.

The aim of the democratic political system should be to establish ways through which antagonism is replaced by agonism, such that the struggle between enemies is replaced by the struggle between adversaries, so that collective passions are channelled through modes of identification where they are obliged to respect the existence of opponents and their entitlement to be political, rather than seeing them as an enemy to be destroyed.

In this way, it is possible to establish a common ground that is predicated on the ethical-political principles of political communication that would help facilitate agreements (or merely temporary arrangements) between adversaries. This means that 'citizenly subject positions' are constituted as temporary respites in ongoing confrontations and the struggle over the meaning of citizenship. In short, the specific virtues that each kind of citizenship mobilizes and articulates are provisional. Indeed, a vibrant clash of different political subjectivities is an indication of the robust nature of a democratic system. In agonistic democracy these confrontations should ideally be staged around diverse conceptions of citizenship, each trying to implement a different form of hegemony and each proposing its interpretation of the common good, the right course of action and the virtue(s) that should be cultivated. We should not regard ecological citizenship as a universal answer but as just one way (perhaps even a variety of ways) of engaging in 'the political' and as a way of inventing subject positions that will be environmentally beneficial, thus enabling us to identify the potential and limits of subject positions that feature in environmental discourses.

Identity and citizenship through gender: engendering citizenship

To develop this argument, we have chosen to consider the important influence of research on gender and citizenship and feminist theoretical responses to the questions and issues that these debates raise, especially with regard to the environment. Rather than start with the theory, the reader may have guessed that we want to initiate the discussion with a feminist intuition – that lived politics draws on everyday experiences and, through this, it is possible to make sense of power relations that affect us in our private lives. So, rather than draw upon the universalistic pretensions of some areas of feminist theory, we recommend attention to the particular detail and context of what women experience in concrete conditions (which, like all experience, is enormously varied). Feminist research has often placed a special emphasis on qualitative social enquiry because ethnographically informed research is a practical starting point that allows us to see and grasp what ordinary women do in their workplaces, in their villages, in the fields (literally) and in political support groups, as well as in their daily practical activities such as child-rearing, household management, mutual supporting, water-carrying and distribution, storytelling, knowledge transmission (including ecological knowledge), caring for the sick and the elderly, and other forms of emotional labour that are vital to sustaining social life.

Ethnographic research essentially provides a more detailed and vivid examination of women's lives, which are often overlooked by other research methods. Qualitative research techniques offer a more 'genuine' attempt to assess localized situations because they involve a free flow of communication between the researcher and the respondent. The approach is one in which the researcher is present not to extract information but to listen and understand, which often more effectively captures subjects' voices and more accurately reflects the actual needs of the respondents themselves. Ethnographic studies thus offer rich, detailed, in-depth analyses that allow us to establish and understand the complex links between the local and the global. Given that so much of social research is androcentric, and focused on male-dominated spheres, how else would we be able to learn of women's social relations, their concerns, the problems they face, and how they go about resolving them?

In terms of citizenship, feminist thinking challenges the discriminatory and cultural prejudices grounded in androcentric assumptions that place an emphasis on the public sphere while also seeing other aspects of human existence as non-political (Prokhovnik 1998). Traditional conceptions of politics as a power relation tended to portray decision-making and the 'mobilization of bias' that formed a particular agenda (around

37

Citizens, citizenship and citizenization

which decisions were made) as those that are empirically visible. Feminist analyses, however, view power as operating across different spheres and take the approach that the personal is indeed political. In addition, they argue that power is visible through its consequences – that even if decisions and agenda formation completely ignored gender issues, then if the status, income and wealth of women were statistically lower than those of men, power was still exercised, although in more subtle ways, such as through socialization and the workings of social structures. Nevertheless, political and social rights (in some cases civil rights, when property ownership has not been gender specific) have served positively in establishing anti-discriminatory legislation, despite its underpinning individualism (Bryson 1999). The historical trajectories of citizenship have tended to exclude women from membership of the political community whether the emphasis was placed upon participation as a civic duty and a route to personal fulfilment (republicanism) or characterized as citizenship in terms of civic or social rights (liberalism and social democracy).

As a result, feminist vocabularies of citizenship have challenged the idea that citizenship was a discourse mainly concerned with rights while, at the same time, taking every opportunity to mine civil, political and social rights as a means to achieve ends that matter to women (from matrimonial property rights to maternity rights). While this demonstrates how entitlements and rights have become a site for struggle, recent interventions have sought to explore how obligations and duties could work in the same way. In particular, feminist advocacy has generated a greater concern for acknowledging the role of women in caring for others (dependency work) and the work of women in many areas that remain unpaid, such as community service (Young 1995). This emphasis on the politics of obligation, with reference to gender, has generated a growing recognition of the role of women in the reproduction of labour (i.e. that the existing social structures depend on women) and, most importantly, the recognition that rights should be seen as a means to an end rather than an end unto themselves. As the debate on obligations has emerged, feminist scholarship has increasingly viewed obligations as a political space that offers opportunities for highlighting a new kind of ethics that has much in common with environmental concerns. To cite one recent contribution concerned with the issues of environmental justice raised in the previous chapter:

> It may be surprising to learn that the environmental movement's next revolution is now being plotted around kitchen tables. In inner cities,

in rural poverty pockets, and on Indian reservations, poor people and people of colour are meeting in kitchens and living rooms, organizing coalitions, and speaking out against pollution that threatens their families and communities. These campaigns, collectively called the 'environmental justice movement', challenged traditional environmental policy, which has too often benefited the affluent at the expense of the poor. (Verchick 2004: 63)

Moreover, these interventions on the *ethics of care* have helped to redefine what obligations mean, challenging the preoccupation with aggregates of individuals, a common assumption in malestream conceptions of obligations (Hirschmann 1996), and posing, in their place, the proposition that atomistic individualism is inappropriate for discussing gender issues. According to Selma Sevenhuijsen, we should think more in terms of the 'self-in-relationship', i.e. that identities are constructed through networks of relationships that pose competing demands in terms of responsibilities (1998; 2000: 5–37). By defining the relationship between the self and others in terms of the flow of communication and mutual redefinition of each actor, these contributions have much in common with phenomenological conceptions of intersubjectivity (where identities are formed through exchanges and other interactions with others and, in so doing, create a common stock of knowledge that enables citizens to manage their various responsibilities).

Moreover, these important questions raise new kinds of concerns regarding the scales appropriate to women's activism, in particular that a transnational dimension should be integrated from the start. Thus, the experience of women in Western industrial societies should not always be the starting point for analysis. As Pangsapa (2007) argues, ethnocentrism tends to lead to the assumption that non-Western women are passive, subject to manipulation, and that their identities are shaped by external forces. In fact, far from being timid, they are a major source of activism and mobilization, even in the apparently powerless situation of being a member of an outsourced manufacturing workforce at the bottom of the global supply chain on the margins of a distant society, a long way from the retail outlets of transnational brand corporations. Such an approach highlights how power relations generate principled resistance even in the least promising and most difficult circumstances.

The concerns of women, especially women engaged in home-based work and other localized forms of productive activity, have often been neglected by international organizations, including the International Labour Organization (ILO), which had primarily been concerned with defending the rights of workers in medium-to-large-scale productive processes (Prügl 1999). Post-colonial feminism has made useful interventions by embracing the complexity in women's experiences with close attention to the mix of factors involved in a specific location and, in the conduct of research, by focusing upon historically and socially specific sexisms, racisms, heterosexisms, and so on. For example, Christine Chin's (1998) ethnographic research, on the role of migrant female domestic labour in Malaysia in the 1980s and 1990s, was based on in-depth interviews with female domestic workers and their employers. In her study, Chin provides a useful insight into how gender processes are at work at the local, national and international level, highlighting how the availability of cheap and plentiful domestic servants from Indonesia and the Philippines liberated the Malaysian middle classes to enjoy the benefits of Westernization, securing active and general consent for a specific form of national development. In her ethnographic study of Thai factory women, Pangsapa (2007) explores the effects of subcontracting and piecework regimes in a peripheral economy within the international division of labour.

As with earlier feminist studies, these investigations seek to establish the resistance strategies developed by women as part of localized emancipatory projects. This can also be seen in recent research on the role of indigenous knowledge in linking local to international developments in research on environmental impacts. One research approach is particularly effective in thinking through the implications of gender identities in relation to the environment – eco-feminism (see Box 2.2).

Box 2.2 Feminist and eco-feminist thinking

Eco-feminist analysis has emerged out of a difficult process of self-criticism in feminist approaches to the social and political order since the 1970s. The feminist standpoint approaches (from radical to socialist) had argued for a transformation of social relations by identifying the real social structures that needed to be changed. They argued that the experiences of women are shaped through social relationships that are oppressive, exploitative and dehumanizing, and that the only way to overcome this is to take the 'standpoint of the oppressed' in patriarchy or capitalism or some combination of the two. In radical feminism, the concept of patriarchy and patriarchal ideology plays a key role in explaining women's experiences. Patriarchy is composed of social structures that regulate appropriate behaviour for men and women and

---

within which women are constrained in certain social spheres. Patriarchy can be defined as a set of social structures that govern social behaviour and within which oppression was made to appear normal. Feminist attempts to secure the emancipation of women from oppressive social relations depended upon mobilizing the women's movement to seek alternative non-elitist forms of social organization and consciousness-raising, with a strong emphasis on the subjective and personal features of women's everyday lives. A key element in this explanation is the idea that power exists at all levels of social existence and that the 'personal is political'.

A great deal of emphasis was placed on controlling biological reproduction for the purposes of emancipation – i.e. that scientific knowledge and technological intervention (contraception and abortion) offered a way of emancipating women from childrearing and its associated social and health implications. This kind of view is now a key part of UN strategies for development. The focus on the varied personal experiences of women by 'black feminism' and lesbian feminism destabilized this approach, however, simply by highlighting problems with the idea that there was a universal experience for all women. In addition, the use of scientific contraceptive technologies to sterilize some black women in the United States, and the use of the female population of many developing societies to test birth control techniques, prompted feminists to reassess the role of science in emancipating women from childbirth. What this highlighted was the important but simple realization that no one formula could account for the complexities of women's experience and, therefore, no single answer could be identified. It became increasingly felt that feminism had simply substituted one set of feminist universal rational categories for androcentric ones. In particular, black feminism raised the prospect that they represented the prejudices of 'colour-blind', white, middle-class feminism in the West, a minority of global womanhood. Eco-feminism developed these arguments into a critique of the interconnections between androcentric knowledge, the domination of women in social relations, and the domination of nature by human beings. In particular, it stressed that the important role played by power relations in everyday life can provide the key to understanding strategies for change. It placed a special emphasis on using the local knowledge and practices of women who have engaged in ecologically sustainable ways of living within the ecosystems they inhabit. Like anarchists, eco-feminists express a preference for decentralized and localized forms of social and political organization, and they have had an important impact on the organizational structures of many green parties (such as in Germany). Nevertheless, they have been critical of everyone in environmental politics from the 'environmental establishment' (established conservation movements) to deep ecology activists for indulging in 'macho-heroics'. They argued that the kind of transformation necessary to resolve environmental problems involves a fundamental shift in human knowledge and values as well as changes in social, political and economic institutions.

Eco-feminism subverts the assumptions of other approaches by identifying the androcentric foundations at work in debates on the environment. Shiva (1989) and King (1989) draw our attention to the close relationship between the domination of nature and the domination of women in the modern world. We should also bear in mind the context of these writings. Shiva and King were writing at a time when the truth claims associated with scientific accounts of the natural world, and the associated beliefs in human progress through mastery of nature, were often taken as authoritative – hence drawing our attention to the close relationship between the assumptions and values we take for granted and how knowledges of the 'natural' and the 'social' are constructed. Joni Seager (1993) demonstrates how eco-feminist arguments apply just as much to the ecological establishment (the conservationist movement and well-known pressure groups), and the 'macho-heroics' of organizations like Earth First, as to the property-based solutions developed by liberal and conservative environmental discourses. Eco-feminist campaigns are also often more low key, linking wider political campaigns to sustainable lifestyles, a kind of politics by example. The Green Belt Movement, initiated by Wangari Maathai, organized poor rural women in Kenya to plant trees to combat deforestation and prevent soil erosion. This movement not only highlights how women's intimate knowledge of the environment is passed down through the generations, it also demonstrates that those communities that can survive and thrive within the limits of their environment are also vulnerable to the impacts of environmental change.

On conservation and biodiversity, Vandana Shiva established Navdanya (which has thirty-four seed banks spread across thirteen Indian states) to support rural women in conserving crops through seed collection and saving and through the promotion of organic farming practices. This campaign is against the reliance on seed monocultures marketed by transnational agricultural corporations (although having the same genetic material, in some cases these seeds do not result in the production of new seed). India also has a long history of indigenous women's movements, not least the Chipko ('tree-hugger') movement that sought to prevent deforestation through commercial logging and maintain traditional subsistence practices – an object neatly captured in their slogan, *ecology is permanent economy*. Similar movements have emerged in Brazil, where women rubber-tappers from forest communities have been engaged in demonstrations to prevent logging of the tropical rainforest. A former rubber-tapper organizer who was appointed as head of the Ministry of the Environment, Senator Marina Silva, highlights how her experiences provide a unique perspective – that responsibility for the rainforests and the freshwater reserves of the Amazon should be seen transnationally, not just in terms of the countries that include parts of the Amazon forest. By focusing on women's role in environmental movements in developing societies, and by paying attention to the close relationship between gender roles and the maintenance of livelihoods, we can see why women's experiences as daughters, wives and mothers need to be linked to political discourses of environmental responsibility. Women are often personally responsible for collecting firewood and water as well as planting and harvesting fruits and vegetables, while, at the same time, they are responsible for transmitting detailed environmental knowledge to their daughters. Consequently, they are often the first to experience the impacts of industrialization and the intensive agricultural practices of modernization. This movement claims unique experiences of the clear link between personal responsibility in a local context and responsibility in the broader global context when understanding justice and obligations.

While Shiva and King were addressing the concerns of the emergent feminist movement in the 1980s, Seager wrote in a different context, where feminism had already worked through some of the difficulties in feminist analysis. Thus, today, it is easier to talk of a variety of feminisms that both acknowledge cultural differences and do not attempt to provide a total solution to the so-called universal experience of patriarchy. At the same time, eco-feminism also addresses the interdependency of the social and the natural and seeks to integrate gender and environment concerns with those of race, ethnicity, social class and national identity (Kirk and Okazawa-Rey 2006). Rachel Stein (2004) asserts that women's

distinct role as caretakers of the family can offer a new window on understanding environmental injustices, one that proposes a new relationship
between political authorities and civil society actors who are female:

> Women are often the caretakers, the daily observers who are the first to
> notice what is amiss in the family, community, and local environment; so
> it is often female relatives or caregivers who mobilize in order to protect
> children and other loved ones from ills such as asthma or lead poisoning
> that are aggravated by environmental factors. These women challenge
> political leaders and health experts who ignore or belittle their suffering
> while blaming mothers for poor care. (Stein 2004: 11)

In addition, this statement highlights an underlying distrust of state
actors and affiliated researchers when dealing with local issues. It has
been suggested that participation in movements for environmental justice
has been politicized, but in a way that conjures up race and class more
than gender (so that the label of feminism is seen as unhelpful). As
a result, the campaigns do not often highlight the gender dimension,
despite the prominence of women activists in high-profile campaigns,
inhibiting the opportunities for broader alliances and the potential for
'movement fusion' (Cole and Foster 2001) Later, we will return to this
problem by addressing how partnerships between citizens and between
state and civil society organizations (based on transparent and inclusive
consultation, active citizen participation and accountable governance) are
essential to establishing workable solutions to a range of environmental
problems.

Gender has not been the only area of social difference that has had
an impact on citizenship studies or highlighted debates on environment
and civic engagement. In the next section we consider contributions on
citizenship and cultural difference as another route whereby identity
politics has opened up to new possibilities.

Identity and citizenship through cultural difference

The emergence of cultural and multicultural citizenship also marks a
significant departure from thinking about citizenship in a universalistic
way. Reconciling the competing demands and desires for respect between
indigenous cultures and the concern to create a broader civic solidarity has been one of the dilemmas for the development of citizenship.
Cultural citizenship has been largely concerned with the construction of
a specific cultural identity through religion, language, habitual customs,
folklore and educational processes that recognize difference as legitimate, whereas multicultural citizenship has been more concerned with

addressing the competing, and sometimes subversive, 'ascriptive identity claims' of ethnic minorities and indigenous peoples (including claims to self-determination), linking these to broader understanding of rights in a specific state. In both cases, temporary (and often undocumented) workers find themselves in a disadvantageous situation. When cultural identity is dislocated from residential location and employment, stateless migrants often find that human rights discourses are more effective in defending their interests than citizenship discourses.

More critically, as Iris Marion Young (1990) has argued, what we have considered to be universal in citizenship has been the disguised particularism of a specific dominant group – i.e. citizenship can cloak the values and interests of those groups that have a privileged place in plural societies. Alternatively, Will Kymlicka stresses the existence of a societal culture (a common history, language and territory) as the context for making meaningful choices. As Kymlicka recognizes, however, liberal institutions are grounded upon certain assumptions, such as individualism, that make minority or group rights difficult to establish. In a context where the language and values of a particular majority dominate, minority claims to be recognized as a people or as a nation demand special consideration. Nevertheless, in this formulation, claims by migrants, by people with disabilities and by gender-specific movements, could only be considered in so far as consideration applied to all citizens or the claims were met through group rights (which may even be discriminatory towards them). For example, group rights for a particular culture may reinforce deeply embedded homophobic, racist and sexist assumptions within that culture.

The shift from recognition of individual rights towards minority or group rights that are particular to group members rather than universal within the territory of a sovereign state (i.e. that are not simply the aggregation of individuals' common interests represented in a procedural process) thus creates new challenges. Group rights have arisen as a way of compensating for disadvantage in plural societies. The most explicit group rights are associated with indigenous cultures – members of the group are subject to a different legal system. A range of rights often described as group rights, however, can just as easily be explained as exceptions to universality (such as rights to healthcare for sexually specific forms of illness or abortion rights). There is always a danger that group rights lead to discriminatory practices, that dominant sectors in the group can control the civil and political processes as well as distribute social welfare unevenly. This raises the question of civic engagement, for the groups that are more effective at mobilization use

45

group rights more effectively; so that a minority group such as the Dalit (the untouchables) in India may not benefit from group rights as much as other castes, although they would offer safeguards against some of the worst forms of discrimination. In another context, the establishment of group rights in terms of religious belief could lead to even greater obstacles to same-sex civil unions being established. Ultimately, rather than protecting minorities, group rights could enable some groups to have greater political control than those intended to benefit or, as in the case of South Africa, could develop into institutionalized segregation on the basis of racial identity. In the case of apartheid this generated attempts to be redefined as a member of another group to facilitate mobility and marriage (see Figure 2.1). In another case, following the Anderson and Wild Report (2007) on alcoholism, drug abuse, domestic violence, child abuse and juvenile prostitution in aboriginal communities in the Northern Territories, the federal government of Australia directly intervened to enforce a ban on alcohol and pornography in 'dysfunc-tional' indigenous communities. This invoked the assertion of human rights and the state's duty to protect children, to regulate groups that had previously acquired self-determination on land rights, although the meas-ures have been criticized for heavy-handedness and for being racist (or at least paternalistic). The situation is complicated by the constitutional status of the powers of the Northern Territories as a devolved governance rather than as a state, and by the shift from self-determination to 'mutual obligations' as part of Shared Responsibility Agreements introduced by the federal government in 2004. Interestingly, in this case, the balance between group rights and human rights is increasingly linked to debates on obligation and duty rather than just entitlements and rights.

Similarly, in Brazil, indigenous people have become more actively involved in all phases of identification and demarcation of indigenous lands. In the past they were regarded as 'minors' who needed assistance from responsible political authorities (Lisansky 2005: 171). Even though indigenous lands are the property of the state, 'the regularization process recognizes and formalizes indigenous rights and specifically guarantees perpetual usufruct by indigenous people of their lands'. Lisansky men-tions, however, that the Brazilian government had expressed reservations about the use of language 'that might imply sovereignty of indigenous areas' and cites an instance where the Brazilian government requested that the World Bank use the term *indigenous people* rather than *indigenous peoples*, because the latter implied sovereignty (ibid.: 176).

When we bring contending groups into the equation, etymology presents particular problems for understanding 'citizenship', i.e. as

1985 had at least 1000 "chameleons"

Political staff

PARLIAMENT – More than 1000 people officially changed colour last year.

They were reclassified from one race group to another by the stroke of a Government pen.

Details of what is dubbed "the chameleon dance" were given in reply to Opposition questions in Parliament.

The Minister of Home Affairs, Mr Stoffel Botha, disclosed that during 1985:

- 702 coloured people turned white.
- 19 whites became coloured.
- One Indian became white.

- Three Chinese became white.
- 50 Indians became coloured.
- 43 coloureds became Indians.
- 21 Indians became Malay.
- 30 Malays went Indian.
- 249 blacks became coloured.
- 20 coloureds became black.
- Two blacks became "other Asians".
- One black was classified Griqua.
- 11 coloureds became Chinese.
- Three coloureds went Malay.
- One Chinese became coloured.
- Eight Malays became coloured.
- Three blacks were classed as Malay.
- No blacks became white and no whites became black.

Figure 2.1 Changing identities under apartheid

a space for establishing rights and the cultivation of identity within the context of 'the city'. As such, the notion of citizen has connoted belonging (*within* the city) and simultaneously conjures up 'the other' (*without* or beyond the city), whether this is constructed in terms of the city, community, region, nation, commonwealth or regional economic integration organization (such as the European Union). As a result, the idea of citizenship has often been articulated within nationalist and racist discourses, linking civil, political and social rights to members of particular political spaces. The experience of marginalized groups has been that it has been more effective to cite human rights rather than citizenship where their claims are not seen as justiciable.

In post-colonial contexts, as Isin and Turner (2002: 5–7) indicate, the status of minorities such as Australian peoples of aboriginal descent has even been subject to retrospective designation as 'aliens'. More often, movements for self-determination (such as the MDFC in Senegal, MOSOP in Nigeria and the OLF in Ethiopia) are seen as threats to national sovereignty from a sub-national group even though they articulated their claims through human rights discourse (Welch 2000: 110). Isin and Turner (2002) also highlight how citizenship has been fixated on rights (in terms of the environment and sexual identity), while obligations to the state or the community have been colonized by authoritarian discourses. Citizenship has also been seen, however, as a space where oppositional social movements can expand rights claims from the civil and political to incorporate social rights (especially when considering gender and racial

Citizens, citizenship and citizenization

identity), and more recently obligations have been seen as essential to campaigns for transformation.

If we focus exclusively on rights, for example the tensions between universal and particularistic or group rights, then the likely result is conflict between different claims and the possibility of the construction of a politics of enemies. Obligations often demand respect for, or at least awareness of, other claims, however – for example, that opponents should be respected as adversaries – so that supporters of group rights claims recognize that certain universal standards can be applicable (such as the respect for life enshrined in the abolition of capital punishment) while also recognizing that the scale and form of punishments may differ within the legal norms of an indigenous culture.

In the Aristotelian tradition, being a good and virtuous citizen has often been tied to active involvement in the community. It is not insignificant that the broadening of meaning of citizenship should also be marked by a move to go beyond the concerns of self-governance and legal status to the way citizens act in and through associations and to the way citizens follow particular norms on the appropriate conduct of those associations. This has also included a widening of the net of responsibilities. Young (2006) argues that we focus too much on blame and not enough on responsibility. Thus we need to move from a liability model that focuses on individual agents who cause harm through aberrant acts that have already taken place, towards the social connection model that shares out responsibility among all participants in ongoing social processes, based on normal structural relations (although the precise form of responsibility will vary). For Young, 'all agents who contribute by their actions to the structural processes that produce injustice have responsibilities to work to remedy these injustices' (ibid.: 102–3). Tackling injustices should be forward-looking rather than just retrospective attempts to establish who is liable for past harms, and take account of the spatial organization of the processes that generate injustices – so that 'agents share responsibility with others who are differently situated' (ibid.: 130). This does not presume that all agents have a common interest in promoting justice (or an equal capacity to do so), as demonstrated when we consider the environmental implications of these developments. Just as knowledge and capacity for acting are socially distributed, so too is responsibility.

Recently, the Indigenous Environmental Network brought together indigenous peoples in North America to develop the Bemidji Statement (2006) to engender respect for the commons and promote the precautionary principle in terms of guardianship responsibility in order to acknowledge the 'Seventh Generation' (i.e. future generations). This

Box 2.3 Between the who and the we: the Bemidji statement of the Iroquois nation

Who guards this web of life that nurtures and sustains us all?

Who watches out for the land, the sky, the fire, and the water?

Who watches out for our relatives that swim, fly, walk, or crawl?

Who watches out for the plants that are rooted in our Mother Earth?

Who watches out for the life-giving spirits that reside in the underworld?

Who tends the languages of the people and the land?

Who tends the children and the families?

Who tends the peacekeepers in our communities?

We tend the relationships.

We work to prevent harm.

We create the conditions for health and wholeness.

We teach the culture and we tell the stories.

We have the sacred right and obligation to protect the common wealth of our lands and the common health of our people and all our relations for this generation and seven generations to come.

We are the Guardians for the Seventh Generation.

development does more than assert obligations from present to future generations. It insists that present conduct has to be carried out with a conjoining obligation to understand the complex interdependency of human and natural relations in the 'web of life' – i.e. we the living have a responsibility to acquire as much knowledge as we can about the water, the forests and the plains, and of the species that inhabit them, and to both repair any damage and report back to other guardians on the current status of the environment.

The Bemidji statement captures one of the essential connections in the current debate on environment and citizenship – strategies for change should be based on the lived experience of citizens and their ongoing relationships with the environment. Above all else, ecological citizenship is grounded through citizens understanding the reasons for change rather than obeying a set of instructions or responding to financial incentives in a utilitarian model of action. This statement also maps on to Agyeman and Evans's (2004: 157) account of 'just sustainability' – we should address quality of life, the relationship between present and future generations, be mindful of justice and equity in resource allocation, and ensure that the results of policy work within ecological limits. If we turn to movements beyond North America, we can see similar kinds of responses emerging. The World Mountain People Association states that their vision of the environment respects and cares for life, ecosystems and future generations. Moreover, they support the recovery and reconstruction of knowledge of the interdependent relations between society and the environment as well as the promotion of environmental education through state institutions to promote this knowledge.

Understanding the circuit of justice: from entitlements and obligations to virtues

In previous sections we have seen how 'citizenship' is a contested space where different social forces seek to articulate it within broader discourses, that the meaning of citizenship depends on its relationship to other concepts such as rights, obligations, the individual and the social. In certain times and places a particular meaning may dominate by becoming part of taken-for-granted common sense, a tacit reference point by which citizens and institutions may know their entitlements and obligations. But in the long and sometimes in the short term, the meanings change and different projects compete to achieve dominance. In addition, the reader will have noticed that justice and citizenship are often connected in political discourses. To prepare the way for the next chapter, this section focuses on how the concept of justice is articulated in environmental discourses and how ethics and politics are intimately related. To this end we have developed the metaphor of the circuit of justice to highlight how its component elements can be understood and also combined in different ways (illustrated in Figure 2.2).

The circuit of justice should be seen not primarily in terms of subservience to the will of the society in question but as a route through which positive qualities of citizens – virtues such as prudence, courage and temperance – can be cultivated so that the development of individual citizens matches the way they respect other citizens. Correspondingly, tendencies that lead to non-virtuous behaviour and failures to respect others (whether these are strangers, non-human animals or the wider components of the biotic community such as trees, land and oceans) generate corrosive effects on the community of citizens. Of course, while neoliberal conceptions are often associated with vices (especially in the rhetoric of anti-globalization protesters), we should not start with a definite assumption, for there are circumstances in which property ownership can have positive effects on subordinate groups (including peasant tenant farmers who acquire land rights or welfare recipients or low-income earners who secure personal ownership in formerly public housing). In situations such as these, farmers can ensure the long-term sustainability of a particular environment for their offspring just as former housing tenants can devote their resources to the improvement of housing stock.

According to Isin and Turner, the 'politics of virtue has a thick rather than thin view of the citizen of a nation, namely of the citizen as a complex, educated and vibrant member of a society' (2002: 8). In addition, John Barry identifies that 'a virtue-based account, unlike rationalist accounts of ethics, focuses on the character of the individual agent ... the cultural valuations of the natural world which form the background and framework within which character formation and individual moral action take place' (1999: 32). This goes beyond the *ecological self* of deep ecology approaches to recognize the 'political' character of virtues and the fact that they have a part to play in all power relations, whether this occurs in the public or the private sphere.

While national conceptions of rights and duties still shape our conception of being a citizen (i.e. the nation-state can offer legal safeguards for individual and group rights), many aspects of human experience, such as cultural identity, scientific knowledge, political influence, economic independence and personal security, are no longer guaranteed through the space of nationhood. This does not mean that the state is irrelevant but highlights how transnational forces are involved in the construction of types of citizenship and how transnational arenas have become the sites of contestation for articulating rights claims and for establishing the ties that bind which have the potential for generating obligations and duties. This argument does not rely on simplistic conceptions of globalization (characteristic of both defenders and the sternest critics of globalization), for the emergence of transnational arenas presents both obstacles and opportunities for promoting environmental responsibility. As will be outlined in Chapter 3, environmental citizenship tends to work within broadly liberal conceptions of rights and obligations. Ecological citizenship goes farther, however, to suggest that the political conceptions are also susceptible to ethical norms grounded in the many and varied traditions of environmental ethics.

Sometimes this is expressed in terms of the contrast between eco-centric and anthropocentric conceptions of justice, but even here we should acknowledge the combination of elements, each of which can be defined in very different ways. As a result, particular ways of thinking about injustice, and the forms of citizenship that emerge or come into being to address them, involve various elements that are defined and combined in different ways. Figure 2.2 presents these in abstract and

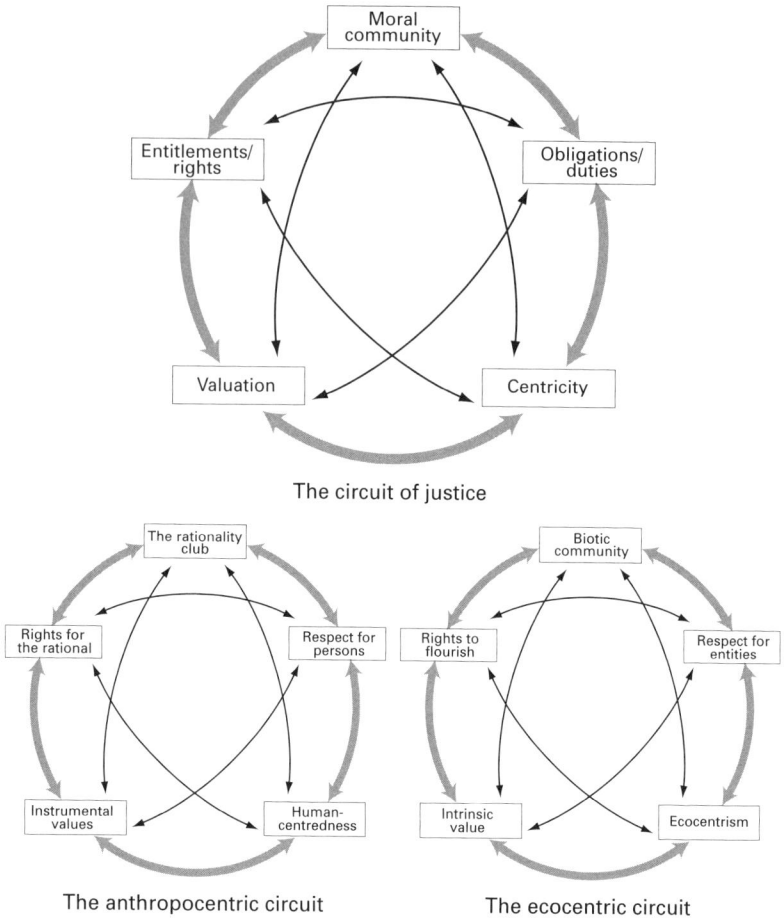

The circuit of justice

The anthropocentric circuit   The ecocentric circuit

Note: The connecting arrows indicate the ways in which specific discourses articulate relations of connection between elements of a discourse.

Figure 2.2 Circuits of justice

provides two commonplace illustrations of how they can be articulated as anthropocentric or ecocentric circuits. We should be mindful that the examples provided here should not be seen as privileged in the current situation, although, at the same time, they did shape the debate over sustainability from the 1970s through to the 1990s.

The hard distinctions between anthropocentric and ecocentric approaches, or even those suggested between strong and weak sustainability, no longer seem so clear and visible. In particular, both intrinsic and instrumental valuation are seen as being open to a variety of definitions

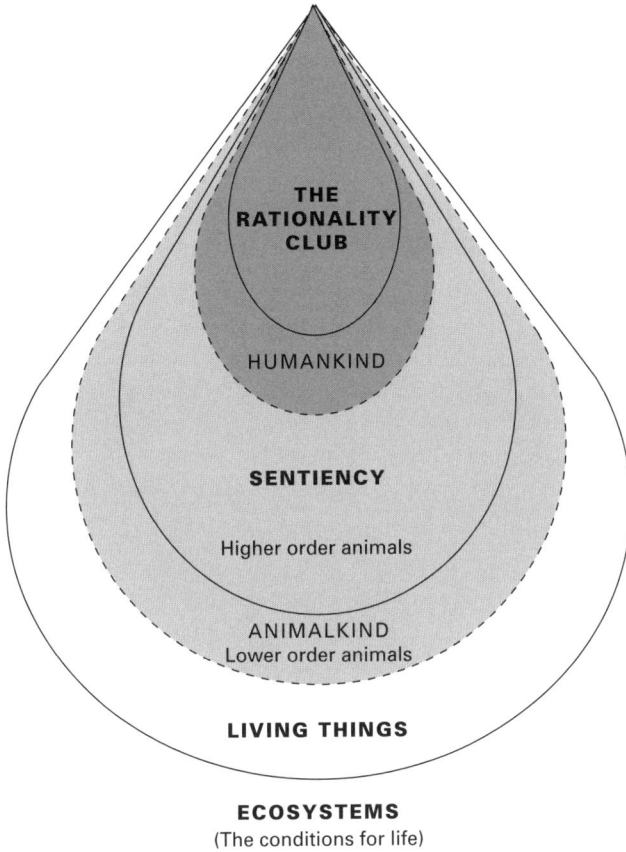

THE
RATIONALITY
CLUB

HUMANKIND

SENTIENCY

Higher order animals

ANIMALKIND
Lower order animals

LIVING THINGS

ECOSYSTEMS
(The conditions for life)

Figure 2.3 The ethical teardrop

while, as will be demonstrated in Chapter 3, the relationship between rights and obligations remains an area of intense discussion. It is also fair to say they reflect the environmental ideologies of what we described in Chapter 1 as the advocacy stage of environmental movements, connoting the desire of NGOs and movements to maintain their outsider status or, alternatively, to influence political decision-making without damaging their position as the sources of impartial authoritative expertise on particular areas of conservation or pollution control.

If we take just one of these elements – the moral community, for instance – and consider how many ways in which this can be defined, then the complexity of ethico-political articulation should become apparent. Each of the boundaries for moral consideration in Figure 2.3 has featured in one or another ethical approach to the environment. If a boundary is defined in terms of species membership then this creates problems in terms of excluding other animals and thus has fixated on what justifies human power over nature. The capacity for human reason, or alternatively imagination or language, has been deployed in many discourses, assuming that human uniqueness exists as a justification for mastery over nature while at the same time demoting some members of the human species (on the grounds of development, gender and/or cultural identity) to being akin to other sentient beings.

If sentiency is regarded as a basis for consideration, this does not automatically mean that non-human animals should have rights, but it does summon obligations of guardianship for active citizens to respect and to take care of animals – animal welfare is analogous to the responsibilities of taking care of children, and people with intellectual impairments or other frailties. Residing within this debate is the unquestioned assumption that *agents* (with full capacities that qualify them for active citizenship) should act for (moral and political) *patients*. So, rather than challenging the 'rationality club', the question then becomes: 'for whom are *the rational* responsible and what obligations do they have towards them?'. For example, interestingly, while a case is emerging for primates to have rights, this has been primarily asserted in terms of their affinity with the human species rather than by undermining speciesism itself. The debate on animal rights and welfare, therefore, has often consolidated rather than challenged the basis of the boundary decisions. Environmental ethics, a tradition that displayed considerable hostility to debates on the status of animals (as opposed to species), has alternatively fixated on what obligations exist for human agents for forests, wilderness areas, mountains, ecosystems, biomes, and what Leopold identified as the biotic community. Consequently, the challenges to traditional moral boundaries, and the assumptions that underpin these, have been plagued by confusion and crossed messages just as much as similar debates on which human beings should count in morals and politics. How then to bridge the presumed gap between ethics and politics? The answer proposed here is not to presume this is the problem at all but to acknowledge the *naming* of this gap as the problem that has inhibited the proposal of solutions.

As Chapter 3 will illustrate, ethicists have often sought to impose answers on political questions while political theorists have sought to impose answers on moral questions. Alternatively, they have disassociated their conclusions from politics or morality respectively. If we start from a different perspective and assume that there is no clear gap, that ethics and politics are always intertwined, then we can avoid these problems.

Take, for example, the debate on the consideration of future generations that lies at the heart of discussions on sustainable development. Political theorists have challenged the idea that it is possible for future generations to participate in political processes on the supposed self-evident grounds that present generations can affect future generations but not vice versa (that a reciprocal relationship does not exist). The power relationship between them is asymmetrical and living people have limited knowledge of what future generations will consider to be in their interests (Barry 1978).

Since the Brundtland Report (1987), few have suggested that concern about future generations should not be considered in environmental policy-making. Is the question merely a spatio-temporal one? Also, we do take account of the past in current political discussions. Traditions are a relevant example. As G. K. Chesterton stated: 'Tradition ... is the democracy of the dead ... [it] refuses to submit to the small and arrogant oligarchy of those who merely happen to be walking about' (1908: 56). So, if we include the past in decisions of the present, should we not also consider the impacts of our decisions on distant future generations? Just like 'the environment' (in the present or the near future), future generations (unborn citizens) lack effective representation in current policy-making. They are presently constituencies rather than stakeholders. Thus the problem is not whether they should be recognized but how best to establish mechanisms to represent them, to ensure that their interests *are* recognized, and to ensure that these interests are taken seriously.

Now, let's take the argument a little farther – and it is not such a new argument, as Kavka and Warren (1983) testify – by posing a question. Is it not also possible to create deliberative contexts in which future generations, primates, trees, forests, ecosystems and even the strangers who man the production lines of outsourced manufacturing in the global supply chain (to name a few examples of unrepresented constituencies) can have representatives to assess the impacts of policy-making on their behalf? If political and corporate decisions have consequences that affect certain interests, then the presence of articulate defenders, stewards or guardians, offers a chance of avoiding significant harm, or at least being able to ensure that potential future harms as well as present harms are mitigated.

The unfinished business of citizenship: towards a theory of citizenization

Environmental movements have often been expressed as transformational projects and, certainly, ecological thought has posed challenges to established political and ethical discourses. In terms of citizenship debates, environmental issues have sought to bridge the disciplinary divides between morality, politics and, to some extent, aesthetics. As demonstrated by the discussion of eco-feminism, transformist movements have moved beyond universalistic assumptions and grand visions of social change. This is a product of women's movements directly encountering environmentalism as a loosely connected 'movement of movements' with divergent diagnoses of the ills of the world and envisioning just as many different solutions. In addition, there is a more diverse set of strategies and tactics in current environmental movements, which is probably associated with the tactical proliferation of the anti-globalization protests. Many environmental movements now use a range of cultural strategies (street parties and discos, quilting societies, poetry readings and storytelling, tea parties, the 'rebel clown insurgent army' using fancy dress and slapstick to disrupt political conference events, as well as the more traditional armoury of speeches, demonstrations and marches) to get their message across in fickle media, and find new ways to win hearts and minds. In addition, cultural strategies have often been safer when addressing environmental issues in more authoritarian regimes, and even in liberal democracies that are more security conscious since 9/11. Cultural performances have thus become vehicles of dissent in environmental politics.

Nick Crossley (2002) also highlights the complicated structure of contemporary social movements using the vivid analogy of a movement as a protest iceberg. At the tip are the highly visible protest events such as the 'battle of Seattle' and anti-WTO protests in Prague, street carnivals like 'Reclaim the streets' as well as mass bicycle demonstrations to produce traffic gridlock. Then there are the less visible protests and organizational events – debates, meetings, magazine and website production, the publication of books such as Monbiot's *Captive State* (2001). Much less obvious in issue-based group or movement politics are the 'social movement organizations and networks' (SMOs), the activists who generate these events, and the wider constituency of citizens who are sympathetic and interested in these kinds of politics (Crossley 2002: 667–73). Incidentally, this does not mean that environmental movements are simply oppositional. Agyeman and Evans (2003) point to the need for seeing them increasingly as a participative mechanism in environmental governance, such as the Dudley Street Neighbourhood Initiative in Boston (a community-based non-profit organization that takes responsibility for the economic, social and environmental health of that community), which has sought not only to facilitate citizens' access to decision-making but also to protect and enhance the quality of the local environment. In this example of 'broad-focus civic environmentalism', environmental injustice is not a result of a lack of access (a narrow-focus approach concentrating on rights) but a result of the inability of communities to be responsible for and develop active strategies that promote economic vitality, ecological integrity, civic democracy and social well-being, so constituting 'just sustainability'. Agyeman is concerned to stress that it is not just affordable social housing which DSNI promotes but energy-efficient affordable housing because the inhabitants are least able to bear energy costs (Agyeman and Evans 2006: 191–2).

Both the changes in tactics and the more fragmented and fluid political structures (both internally but also in partnerships with business and governments) point to three new features of environmental politics. First, a clearer focus on the informal, unorthodox mechanisms of participation and dissent. Second, an awareness of the need to address human duties, responsibilities and obligations as well as rights in a way that links personal and community experience to governance. Third, a sensitivity to the importance of everyday meanings in shaping the agenda on the environment and in helping people understand the reasons for ecologically beneficial activities. All three of these concerns are brought together in the ongoing debate on the precise meaning of citizenship, on how forms of citizenship come into being, and the ongoing debate on what it means as a 'politics of obligation'.

Clearly, something deeper is under way, and it is the contention of this book that it is the recognition that entitlements and obligations (or more formally, rights and duties) work in tandem though not necessarily reciprocally which has changed the way in which citizenship is understood. We also need to acknowledge, however, that the precise configuration of each manifestation of this relationship is shaped by culturally specific circumstances, the modes of regulation through the construction of political subjectivities and the space–time character of the problems under consideration. Even though these will be addressed in more detail in the conclusion, it should already be evident that citizenship invokes more than legal statutes and political recognition. While these are important aspects of how we think of ourselves as citizens, they do not capture the contestation over the meaning(s) of citizenship (some examples of which have been developed above). Citizenship is a space or site of contestation where new configurations of entitlements and obligations can be articulated through different agents. Citizens and new ways of thinking about citizenship come into being through the development of civic engagement strategies that link awareness of injustices to responsibility. It is in that sense that we also need to think about *citizenization*, for the way we define and articulate what it means to be a citizen is in process, provisional and never completed.

Since much of the twentieth century was taken up with the specification of entitlements and rights, the other side, that of obligations, duties and responsibility, has been neglected and, probably worse, left to the activities of traditionalists, conservatives and sometimes fascists. The challenge facing us in the twenty-first century is to find ways of making obligations transformational. In the context of this book, the debate on the environment and citizenship forces us to rethink the relationship between entitlements and obligations and question the assumption that other members of the biotic community can be protected only if they have rights. As this debate has unfolded so far, two currents have emerged: one that tries to maintain a distinction between morality and politics, conceptual clarification being the prime objective, and another that treats the questions in a more strategic way and argues that the lived experience of environmental politics demands that we see ethics and citizenly relations as intertwined. This will now be addressed in Chapter 3, which explores contemporary debates on the construction of ecological citizenship in much more detail.

3 | Rethinking environment and citizenship

Questioning the starting point

The debate on environmental and ecological citizenship provides an important opportunity for us to explore the relations between ethical and political discourses and to consider how the ideas of moral community and political community are articulated. Two options for exploring the relations and ideas have emerged. First, privileging philosophy, particularly environmental ethics, as a guide to the normative conduct of politics, alongside suggestions for expanding the moral community so that future generations (Kavka and Warren 1983), non-human animals (Regan 1984), living things (Goodpaster 1983) or varying conceptions of broader ecosystems (Leopold 1949; Naess 1973; Devall and Sessions 1985) receive moral consideration. Grounding ecological citizenship in the application of a specific tradition of environmental ethics, such as utilitarianism or deep ecology, however, often assumes that there are universalistic principles that can be applied to all cases (for example, future-thinking felicific calculus or biocentric egalitarianism respectively). The second option draws from political theory and develops conceptions of the political community to establish realistic objectives through which environmental or ecological citizenship can be achieved while also squeezing the gap between 'law and justice' (Dobson 2003a; Bell 2005). The advantage of this focus is that it draws us away from the empirical fixation on the gap between attitudes and behaviour (which often generated a concern with rational assumptions susceptible to incentives and disincentives), and pushes us towards a concern with the gap between values and action.

The character of these debates on environmental responsibility mirrors discussions about epistemology, where the search for the truth, objective knowledge or perhaps verisimilitude has taken precedence. Such accounts were described as 'idealized reconstructions' of the scientific method rather than as 'logics in use' (Kaplan 1964). Detailed ethnographic studies on the actual practices of scientists have demonstrated how knowledge is a social product regardless of whether these practices are conceived as disciplinary matrices (Kuhn 1970), produced within organized academic communities (Knorr-Cetina 1981; Latour and Woolgar 1978; Mulkay 1991), generated by research programmes (in one case, grudgingly conceded, minus the 'mob psychology' of normal science, by the critical rationalist, Imre Lakatos 1970), or in schools and intellectual circles. So, just as scientific judgement is bound to social context, so too is ethical and aesthetic judgement.

Conceptual clarification and the generation of theoretical and empirical tests are important tasks but no more important than the task of understanding the concrete circumstances on the ground and the strategic considerations that arise through practical action. For this reason, we want to persuade readers to think in terms of the relationship between the *first-order constructs* of the people at the heart of an environmental problem (whose responses and activism so often provide an object for investigation) and the *second-order constructs* of researchers in this field. Researchers have a responsibility to find these connections and negotiate a balance between explaining and understanding as well as between detachment and involvement. In addition, this strategic orientation prompts recognition that complex (social, natural and socio-natural) relations and processes should not be artificially reduced to simple causal relationships.

Consider again the example in Chapter 1. Responsibility for the Love Canal incident should be seen as distributed widely, but most accounts of this event tend to emphasize two explanations – that the event was a classic example of corporate irresponsibility or that it was the effect of political decisions to enact policy without consideration of the consequences. Both the decisions of corporations and political authorities are important but this does not take us far in addressing or preventing similar problems elsewhere. Ethical concerns are also better understood in the context of application. The actors involved may subscribe to a heady mix of religious values, utilitarian logic, a Kantian sense of injustice (i.e. 'why should I not be treated like everyone else'), ecological consciousness, and may even endorse a range of virtues from prudence to temperance. The ways in which these are manifest are often hybrid and analytically inconsistent – utilitarian logic emphasizes aggregate consequences while Kantian assumptions highlight how the infliction of environmental harm on a few should never be outweighed by the benefits for the many. Nevertheless, the hybrid expressions of ethical judgements can be just as effective as a basis for action and as a basis for achieving change in environmental policy.

As outlined in more detail in the latter part of this book, environmental policy and action seek to use levers that discourage particular actions while encouraging others. Less attention, however, is paid to whether citizens understand the reasons for acting responsibly.

Similarly, academic researchers often impose rationalist conceptions of actual or ideal political or moral communities, where everyone has the same opportunity to initiate speech acts, interrogate, open debate, or make judgements in the 'original position'. These approaches relegate concern for the environment in terms of 'content' rather than form, however, and neglect the actual processes of civic engagement in the concrete strategic situation. In addition, they rest their case on a conception of the citizen as a rational 'minimaxing' actor who makes decisions according to rational calculations and who assumes that other actors will do likewise. This simplification of human action to one ideal type, rational action, is a simplistic exaggeration of one human trait. Certainly, the application of incentives has led to greater compliance with certain environmental policy measures, but it has not always generated a sense of responsibility that leads to changes in other aspects in the lives of citizens. The assumptions behind these measures not only present us with an unrealistic account of how citizens behave, but also neglect a range of so-called 'non-rational' motivations that can have environmentally beneficial effects. Many environmental actions are seen as being in the self-interest of citizens, such as installing energy-efficient light bulbs and solar panels in households or utilizing other energy conservation measures. The adoption of similar measures by companies, applied to the whole life-cycle of their products and services, is part and parcel of ecological modernization. Yet many of these actions do not lead to changes in understanding. Citizens may adopt energy conservation techniques simply as a way of reducing their fuel bills rather than out of a real concern for the environment and may not even be aware of the causes and far-flung effects of climate change. Likewise businesses may adopt life-cycle analysis and promote recycling of their products but do so to cut costs and improve profitability. Moreover, these measures do not necessarily affect other activities by citizens or corporations unless immediate interests are at stake.

Many approaches to environment and citizenship tend to use a disciplinary knowledge as a launching pad rather than adopt an explicitly transdisciplinary approach that is object-oriented rather than procedure-bound (an issue to which we return at the end of this chapter). Consequently, this chapter challenges both philosophy-centred and politics-centred approaches in favour of a strategic orientation that focuses on how ethical and political *elements* are articulated in 'modes of citizenship', whether these are civil, political, social or ecological (Roche 1992; Christoff 1996; Smith 1998a, 1999) and transformed into *moments* where these conceptions have the temporary appearance of permanence. In challenging both disciplines, the approach proposed here considers how the elements articulated through 'modes of citizenship' regulate the production of meaning on entitlements and obligations and generate 'subject positions' in which individuals can invest their identities. Rather than treating *citizenship* as an abstract conceptual device, we argue that it is better understood as an ethico-political space where the right, the good and the virtuous are acknowledged as provisional, open to contestation and subject to deliberation. Conceptions of community, justice, rights, obligations and citizenship need reappraisal in order to provide an adequate vocabulary that can address the many difficulties created by environmental problems. The *return to virtues* in ethical and political discussions on the environment (Barry 1999; Dobson 2003a) offers interesting ways of rethinking the meaning of obligation, where the cultivation of the character of the self acts as a route for the regard of others. This chapter, however, argues that we should not treat one kind of virtue – compassion or justice – as the basis of all other virtues. Subsequent chapters highlight how these discussions manifest themselves at a practical level in relation to policy formation.

Minding the gaps: from 'attitudes and behaviour' to 'values and action'

Opinion research has often indicated that individuals have broad commitments to addressing climate change, the safe storage and disposal of hazardous wastes, promoting renewable energy sources and reducing pollution levels. At the same time, studies of behaviour often do not demonstrate how attitudes generate activities that lead to environmentally responsible actions, especially when the means of resolving a problem (waste incinerators, wind farms, nuclear waste storage facilities, highway construction projects to reroute traffic from population centres) or indirect impacts such as the fall in employment opportunities are perceived as having an adverse effect on a particular community. Localized or regional NIMBY ('not in my backyard') responses account for part of the difficulty (especially on issues such as nuclear waste). They do not, however, account for the gaps between knowledge and understanding of the processes of climate change and personal decisions to invest in motor vehicle transportation over long distances between home and work or in holiday travel that requires long-haul flights to different parts of the world.

Indeed, environmental awareness is often associated with the desire to be closer to nature, to have access to green spaces and experience environments that are unlike the ones with which we are familiar. Parents move their families from urban areas to suburban or rural ones in the desire to have a better environment for their children to grow up in, consequently having to commute long distances to workplaces in order to maintain their 'nouveau-environmental' lifestyles. These privatized ways of ensuring access to environmental 'goods', for those who can absorb the costs, are based on the same attitudes that are recorded in opinion surveys that attempt to quantitatively and qualitatively measure environmental knowledge. Similarly, awareness of biodiversity may be stimulated by an expensive long-haul flight to an African safari resort or to an eco-tourist haven in South-East Asia, implying that awareness can also have a price in terms of leaving a larger ecological footprint. If we consider travel use, regulating fuel and engine capabilities and tax incentives on efficient vehicles, these have achieved some good results. Jillian Anable (2005) identified how reductions in energy demand have to take into account the motivations of citizens in choosing the means of achieving their eco-friendly objectives – using less energy-intensive transport, ensuring that consumption does not depend on goods and services that have high energy uses, improving access to environmentally enhanced activities in the locality, and ensuring that groups experiencing higher levels of environmental bads and lower levels of environmental goods, do not find themselves in a worse situation than before. For Anable, as well as the Smarter Choices research team at the Department of Transport (UK), voluntary 'soft', 'smart' or 'bespoke' measures are underexploited, even though they could be promoted in simple ways such as providing households with information about public transport or opportunities for car pooling, providing travel planning tips, creating opportunities for teleworking and teleconferencing, and taking advantage of the Internet and local shopping services (Cairns et al. 2004). Anable's high-intensity scenario projections raise the possibility that these kinds of measures can generate an 11 per cent reduction in traffic (including reductions of 21 per cent in urban peak traffic, 13 per cent in urban off-peak traffic, 14 per cent in non-urban peak traffic and 7 per cent in non-urban off-peak traffic). She also highlights different kinds of psychological responses to the issues.

- *Malcontented motorists* accept that they have responsibility to restrict their car use and thus experience stress when driving but doubt that there are more feasible forms of travel.
- *Car complacents* do not make the connection between their travel practices and congestion and do not feel the need to restrict car use.
- *Diehard drivers* are psychologically dependent on car use and are therefore unwilling to sacrifice for environment.
- *Aspiring environmentalists* see cars as having a practical use,

acknowledge environmental responsibility, and have already reduced or are willing to reduce car use.

- *Car sceptics* have strong environmental awareness and sense of responsibility, and thus avoid car ownership, use alternative modes of travel, and view public transport positively.
- *Reluctant riders* use cars when they have opportunity, prefer access to motorized vehicles unless restricted by lower incomes (for example, the elderly), and are motivated by thrift rather than environmental awareness.
- *Car aspirers* tend to use public transport and see cars as an object of desire but are not motivated by environmental awareness. (Anable et al. 2005)

While these typifications serve as a useful set of categories for highlighting different kinds of responses to car use, they also highlight the socio-economic factors involved (such as those discussed in Chapter 1 when exploring the environmental justice movement). Much depends on the capacity to act as well as a willingness to act, especially when given access to recycling facilities or green market networks, or depends on the availability of employment that facilitates home working. In many developed societies, researchers and governments often simply equate the problem of a lack of civic engagement on environmental issues with a lack of awareness of environmental issues (Barr 2003), and point out that knowing the facts often leads to attitudinal change and, in turn, to more responsible behaviour in a linear way. Certainly, the possession of practical knowledge (such as 'knowledge of' vegetable gardening and animal husbandry in the slow food movement) provides a basis for responsible action, and this can be a significant factor, as opposed to 'knowledge about' (James 1890), i.e. general abstract knowledge of climate change or the effects of toxic chemicals. This ignores, however, two important issues: that a range of other factors may be involved; and that citizens accept, modify and reinterpret the information provided by scientists, governments, NGOs and other sources, in the everyday discourses through which they make sense of the world (Burningham and O'Brien 1994). Barr (2003: 229–30) suggests that empirical research has identified three continua of values:

1 from egoistic to altruistic values and from being conservative to being open to change (with the latter, in both cases, prompting environmental responsibility);
2 from anthropocentrism to biocentrism (including instrumental and intrinsic valuation respectively);

3 from technocentrism to ecocentrism as 'belief driven values' in response to environmental problems.

Environmental psychologists have considered these (when, in fact, they are simplistic, ideal-type oppositions) and other factors as independent variables, as empirically real and as causally relevant. In addition, they suggest that they can explain environmental activism as a consequence of personality types, identities (gender, religious affiliation, ethnicity and social class), intrinsic motivation (i.e. the degree of personal satisfaction achieved through environmentally responsible actions) and social pressure (especially where the behaviour is visible to peers, and when reputations are at stake). Interestingly, Barr sees variables involving 'norms' as synonymous with citizens feeling moral obligations, but, as with studies of criminality, fears of the loss of status or regard for others should not be confused with citizenly acts that demonstrate that actors understand the reasons for the act or that they genuinely feel obliged to act in a certain way. So, rather than just focus on the search for empirical regularities between attitudes and behaviour, it is crucial to examine the intentions of actors and the tacit knowledge or the taken-for-granted assumptions of citizens. In addition, psychological approaches tend to consider actors in individualistic terms rather than as citizens who may be individuals, corporations, NGOs, unions or movements. All these 'citizens' should not be viewed as solely operating in the private sphere but also as making interventions in the public sphere, participating in partnerships with political authorities while also simultaneously engaging in self-regulation. Such studies tend to focus on actions in a way that could be interpreted as suggesting the privatization of environmental responsibility (i.e. an abdication of responsibility by political authorities) rather than challenging the distinction between public and private. The construction of ecological citizens is better seen as involving new ways of producing the meaning of entitlements and obligations, whereby values and action inform one another in culturally specific ways but are also shaped by open and tolerant discussion that does not ignore the passions and commitments involved in environmental activism.

The indeterminacy of culture, as an 'everyday laboratory of civilization' (Beck 2000: 147) where we can make up meanings as we go along, has also been presented as a key feature of environmental cosmopolitanism. While this recognizes and even celebrates cultural diversity and innovation, however, ironically it displays an abhorrence of bio-invasion and trans-boundary pollution, when confronting the fact that natural and socio-natural processes can be unruly too. As a result, environmental

65

Box 3.1 Educating environmental citizens in the UK
(*source*: Dobson 2003/04)

Do we have a right to an environment adequate for our health and well-being? Citizenship is key to both environmental sustainability and social justice. It is the statutory responsibility of secondary schools to teach citizenship ... and offers the chance to expose students to environmental citizenship. Broadly, there are two kinds of reasons why people might have to move to more sustainable forms of behaviour – because of incentives and disincentives associated with doing or not doing so, or because they regard it as the right thing to do. The Government's sustainability strategy is based almost entirely on the former. Faced with the task of complying with EU regulatory demands to reduce the volume of biodegradable municipal waste sent to landfill by 2010, the Downing Street Strategy Unit charged with proffering policy alternatives noted that 'there are few financial incentives in place for either industry or households to seek alternatives to landfill'. With this premise established, the solution to the problem is obvious and the Unit predictably recommends, 'Greater freedom for local authorities to develop new financial incentives for householders to reduce and recycle their waste. Householders currently pay the same Council Tax no matter how much waste they produce or whether they recycle or not. This means that they have no incentive to manage their waste in more sustainable ways'. A concrete suggestion floated in the summer of last year was to charge people for taking over-quota sacks of rubbish away – say £1.00 per sack or £5.00 per month.

From one point of view ... people will want to avoid paying the rubbish tax and so will reduce the amount of waste they throw away. But critics of the proposed scheme immediately pointed out that this model contains the seeds of its own demise. People uncommitted to the idea behind the scheme will take the line of least resistance in a way entirely consistent with the model of behaviour on which the scheme depends – but entirely at odds with its desired outcomes. As a *Guardian* newspaper leader pointed out, 'Rather than pay up, the public are likely to take their rubbish and dump it on the pavement, in the countryside or in someone else's backyard' (12 July 2002). No thought was given to the 'long haul' approach whereby more deep-seated commitments to sustainable living are encouraged, developed and enabled. This is where environmental citizenship comes in.

We are used to thinking of citizenship in two different but related ways. On the one hand there is the liberal tradition of citizenship according to which citizenship confers upon citizens, certain rights which citizens claim against the constituted political authority. ... Then there is a tradition of citizenship which stresses its obligations – usually obligations to the state (to pay taxes, to do military service where required, to vote, for example), but sometimes these obligations are regarded more generally as responsibilities to work towards the public good. Both of these dimensions of citizenship are connected with environmental sustainability and social justice in important ways.

First, we are by now well acquainted with the idea of civil, political and social rights, and we expect them to be upheld. Citizenship in this context is about defending these rights and ensuring that they are made good. Recently, the existence of another set of rights has come to be canvassed: environmental rights. One common formulation is that, 'All human beings have the fundamental right to an environment adequate for their health and well-being'... Poor people are so often denied their environmental rights as a direct result of their poverty. This makes them vulnerable to the imposition of 'bad' environments, such as landfill sites.

Second, we know that each and every one of us makes an impact on the environment in living our daily lives. We also know that individuals make different impacts – the impact of a wealthy Briton is much greater than the impact of a poor Angolan. We have, in other words, different sized 'ecological footprints'. The question for the environmental citizen is whether some of our ecological footprints are too big, in the twin sense of (a) being unsustainable and (b) robbing others of their just proportion of ecological space. If we come to the conclusion that they are too big, then we have a citizenly duty to reduce their size. We should ... compost our domestic organic waste not only because the government will charge us £1 per week if we don't, but because it is unjust to others not to do so (those who live near the landfill site where our waste is taken).

Importantly perhaps, the key questions are not technical in any case – they are normative.

cosmopolitanism makes the mistake of combining environmental awareness with a determinate conception of nature (Clarke 2002). In its place, we need a stronger sense of the interdependency between the social and the natural in order to understand environments as diverse as the Antarctic and downtown Manhattan. On the other hand, by highlighting cultural and political transiency, cosmopolitan approaches emphasize how practical concepts, such as citizenship, can evolve and be transformed in startling ways. At a more abstract level, *modes of citizenship* regulate the production of meaning on entitlements and obligations and generate 'subject positions' in which individuals can invest their identities (Foucault 1980, 1982). In more concrete terms, the precise configuration of entitlements and obligations (and whether these should be reciprocal) will be subject to negotiation. And in the strategic context of ethico-political discourses, subject positions provide the means through which politics is lived. It should be added that genuinely transdisciplinary accounts of environmental issues (Smith 1998b, 2000a, 2000b) also relate *ethics and politics* to cultural diversity and the unruly characteristics of 'the natural', as indicated in Box 3.2. As stated earlier, but relevant here also, preoccupation with the specification, clarification and elaboration of entitlements and rights has

Box 3.2 Transdisciplinary research and the environment

The knowledge produced by researchers and the institutional context of its emergence are interdependent (Gibbons et al. 1994; Jacob and Hellstrom 2000; Nowotny et al. 2001). There is a sharp contrast between Mode 1 and Mode 2 forms of knowledge production; alternatively between disciplinary and transdisciplinary knowledge. Mode 1 knowledge production in university-based disciplinary science claims that accountability is secured through peer review. The criterion for assessing disciplinary knowledge is whether the empirical tests corroborate the assumptions and hypotheses of scientists, that is to say reliability (with the boldest conjectures and strictest tests) provides epistemic value (see Table 3.1). In environmental studies, diverse knowledges and the increasingly competitive criteria by which we judge what is worthwhile and valued in academic output have generated interdisciplinary (asking questions from beyond the discipline before returning to conduct new work in the disciplinary matrix) and multidisciplinary studies (bringing together expertise from various disciplines in a bolt-on way). Trying to understand climate change as a product of interconnected systems has fostered this process.

Mode 2 is non-hierarchical, operating within a context of application where research problems are not set in the disciplinary matrix but arise from elsewhere. As a result, Mode 2 is characterized by a transdisciplinary approach and heterogeneous organizational forms constructed for the purposes at hand. It involves collaboration on a localized problem, and a range of actors with greater opportunities for accountability within and beyond the academy. Thus quality assurance uses the wider criteria of social robustness (supplementing reliability with, for example, efficiency, justice, practical adequacy or value relevance, or providing a solution for a specific problem) and knowledge users act as stakeholders. The debate on environment and citizenship has often been shaped by Mode 1 and, like other areas, is being prompted to reorientation towards transdisciplinarity within the context of application; with regard to more localized qualitative inquiry, it encourages participatory research. Mode 2 knowledge is:

1 intentionally useful in business, government, among institutional clients, activist networks and a variety of wider audiences;
2 formed through a process of negotiation between different agents with different interests (contrary to the pretence of disinterested detachment in disciplinary knowledge);
3 originates in diverse institutions, i.e. think tanks, research institutes, NGOs, research centres, consultancy networks and community participation, as well as departments and laboratories;
4 has a variety of applications, not just in the traditional sense of applied knowledge.

This approach recognizes the social distribution of knowledge (i.e. widely dispersed and unevenly distributed), drawing on the phenomenological account of conditions for *intersubjectivity* (Schütz 1932 [1967]). Transdisciplinarity adopts the *postulate of adequacy*, stating that the second-order constructs of social scientists should draw from the first-order constructs of lived experience, and that the knowledge produced should be intelligible to those people and the environments studied.

neglected obligations, duties and responsibility. There is a tendency to assume that obligation takes us down the road to obedience (eco-authoritarianism). These concepts have 'internal complexity' (Freeden 1996), though it is the conceptual specificity of obligation which needs to be more adequately elaborated. The *return to virtues* in ethical and political discussions on the environment (Barry 1999; Dobson 2003a) offers interesting ways of rethinking the meaning of obligation, where the cultivation of the character of the self acts as a route for the regard of others. This chapter argues, however, that we should not treat one kind of virtue – compassion or justice – as the basis of all other virtues. There are plenty to chose from that are directly relevant to environmental problems.

TABLE 3.1 Contrasting Mode 1 and Mode 2

Mode of knowledge production	Mode 1	Mode 2
Problem-solving	Problems are set and solved in an academic community	Problems are set and solved in the context of application
Knowledge base	Disciplinary	Transdisciplinary
Extent of organizational unity/diversity	Homogeneity	Heterogeneity
Organizational form	Hierarchical	Heterarchical and transient
Communication of knowledge	Dissemination through established institutional channels (peer review journals, conferences)	Diffusion through problem-solving and in new contexts of application (communication networks)

Source: Smith and Pangsapa (2007)

Globalization and citizenship

The new benchmark in these debates is Andrew Dobson's *Citizenship and the Environment* (2003a). For Dobson, the transformationalist view of globalization developed by David Held (2002) overemphasizes interdependence and the assumption of a common future. Cosmopolitanism builds on this account to stress the virtue of 'equal and open dialogue', emphasizing reciprocity, with political communities assembled through social bonding. Drawing on the work of Vandana Shiva (1992), Dobson argues that the constitutional asymmetries should be factored into globalization processes at the start, and not added to a picture of a more interconnected world. The effects of social and economic changes in advanced countries are global, but this does not necessarily mean that the processes work both ways. In addition, the focus on networks and flows tends to ignore the differential power of the actors in negotiations and bargaining at the international level – the experience of time–space compression is enjoyed by those who have the privilege of belonging to the gated communities of industrial societies (the globalizers) rather than those on the outside (the globalized). These asymmetries within current generations and the lack of reciprocity are analogous to those identified in debates on obligations to future generations (Barry 1978) and on harming our reputations in the future (O'Neill 1993).

Dobson suggests that cosmopolitanism offers the hope of resistance to the asymmetrical tendencies of actual globalization and explores dialogic and distributive forms to develop his argument. *Dialogic cosmopolitanism* (developed by Linklater 1998) heralds the possibility of constructing political communities beyond the nation-state which can be achieved through social bonding and a commitment to open dialogue (with the creation of institutional conditions for realizing this), so that all participants are recognized and can voice their concerns. This approach focuses on the human community, assumes that impartiality is the modus operandi, and posits that greater or more intense dialogue is the democratic objective. Bonding develops the sense of belonging to the human community and the duties this entails. We are obliged to act with regard to the needs of strangers out of *compassion* and charity – the 'good Samaritan' principle of global citizenship. For Dobson, this not only leaves obligations hanging (as charity can be withdrawn or even reproduce the vulnerability of the recipient), it lacks a specific mechanism for addressing environmental harms, even if transnational dialogue can help crystallize the duty of protecting the vulnerable. What Dobson has in mind is a focus on specific communities of obligation, in other words obligation spaces with their own injustices and coerced dialogues. He argues that partiality is crucial for effective strategies to achieve more justice, so the objective should be to change the reasons for acting. Being obliged to do justice, to act in a way because it is *binding* rather than just bonding, is, for Dobson, a political rather than a moral obligation. Justice is thus portrayed as a *binding* relationship between equals rather than the one-way and revocable consequence of humanitarian obligations. In short: 'if citizenship is to have any meaning at all, then the condition of being a citizen must be distinguishable from being a human being. In other words, there must be a difference between the community of citizens and the community of humanity' (Dobson 2003a: 27).

Distributive cosmopolitanism has the first virtue of more justice in response to harm, in addition to the commitment to open and uncoerced dialogue. Drawing on the work of Simon Caney (2001), Dobson highlights how a theory of distribution can be defended by reference to a theory of moral personality, whereby entitlements to an equal share can be established *prior to* inhabiting culture, national identity or ethnicity. Such entitlements are viewed as being grounded in human autonomy or the possession of rights; the selection of which lends plausibility to his contention that this is 'a specifically political type of obligation as opposed to a more broadly moral type' (Dobson 2003a: 29). This reasoning is portrayed as a more convincing basis for thinking through citizenship beyond the state, dealing in the *currency of justice rather than compassion*, but distributive cosmopolitanism still lacks a clear idea of the reasons *why* we should act. This treatment of the virtue of justice is comparable to the unification of virtues developed in Christian accounts privileging compassion or charity (along with faith and hope) over the classical virtues of courage, practical wisdom (prudence), justice and temperance. This kind of unification process is questionable. Instead, we need a more flexible framework that recognizes the co-dependence of and overlaps between virtues. Being compassionate depends on having courage, while being *just* depends on temperance – restraining materialistic appetites – as implied in Dobson's endorsement of ecological footprint analysis. In place of these thin and non-material cosmopolitan accounts of the 'ties that bind', he proposes post-cosmopolitanism, whereby the ties are materially (re-)produced in daily life within an unequal and asymmetrically globalizing context. As a consequence of globalization, relations once considered a matter of compassion are increasingly citizen relations. The provision of 'aid' in response to natural hazards should be seen not as a benevolent act of charity but as compensatory justice, for the harm inflicted by industrial societies on others is a result of human-induced climate change, altering the nature and the source of obligation.

Dobson makes a distinction between moral obligations as a non-reciprocal commitment to others and political obligations as grounded in binding relationships based on some degree of parity (although the degree can vary), as well as between *specifically* political obligations and *general* moral obligations, with politics and morality distinct in terms of scope. By grounding entitlements in autonomy and the possession of rights, this already assumes some understanding of rationality or species membership. The line drawn between politics and morality is asserted but not substantiated, suggesting that politics is ethics free. Analytic distinctions clarify the precise kinds of ethical and political judgements, but assuming that they can be separated in substantive terms within everyday life is misleading. This also leads us back to the importance of the cultivation of characteristics that are virtuous. When we live in a 'community', we are simultaneously human and a citizen – what matters then is how these are defined and how they are articulated in the concrete situations of 'ineradicable antagonism' (Mouffe 2000, 2005; Smith 2005b). Citizenly 'subject positions' are temporary respites in ongoing confrontations over the meaning of citizenship and the virtues each subject position mobilizes are provisional. In agonistic democracy, struggles are staged around diverse conceptions of citizenship, with each proposing its interpretation of the common good, right courses of action and virtues that should be cultivated. Ecological citizenship is just one way of engaging in 'the political'. The key task is to identify the potential and limits of subject positions that feature in environmental discourses following the *postulate of adequacy* outlines in Box 3.1. Artificially separating morals and politics smacks of the *attachment to detachment*, a key feature of disciplinary knowledge (Smith 2000a, 2001).

Citizen types

When specifying citizenship, Dobson builds on Peter Reisenberg's (1992) characterization of the declining influence of republican conceptions of citizenship in the face of a triumphant liberal conception (rights claims replaced civic virtue while passive subjects replaced active citizens). He constructs a model wherein liberal citizenship stresses rights and entitlements and the absence of foundational virtues as a basis for action, while republican citizenship emphasized duties, responsibilities and virtues. Both are grounded in contractual relations between state and citizen, and both operate in the public sphere within a given territorial space. Cosmopolitanism acknowledges the unbounded diaspora of the political community but retains the insistence on the importance of an incipient discursive democracy, a cosmopolitan political sphere, alongside the commitment to treating the vulnerable with compassion. His proposed *post-cosmopolitan* citizenship is non-contractual (dropping the vocabulary of reciprocity), non-territorial and operates in both public and private spheres, with affinities to the republican emphasis on duties, responsibilities and virtues – although it rejects the masculine virtues of republicanism in favour of feminine virtues (an ethics of care). Citizenship is often understood as based on a contractual relationship between state and citizen – as a bargain or settlement whereby the citizen loses a little bit of liberty to enhance personal security, or, as Ignatieff (1995) puts it, 'a bad bargain'. In proposing post-cosmopolitian citizenship, Dobson asks why contracts should be definitive of citizenship (as opposed, we could add, to conceptions of friendship).

This approach asks the legitimate question of why contracts should be seen as definitive of citizenship and raises the possibility of unreciprocated and unilateral citizenship obligations, i.e. the changes we attribute to globalization may herald a shift in the structure of obligation which parallels how the scale of democratic involvement laid the grounds for a movement from republican to liberal citizenship. Dobson substantiates this by claiming that we are trapped between extreme opposites with discrete contractual exchanges between equivalent actors on the one hand, and unilateral and unreciprocated acts of charity on the other. Contracts, in the sense described by Nancy Fraser and Linda Gordon (1994), as civil citizenship relations voluntarily entered into, are presented by Dobson as ideological rather than just a definitional feature of current conceptions of citizenship. Reciprocity provides a motive for action because of the possibility of a penalty should one break a contract. Dobson makes a significant step towards challenging the cast-iron certainty of reciprocity by highlighting the contingencies between entitlements and obligations. He insists that there should be a mechanism for distinguishing the obligations of citizens from humanitarian obligations.

Drawing on the work of Judith Lichtenberg (1981), Dobson claims that a *moral view* involves A helping B because they are willing and able to come to someone's aid and alleviate their plight when A has no causal role in their plight. In the historical view A *owes* B as a result of a prior action, undertaking, agreement or relationship binding on the actors involved. Dobson argues that the recognition of such 'bindings' in the context of increased awareness of environmental issues and globalization calls forth the virtues and practices of citizenship. This takes little account, however, of the difficulties of persuading citizens, companies and government authorities within industrial societies that their activities are responsible for environmental impacts elsewhere, just as it took the UK government and energy companies a decade to accept responsibility for the acid rain effects of sulphur dioxide emissions in western Europe. The refusal of the US government to accept the Kyoto Protocol, for example, demonstrates how states continue to deny their responsibility for trans-boundary effects (in this case, on climate change) in order to protect interests within territorial boundaries. Nevertheless, there is movement on the acceptance of climate change as a human effect in the USA, such

TABLE 3.2 Dobson's three types of citizenship

Liberal	Civic republican	Post-cosmopolitan
Rights/entitlements (contractual)	Duties/responsibilities (contractual)	Duties/responsibilities (non-contractual)
Public sphere	Public sphere	Public and private spheres
Virtue-free	'Masculine' virtue	'Feminine' virtue
Territorial (discriminatory)	Territorial (discriminatory)	Non-territorial (non-discriminatory)

as the 'mission statement' (1 August 2006) agreed between the UK and California to work towards cutting greenhouse gas emissions.

Dobson also draws on the feminist ethics of care, rather than treating the public sphere as the site of freedom and the private sphere as the site of necessity. He directs us to consider how feminists see progressive potential in the concept of citizenship by problematizing the discriminative assumptions that privilege the public and subordinate the private, suggesting that the 'citizenly ties that bind' are present in both private and public spheres (Prokhovnik 1998). In the private sphere, parental obligations should be acknowledged as ethically grounded civic obligations, and attempts to encourage 'responsible personal lifestyle decisions' have citizenly characteristics. Appeals to take regular physical exercise, diet, stop smoking, reduce alcohol intake and ensure one's teenage daughter does not become pregnant are couched in terms of the duty to not waste the time and resources of a medical or welfare system. On the environment, the decisions that matter most are those we face in our private lives: responsibility for waste and litter, choosing less resource-consumptive means of transportation, energy conservation measures, voluntary conservation activities or local biodiversity monitoring – effectively reducing the impacts of our ecological footprints. Thus post-cosmopolitan citizenship renegotiates the meaning of 'the political' (Mouffe 2000), yet the disciplinary framework of political theory inhibits Dobson's accounts of the relationship between ethics and politics. Before we consider how to move beyond these limits, we need to deal with the liberal response to Dobson's case, in particular his use of the ecological footprints approach and his claim that justice will involve a 'fair share to ecological space', both in terms of the resources we use and the extent to which the environment can operate as a sink.

Liberal environmental citizenship

Dobson's distinction between *environmental* citizenship (the extension of liberal rights such as civil, political and social rights to include access to environmental goods or to prevent environmental bads) and *ecological* citizenship points the way to the development of a new political imaginary or space. For cosmopolitans, rights are established by virtue of being located in an imagined territory constituted by membership of a common humanity. Post-cosmopolitans create ecological space by acknowledging their causal and material relationship with other citizens in terms of resource use and pollution (the primary example being how the globalizers impact on the globalized – a relation of *victimization*). The key obligation of ecological citizenship is to ensure that our ecological footprints do not 'compromise or foreclose the ability of others in present and future generations to pursue options important to them' (Dobson 2003a). For Dobson, the first virtue of ecological citizenship is justice, or that all virtues should contribute to the eradication of environmental injustice.

Derek Bell (2003, 2005) offers some interesting insights on how rethinking citizenship can aid the promotion of sustainability, suggesting that Dobson's account is a merger of liberalism and ecologism. For Bell, law represents an actual state of affairs (subject to the proviso that most citizens comply with the law and transgressors are subject to prosecution within due process) whereas justice represents an ideal situation where environmental objectives are realized. Bell (2003: 10) draws on the metaphoric devices of liberalism (Rawls 1993, 1999) to specify the different causes of this gap.

1　The state or other institutions lack the power to enforce certain laws to secure for everyone the right to a fair share of ecological space and redistribute ecological space from the 'globalizers' to the 'globalized'.
2　The necessary laws will be too unpopular to be approved in democratic society, and could undermine the rule of law so that forcing through policies without consent undermines the social and political fabric.
3　Many of the necessary laws and the means of enforcing them will involve imposing restrictions that are inconsistent with liberal values, as with compulsory population control (Malinas 1980; Young 1980).

While Dobson is preoccupied with a just distribution of ecological space, for Bell the key issue is broadly one of distributive justice. He claims that environmental rights (to clean air and water) already include the just distribution of ecological space as a subsidiary assumption. In addition, if we limit ecological citizenship to those acts that involve sacrificing part of one's own ecological footprint and redistributing space to others with less than their fair share, then many environmental activities (from local conservation volunteering to participation in local Agenda 21 consultations) are excluded. Bell finds it odd that all we achieve here is a different way of describing archetypal environmental activisms, shifting the classificatory practices without providing a more adequate explanatory framework. Bell's main concerns are as follows.

1 Eco-authoritarianism – liberals prioritize justice over the good, such that citizens have a duty not to pursue their own conception of the good in an unjust manner.

2 Over-restriction – why should we worry whether environmentally beneficial practices are motivated to redistribute ecological space.

3 Liberals are committed to both negative and positive duty already – limiting duty merely to not violating others' right to a fair share of ecological space ignores how we also have a duty to secure a fair share for all citizens in the first place.

4 Narrow focus of complicity – limiting duty to when an actor is personally complicit could let us off the hook if environmental injustice occurs in other societies, committed by other states, or between citizens with whom we have no contact.

Where states lack legitimate enforcement powers, Bell acknowledges that Dobson's approach may help redress some injustices and help to close the gap between law and justice. He suggests, however, that this must involve voluntary (non-coerced), morally and politically required self-regulation. The question becomes how to persuade many citizens to make the necessary sacrifices. For Bell, voluntary self-regulation will not fill the gap, and Mill's combination of legal and moral regulation may provide a better answer. We should remember that for Mill both the physical force involved in legal penalties and the moral coercion of public opinion are potentially tyrannical if used unjustly. They can be used to establish a climate of expectations, however, so that non-compliance is judged harshly by other citizens.

Dobson's approach prompts liberals to address the cultural expectations that underpin effective environmental strategies. But if ecological citizenship is not simply an extension of liberalism, why did it come into being? Advocates of ecological citizenship from the green movement question the need for a clear line in the sand between political analysis and ethical investigation, since, even when the line is drawn, there is still sand on both sides. In particular, the division inhibits strategic thinking and fails to acknowledge that the kind of change required will be an ethico-political one. In addition, if morality is about establishing the good or the right course of action (depending on whether one endorses some form of consequentialism or deontology), then, given the centrality of these concerns in policy-making, to pretend that politics is an ethics-free zone seems to be doomed to partiality and one-sidedness. Analytic accounts aid, conceptually, clarification of ethical and political judgements at work, but to assume that they can be separated in substantive terms on the ground is misleading. When we live in a 'community', we are simultaneously citizen, human and ecologically situated; what matters is how citizenship is defined, what obligations humans have to others (from strangers to ecosystems).

The rather stark contrast of binding with bonding presented by Dobson is not always helpful. The demarcation of politically binding relationships from human bonded relationships misses the possibility that environmentally positive results can follow from an attachment to the specific community. So, by pushing Dobson's approach in the direction of an ecologically guided ethico-political project, we can escape these limits, avoiding the fate of being reterritorialized by liberal environmental discourses and ensuring that we deterritorialize the assemblages constituting citizenship (Deleuze and Guattari 1987, 1994). Three steps are needed to achieve this: a keener awareness of political subjectivities so that citizenly subject positions can be established which avoid the pitfalls of liberalism; conceptual clarification of 'obligation'; and an endorsement of virtue ethics to bridge the gaps between attitudes and behaviour and between law and justice.

Subjectivities and the discursive territory of ecological citizenship

Ecological citizenship focuses on understanding the motivations and reasons for responsible actions. Responsibility, duty and obligation have resurfaced in other areas of public policy such as welfare and criminal justice, but the ban on smoking in public places is a particularly useful parallel. In Norway, there was a qualitative difference in approach that made substantive contributions to its effectiveness. Prior to the legal change (April 2004), concerted media campaigns were launched in conjunction with projects in schools, workplaces and cultural events to enable citizens to volunteer to change their behaviour. Besides legal penalties, to help avoid potential areas of conflict, an emphasis was placed on the subject position of 'the considerate smoker', to avoid situations where others (children and retail staff) are vulnerable to passive smoking, and hence manage the contradictory discursive elements that being a smoker entails. This provides an analogue for strategies seeking to alter behaviour in relation to ecological space. Dobson provides the example of the problems of biodegradable waste dumping in the context of the EU Landfill Directive, where local authorities have sought to use incentives to ensure pre-disposal waste sorting by households. The logic underpinning waste reduction strategies sees motivation in terms of the intentions of the 'minimaxing' actor, rationally maximizing benefits and/or minimizing costs or harm. Conservationist policy and environmental valuation have long been associated with such utilitarian calculations to discern the 'greatest good for the greatest number for the longest time' (Pinchot 1901). Rather than rejecting 'minimaxing' as an explanatory account, the rationalities produced can be translated into subject positions in which citizens have or could invest their identities, and can help us identify some of the unintended consequences of environmental regulation. The following subject positions, or alternatively *typifications* (in the phenomenological sense), are not real, just means of representing ways in which citizens act, in this case with underlying assumption of rationality.

1 *The CABWITH (can't be bothered with the hassle) citizen* – some citizens will do the minimum necessary or avoid sorting waste diligently, using their capacity and taking additional unsorted waste directly to the tip (with transport costs), defeating the objective of kerbside collection.
2 *The furtive dumper citizen* – dumping in the skips of neighbours, car parks, building sites, redundant petrol station forecourts, waste land or any location beyond surveillance as a response to the costs of recycling obsolescent consumer durables in the absence of local recycling facilities (cars and fridges are processed in designated facilities) or when financial cost means citizens are unable or unwilling to pay.
3 *The passer-by citizen* – taking account of citizens who decide to ignore furtive dumping, 'CABWITHing' or more visible forms of damaging behaviour based on rational calculations.
4 *The entrepreneurial neighbourly citizen* – households who sort effectively can sustain unfilled capacity in their household waste bins and can sell their landfill disposal space to neighbours who do not recycle, in order to realize small financial gains (while their CABWITH neighbours perform an opportunity cost calculation on their time and costs of waste disposal).

CABWITH and furtive dumper citizens can be understood in terms of individual intentions, but the other subject positions highlight citizen-to-citizen relations. The liberal split between public and private spheres is

Box 3.3 Thinking through ecological citizenship

If we recognize the intrinsic value of living creatures and other natural things as ends in themselves rather than as the means to some human end, we displace humankind from its dominant position within the ethical 'pecking order'. Moral governance is concerned with what is appropriate within complex ecosystems in definite situations; ecological citizenship questions the relations of rights and obligation within the species barrier. Ecological citizenship presumes that human beings have obligations to animals, trees, mountains and the biotic community; it also means that we have to be cautious about embarking upon any project that is likely to have adverse effects upon ecosystems. In one sense, developing the idea of ecological citizenship is the first attempt at developing a new political vocabulary to articulate this relationship between society and nature; a new 'politics of obligation' that questions the theoretical boundary between public and private spheres and undermines their institutional embodiments of the state and civil society that remain so central to liberal thinking. Beck argues that we face two

problematic – especially where individualism is deeply embedded and the 'moral coercion of public opinion' is viewed as a dangerous intrusion into privacy. The fourth hypothetical example, assuming higher costs for waste disposal and stricter limits, is a rational response analogous to pollution permit trading (where companies discover ecological modernization prohibitively expensive and purchase unused ecological space). Moreover, small gains (5 cents a bottle) can motivate 'urban street scavenging' of recyclables on waste collection day, for example across New York State in the USA.

While the total volume of landfill disposal is reduced, the examples presented mean that significant recyclable materials will still be dumped. Ecological footprint analysis suffers from the same flaw – ecological space trading is a feasible market for citizens as well as private corporations, and citizens of advanced industrial societies could be deemed to have compensated citizens outside this context for a portion of their ecological space through overseas aid, charitable donations and knowledge transfers. Such results are (or would be) direct responses by citizens to environmental regulation based on rational decision-making. Of course, many citizens who sort waste would otherwise feel no compulsion to do so, which still does not ensure that most citizens will engage in the choices, one where 'the state absorbs civil society' and the other where 'civil society absorbs the state' (respectively, authoritarian or democratic ways of addressing ecological problems). Proposals for sustainable society point to the simpler, more localized division of labour that often features in different forms of socialist and anarchist assumptions, as expressed by the bioregionalist movement. Perhaps Peter Saunders, a staunch defender of individual freedom and market-based systems, is right to see environmental movements as the next big threat to capitalism; as he stated once, 'now we have Karl Marx with dreadlocks and a baggy jumper'. Nevertheless, we should also remember that small can be ecologically ugly as well as beautiful; there are no guarantees that reducing the scale of production is the best remedy for many environmental issues. For instance, much of the timber in China during the 1950s was cleared in a very wasteful way for use in small-scale, village-based iron and steel forging. At the end of the day, it is the impact of social practices on ecosystems, rather than the scale or a particular political affiliation, which matters.

desired behaviour, and it may be counterproductive to make such an assumption, for this neglects the non-rational motivations for securing personal satisfaction and well-being, based on ethics, community spirit, affective attachments to the environment, even guilt feelings if they do not recycle.

More effective is persuading citizens that there are sound reasons for recycling waste and limiting environmental damage which they can endorse. As Dobson highlights, the Durham city road pricing scheme can have dramatic results, but it is questionable whether the changes would be sustained if congestion charges were terminated. It is also questionable whether behavioural changes in one area would be translated into

TABLE 3.3 Classifying citizenly relations

	Capacities to act (enablement)	Liabilities to others (based on binding constraint)
Formal	Rights	Duties
Informal	Entitlements	Obligations

changes in others. If we assume that citizens are simultaneously bearers of entitlements and obligations (some of which may be more formally or legally prescribed as rights and duties – Table 3.3 – some of which may be reciprocal), specified through the relations between citizens, then we can move away from a rights-centred approach (and financial incentives) to acknowledging that entitlements provide capacities to act and obligations indicate susceptibilities to the concerns of others. Since duties and obligations are used synonymously in the literature we now draw on the morphological analysis of concept formation to explore the meaning of obligation.

Clarifying obligation

Concepts have different meanings in each theory or ideology but also have internal complexity with three kinds of elements that have different purposes.

* *Ineliminable elements* – are the core definitions of the concept that cannot be eliminated or it would not be the same concept.
* *Adjacent elements* – clarify the precise use and purpose of the concept.
* *Peripheral elements* – make the concept relevant for political practices in a particular time and place or in specific institutions.

For Freeden, 'liberty' has the ineliminable element of 'non-constraint' while 'self-determination' is logically adjacent (summoning democracy or self-government), and 'community' culturally adjacent. These are shaped by the beliefs, values, institutional patterns and ethics that have intellectual and emotional significance. Peripheral elements for liberty besides 'natural rights' or 'order' include aphorisms like 'dog eat dog', 'charity begins at home' or 'you have no one to blame but yourself'. The elements of a successful political assemblage are defined and arranged to ensure that concepts are *decontested*, and appear fixed and certain in a specific location (Freeden 1996: 47–95). Describing elements as core or peripheral, however, connotes that the peripheral is dispensable. From a strategic orientation, 'peripheral' analogies and metaphors, by which citizens think through motives and communicate meaning, have a greater importance. It is helpful to understand the ineliminable element of obligation, as being the presence of *ties that bind one agent to another or other agents and things*, taking account of the various ways in which an agent feels they owe obligations.

Focusing on binding excludes legitimate ways in which obligations can be justified through compassion. Environmentally beneficial practices can be rationalized in a variety of ways – what matters in environmental activism and civic engagement is whether citizens understand why such actions (or their avoidance) need to take place. When gains for donors are not evident, reciprocity may not be adequate and humanitarian efforts (even though they can be withdrawn) may provide the necessary motivation. Attributable causality on trans-boundary environmental impacts, despite 'some antecedent or prior action, undertaking, agreement, relationship', is not always persuasive. The reasons for having obligations are context specific, just as 'the others' to which we owe obligations may alter depending on the precise form of an environmental problem.

To illustrate, the effects of deforestation highlight the reconciliation of justice between and within generations (Humphreys 1999), water quality issues prompt an awareness of our immediate successors (Blunden 1999), while the disposal or storage of nuclear waste raises obligations to distant future generations (Blowers 1999). Each environmental issue raises different questions about obligations to present and future generations as well as the present and future effects on non-human animals, habitats, mountains, streams, trees and the biotic community. More research is needed on *why* citizens endorse specific bundles of obligations and how they are articulated with entitlements in modes of citizenship.

Agnes Heller's critique of morals as a sphere treats the ethical component of citizenship as the 'good citizen practising the citizen's virtue', i.e. 'the subject of the good life is the righteous person' (1987: 274), human bonds are constituted by internalized morals (virtues, norms, values and principles). All relations and processes have a moral dimension. Similarly, this chapter considers every sphere of existence as moral, political and cultural, simultaneously. Distinguishing politics and morality as separate spheres follows disciplinary knowledge formations rather than concrete experience (Smith 2005a). Heller suggests that the presence of ideal objectivations (abstract norms or terms of virtue) does not mean that a moral sphere exists – that we should not treat the principles of justice as pre-existing essential categories or clusters to which rules should apply.

Heller's analysis helps to clarify the components of obligation, distinguishing 'rules' followed in a single and definite way (without deliberation or reflection) from two types of 'norms': *concrete norms* on *how to act* in particular situations and *abstract norms* providing standards or virtues to cultivate or live up to (see Table 3.4). Heller highlights the contingencies involved in moral judgement – citizens can exist in more than one cluster simultaneously and, in each cluster, norms and rules are usually applied inconsistently. Even when norms and rules are consistent, they can still

TABLE 3.4 Rules, norms and obligations

Claiming/obedience	Rules	Assumes compliance is normal, for example that all strangers must be respected
Rights/duties	Concrete norms	Norms on how to treat a visitor
Entitlements/ obligations	Abstract norms	Living up to virtue of acting with civility to strangers

be seen as unjust, highlighting how alternative norms and rules have the potential to constitute a social cluster (Heller 1987: 275–6).

Analytic distinctions between moral and political elements have critical purposes and ethical analysis can specify how particular conceptions of the moral community are articulated with ways of thinking about the good, the right and the virtuous. Contrasting philanthropy with justice, however, avoids the key issue for addressing the law–justice gap – enabling citizens to feel obliged to act in environmentally responsible ways without resorting to the exercise of some mechanism for compulsion. It is crucial to ask whether the binding nature of citizenship is sufficient to achieve environmental objectives and whether the contrast of binding with bonding is helpful. If the distinctive feature of citizenship is its binding nature, failure to fulfil duties can be remedied through due process; we are limited to the formal-legal aspects of citizenly behaviour. Local authorities in the south-east of England incurred £1.2 million costs in addressing organized illegal fly-tipping in 2003/04, and while thirty cases were successfully prosecuted the penalties imposed do not deter. Stiffer penalties may affect the behaviour of some but it is widely accepted that they will not address the problem fully. This highlights the weaknesses of depending on penalties as a motivational force in reciprocal contractual relations where actors simply feel no overriding sense of duty. Much more effective is changing the obligations that inform dutiful citizenship and the cultivation of environmental virtues. Dobson's account is valuable, shifting us away from sterile preoccupations with reciprocity and compassion and opening up a terrain of multiple motivations that can come into being through the active civic engagements and citizen–citizen relations. Nevertheless, Bell's critique highlights the limits of Dobson's approach, especially in addressing the transformative implications of ecological citizenship. Contrary to Dobson, demarcating politically binding relationships from human bonded relationships misses the point that environmentally positive results can follow from attachments to the specific community. Commitment towards projects with a social and environmental purpose, such as the *'dugnad* (let's-do-it-together) culture', benefits the community through voluntary action, for example painting a school during the holidays, or cooking weekly meals for residents (Haugestad 2003). These are not formally binding contracts but are informally binding arrangements while, at the same time, providing an expression of bondedness; non-participants may feel guilt and be treated differently but without legal retribution. In a similar example, Maria Mies outlines the subsistence perspective as a way that links the maintenance of sustainable livelihoods grounded in the every-day practices of women while also preventing ecological damage (Mies and Shiva 1992). We therefore need to pay much more attention to the informal, everyday reasons and motives for environmentally beneficial acts if there is any chance of bridging the gaps between law and justice and between values and action.

Conclusion: towards ecological virtues

The arguments above alert us to the difference between obliga-tions and duties as well as identifying the informal kinds of binding and bonding through which obligations are sustained. This approach avoids privileging one virtue, such as justice or compassion, over the range of different virtues (often combined) that may be relevant in each manifestation of citizenship (including environmental and ecological varieties). Practical wisdom (or prudence) is more compatible with the precautionary principle and notions of environmental stewardship than justice. Potential exists in using the virtues of temperance, kindness, generosity, humility, simplicity, gentleness, tolerance, forgiveness, self-sacrifice and even sadness (being resigned to one's fate). The list could be longer, but a brief scan of these should immediately demonstrate that they may or may not be articulated in terms of Dobson's case for justice as fair shares of ecological space. The key point is that notions of virtue are not simply imposed, they are cultivated as deliberate attempts to live up to regard for others (whether they are our adversaries or our friends). Fulfilling obligations is also an honourable act of self-regard, completing one's side of an agreement, living up to a mission, feeling good about one's reputation, being a 'good human being' or leading a flourishing life. There will be dilemmas when adjudicating upon the relative importance of one species compared to another (including the human species), but then ethical dilemmas are not absent from other approaches and we should not anticipate their absence here. We started out by stressing that citizens often articulate ethical and political ideas in hybridized and analytically inconsistent ways, so by focusing on concrete manifestations of 'the virtuous', 'the good' or 'the right' – along with the use of epistemological and aesthetic judgements – we can begin to understand how culturally specific antagonisms affect environmental debate and encourage us to treat other political subjects as adversaries we can respect rather than as enemies to confront.

Once we acknowledge that moral traditions, such as utilitarianism and Kantian contractarianism, simply offer guidance on particular problems in specific circumstances, rather than absolute solutions, then ethical standpoints can be understood as being relevant to definite spheres of existence, rather than suggesting that one form of morality is applicable across all forms of existence. As Christopher D. Stone suggests, the ethical act of becoming a vegetarian or preserving an acre of wilderness does not follow from the application of a single principle but makes sense only when it becomes part of an integrated 'network of mutually sup-portive principles, theories, and attitudes toward consequences' (Stone 1987: 242). The environmental priorities of each situation vary. Different ecological and cultural conditions prevail within a particular biome, so we should be suspicious of universal solutions and perfect answers; they are unlikely to be effective. We do not require a 'blueprint' – an ideal 'ecotopia' – worked out to the last detail, but we need to work towards a 'greenprint' – that is, a set of working principles that acknowledge complexity, uncertainty and interdependency between society and nature – in order to develop flexible strategies for change. It is with this in mind that the subsequent chapters focus on the scales and sites for developing ecological citizenship within the terms of environmental policy.

PART TWO

Practice informed by theory

4 | Environmental governance, social movements and citizenship in a global context

Introduction: from regulation to obligation at a global level

The hollowing out of the state combined with the transformation of the global economy has led to a shift from a concern with 'government' policy to an interest in 'governance' networks across different levels and between different sectors, issues and policy communities. This chapter considers the emergence of environmental governance at intergovernmental, regional (in particular the EU), national and sub-national arenas. Sometimes, governance is described as 'government without statehood' (Weale et al. 2000: 6), although this misses the point that national policy is still part of the complex relations through which environmental policy emerges. This chapter brings together case studies of international regime formation on global environmental commons (such as forestry and climate change) with a specific focus on the interaction between NGOs and national governments. It is difficult to identify exact benchmarks for the growing importance of environmental policy in this context – although those often highlighted range from the Stockholm Conference 1972 through to the Earth Summit twenty years later, in Rio de Janeiro.

What we can state is that, in the 1970s, environmental policy was concerned more with environmental protection (conservation, air pollution and water quality measures), but by the 1990s had shifted more towards standard-setting and assessing performance. In addition, since 'globalization is first and foremost a creation of business, devising a policy will necessarily require the contribution and support of those actors who generated it and remain its primary movers' (Tesner 2000: 145). The structural changes in the global economy mean that nation-states are less capable of regulating the behaviour of corporations and the effects of capital mobility. This means that other ways of influencing the activities of international capital are seen as more effective, hence the rise of NGOs and transnational networks concerned with sweatshops, human rights abuses, labour standards violations and unsustainable environmental impacts.

Environmental concerns over pollution or resource depletion can potentially lead to serious conflicts. Even when environmental problems

Box 4.1 Potential conflicts over environmental resources in the Arctic region

With the rise of oil prices to over US$130 a barrel in 2008, attention has been redirected to potential fossil fuel resources in the polar regions. The knock-on effects include new designs for icebreaking supertankers and funding for military vessels in nations with a territorial interest in the Arctic, even including Canada. Russia has even planted its national flag on the seabed at the North Pole. Ownership of fossil fuels and other resources in the Arctic will result in conflict 'fought in temperatures below 40°C, amid bone-chilling blizzards and unrelieved winter darkness. The political powers of the northern hemisphere are suddenly facing tense negotiations over who gets what in an oil- and gas-rich polar territory twice the size of France' (Mills 2007).

In some cases, the rush to the North Pole is as much an expression of national pride as driven by necessity in terms of environmental security. According to Mills, 'Artur Chilingarov, a Russian explorer and politician, dropped a rustproof titanium flag from the hold of a mini-submarine to prove that while Moscow lost the space race, it is determined to win the ice race ... access to what geologists believe are a quarter of the globe's oil and gas reserves – in short, the solution to the crippling energy shortages that will begin throttling Western economies within the next two decades'.

The rush to the pole is also precipitated by the effects of global warming and the Arctic melt, making regions of the globe more accessible to exploration as well as to potential shipping routes that were previously ice-bound. The putative North-West and Bering Strait passages linking the Atlantic to the Pacific also offer new routes for trade in fuel that would link available resources in the Arctic to the rapidly developing Asian economies, while the high fossil fuel prices make the high costs of polar oil and gas exploration in the Arctic more economically feasible, that is, profitable, in business terms.

are located within national boundaries (as with the nuclear accidents in Japan – at Tokaimura 1997, 1999; Kashiwazaki-Kariwa 2007) or affect a limited number of countries (such as the nuclear fallout from the Chernobyl meltdown or acid rain deposits in European countries in the

1980s), the response to such hazards is often conducted in what has been come to be called the world community. Acid rain problems are not limited to Europe but are well documented in Korea, Japan, South Africa and Brazil. The same can be said of the slash-and-burn activities of Indonesian farmers, which have created significant air pollution problems for other South-East Asian countries such as Malaysia and Singapore. This region, along with China, is also displaying the early signs of significant acid rain problems. In particular, the rapid industrialization of areas of India has produced what has been dubbed the 'Asian Brown Cloud'. In addition, concern about regional atmospheric pollution is closely related to international negotiations on deforestation.

On the resource depletion side, resolving conflicts of interest presents difficulties when they concern scarce resources such as oil and water as well as minerals. Commodity prices for these resources have appreciated considerably since the start of the twenty-first century as a result of the rapid industrialization of China and India. In addition, it is expected that oil and gas production will peak some time in the second decade of this century (see Box 4.1). These examples highlight the critical importance of environmental negotiations and the development of coordinated responses to environmental problems that go beyond the local and the national arenas, highlighting the relations between state actors and transnational NGOs. It is to these we now turn in the next section.

Global commons and international environmental regimes

One of the most influential studies of the politics of the international environmental issue, John Vogler's *The Global Commons* (2000), provides a useful framework for understanding international environmental regimes. Regime analysis emerged in the study of international relations during the 1970s and 1980s during a period that witnessed the relative decline of the dominance of the USA in international relations, the development of transnational cooperation on formal legal instruments, and the proliferation of informal networks through which agreements can become effective. Vogler argues that the shift in relationships between states and the growth of institutional relations below, alongside and above national governments demanded a very different approach in order to make sense of the complex evidence involved. Vogler highlights Krasner's definition as a baseline for understanding regimes:

Sets of implicit and explicit principles, norms, rules and decision making procedures around which actors' expectations converge in a given area

Four

of international relations. Principles are beliefs of fact, causation and rectitude. Norms are standards of behaviour defined in terms of rights and obligations. Rules are specific prescriptions or proscriptions for action. Decision making procedures are prevailing practices for making and implementing collective choice. (Krasner 1983: 2, cited in Vogler 2000: 20)

The concern here is as much with the flexible and constantly re-negotiated informal rules of conduct as with the formal legal rules regulating actors in international relations. While the research litera-ture tends to focus on legally binding instruments as tangible objects of analysis (Porter and Brown 1991), this neglects the role of tacit knowledge and the effect of shared experiences through which trust has been established (and sometimes damaged) in past practices. In-evitably, legal documents at this level are often broad in scope, making the achievement of specific outcomes difficult without a shared com-mitment and common understanding of what objectives are desirable, especially when success requires wider support from a range of non-governmental actors such as private corporations and NGOs. This may also involve the need to reconcile the objectives of state and non-state participants before any specific agreement, once drafted and accepted, can prove workable. It is these issues which make the careful analysis of environmental regime formation and implementation so pressing. When considering *issue areas*, always central to defining the scope of a regime, we are concerned with how an increase in average atmospheric temperatures or the preservation of the Antarctic wilderness can become objects for common negotiation. These examples are also useful for highlighting how issue areas overlap; for example, how climate change or ozone depletion is intimately connected to the polar regions or how deforestation and marine acidification are relevant to understanding global warming. Hence adequate analysis has to take account of how changes in bio-physical processes (often as a result of anthropogenic impacts on environments) in one issue can generate causes that have consequences in other issue areas. Vogler presents two useful illustra-tions with reference to space and marine environments as global com-mons:

• separate regimes exist for the safety of astronauts, information flows, military uses and the geostationary orbit (GSO) frequency essential for communication links;
• the hunting of whales is subject to the International Convention on the Regulation of Whaling (1946) but since whales migrate back and

forth across the Antarctic convergence (roughly 60 degrees south), they are also regulated by the Antarctic Treaty System as well as regimes specific to the high seas.

Environmental negotiations can also be partitioned off from the regulation of other aspects of international relations, such as trade relations. For example, restrictions on the importation of particular goods for health and environmental reasons, such as beef involving the use of hormones, have been ruled to be a barrier to free trade by the World Trade Organization (WTO). Similarly, when the WTO met in Seattle in 1999 to consider the uses of biotechnology (specifically, restrictive practices primarily by the EU on the trade of products containing genetically modified organisms, GMOs), it set in process a claim by the national governments of the USA, Canada and Argentina. This resulted in a WTO ruling on this dispute in 2006, to the effect that the six-year moratorium on approving GMO food products by a number of countries in the EU was in breach of trade rules (it applied a de facto moratorium), which marked a significant shift, but the European Commission claimed that this did not affect the existing procedures in place. As a result, since the WTO found that the EU was creating undue delays in approval of GMO products, discussion has focused on speeding up the process for approval. Environmental NGOs in Europe were particularly unsatisfied that the European Commission did not appeal, asserting that sovereign territories should have a clear right to reject food products that posed potential risks.

When it comes to actors and their interests, as the GMO case highlights, states are still important in environmental negotiations. States have difficulties in representing the diverse views and interests of their citizens, however, and they cannot guarantee the compliance of actors responsible for environmental degradation. Meanwhile, non-state actors (whether they are for-profit or not-for-profit) are also increasingly significant in environmental negotiations in terms of both the formation and implementation of agreements. In the global marketplace, as a result of increased capital mobility, private corporations are able to secure considerable concessions from governments, in the form of weak regulation as well as tax breaks and subsidies within their territorial boundaries. Besides states in the conventional sense, these actors can be divided into organizations or coalitions of states, UN bodies, private corporations and NGOs. For example, the interests of developing societies have been represented by the coalition Group of 77 (most often designated as G77).

Coalitions of states may act in a way that contradicts the stated objectives of member states or international bodies in which states play a part. By way of an example, the EU (or its predecessors before 1993) is a unique actor in that it is the sole example of a Regional Economic Integration Organization and is often cited as an important agency for developing international environmental agreements. Nevertheless, developing a common environmental policy within the EU is never easy. While in formal terms the EU negotiates as a bloc, internal negotiations can lead to problems in effectiveness. During the final session of the UN's Intergovernmental Forum on Forests held in February 2000, when considering the possibility of an International Convention on Forests, representatives of the EU member states could not agree internally and so became ineffectual in the discussions. Spain and Finland aligned themselves with the opinions of representatives of countries favouring a convention. Meanwhile other states, including the UK, were against. The result was that the EU played an increasingly peripheral role as the negotiations unfolded. This kind of immobilism means that when a policy proposal arises, majority support among members is not evident, and when a majority begins to emerge, the disagreements on substantive aspects of policy get in the way of united action, which could be a recurrent pattern if the global system becomes divided by regional blocs.

While the UN is formally and primarily a negotiating arena, the programmes and organizations that have been established also operate as actors in the processes of environmental negotiations. The United Nations Environment Programme (UNEP) and strategically located individuals in other UN institutions have coordinated state and non-state actors to achieve specific outcomes – for example, in dealing with ozone-depleting chemicals such as CFCs. In addition, private corporations and environmental NGOs have sometimes had a place in national delegations by virtue of the specialist expertise and technical competence they can provide. Such involvements also create opportunities for civil society organizations to act as transmission belts for disseminating information within nations, as well as transnationally through organizations such as the Environmental Liaison Centre International, itself a key member of the broader Sustainable Development Issues Network, which seeks to use knowledge-sharing for NGO capacity-building.

While the focus on rules in the operation of international regimes is crucial, the changing circumstances, shifting perceptions and emergence of new scientific evidence regarding environmental problems mean that it is just as important to consider the principles and norms that underpin the rules. Vogler suggests that regimes operate according to certain foundational assumptions as to the physical character of the issue area, the kind of environmental problem that should be subject to regulation, the scientific theory and evidence through which the 'problem' is constructed, and the identification of specific measures for producing better outcomes. For example, regarding climate change, these assumptions include the problem of global warming, the aggregate level of CO_2 and other emissions, the scientific consensus established through the Intergovernmental Panel on Climate Change (IPCC), and the targets for limiting emissions, alongside mechanisms such as carbon trading. As a result, he defines principles as beliefs of fact, causation and rectitude, while describing norms as standards of behaviour. Regarding norms, Vogler does not distinguish between abstract and concrete norms (see Chapter 3), generalizing that norms are defined in terms of rights and obligations. Principles provide the broad framework for working through the relationship between property rights and the responsibilities of actors to others, such as taking care with common sinks by maintaining air quality, not polluting the oceans, and ensuring a stable climate.

In addition, there are what Vogler defines as allocative principles, market-based or centralized resource planning, which provide ground rules for rights to extract resources and rights to discharge waste. If in an open-access commons, when initial exploiters discover a new location of a resource or develop technologies for extraction that were implausible before, then 'first come, first served' works as the allocative principle. Norms involve the application of principles to specific global commons, ensuring that rights to use the commons are moderated by duties (although it is often the case that rights exist here alongside obligations, i.e. an informal sense of commitment at best, and very narrowly defined duties). For example, members of particular nations can enjoy rights within territorial waters to fish stocks, crustaceans and sea mammals. Overfishing has resulted, however, in declining fish stocks in many cases, leading to the collapse of particular species in certain areas when stocks fall to unsustainable levels. State and EU regulations have restricted harvesting in this context with fishing quotas, hence translating obligations into duties. In 2006, the International Council for the Exploration of the Sea (ICES) recommended a total ban on cod fishing in the North Sea and other waters surrounding the British Isles so that stocks can rise to the minimum desired level of 70,000 tonnes, though this falls short of the agreed target of 150,000 tonnes made between the EU and Norway a year earlier.

Using these terms poses difficulties. Norms can be prescriptive and proscriptive (indicating what can and cannot be done) or they can be used in straightforwardly normative ways to signify good and bad outcomes, the right and wrong course of action, or the virtuous and unvirtuous forms of behaviour. In addition, many statements on sustainable development simultaneously imply principles and norms. To add confusion, international agreements often describe norms as principles. For instance, in the Earth Summit declaration (1992):

> *Principle 15* – that the absence of scientific certainty should not postpone action to prevent environmental degradation (the precautionary principle);

> *Principle 17* – that environmental impact assessment (EIA) should be introduced on all projects where environmental impacts follow.

Decision-making procedures and the organizations that make decisions attempt to provide a mechanism for transforming collectively agreed choices and commitments into effective actions in particular locations. The procedures vary from ad hoc meetings without sustained secretarial support (such as in the case of the Antarctic Treaty System) to regular meetings organized with bureaucratic and research support. Vogler's framework, rather than defining institutions in narrow terms, is useful, for they are portrayed as structures as reproduced, modified and transformed through strategic agency and simultaneously enabling and constraining the actors working within them. Institutional formation at the intergovernmental level is also a response to the complexities of the issues, the problems of reconciling diverse interests and claims, and the need for frequent decisions in a context of rapid change, especially when effectiveness can be achieved only through close and sustained monitoring. Another key reason is the need to coordinate the decisions and actions of a range of intergovernmental bodies. The mandate for the meta-coordination body the Commission for Sustainable Development (CSD), formally a subsidiary body of the UN's Economic and Social Council (ECOSOC), does overlap with that of the UNEP. While the latter coordinates and acts as a catalyst for environmentally focused projects across UN agencies, the CSD has been responsible for implementing Agenda 21 and the Rio Declaration on Environment and Development and for following up the Johannesburg Plan of Implementation by developing partnerships and strengthening the institutional links between governments, international bodies and key actors such as corporations, NGOs, scientists, trade unions, local authorities, farmers and indigenous peoples.

Intergovernmental bodies tend to adopt internal voting procedures that operate on a 'one state, one vote' principle, but this often creates conditions for powerful states that feel their interests have not been accommodated to not implement the policies. An alternative voting mechanism is quota voting, whereby the voting share of the state is determined by its contributions to an organization, together with the special privilege of being able to appoint to key positions. For example, the World Bank and the International Monetary Fund (IMF) have votes weighted by the financial contributions of members, and the president of the World Bank is appointed by the USA while the EU appoints the managing director of the IMF. The International Tropical Timber Organization (ITTO) has a system whereby the share of votes is allocated according to a country's share in the international trade of tropical timber. Quota voting tends to result in excessive influence on the part of the most powerful states, while one state, one vote often only works when the most powerful states agree with the policies developed.

Finally, when considering intergovernmental environmental negotiations, we need to consider rules. These are the concrete applications of principles and norms in concrete circumstances, i.e. situations where international regimes overlap and can generate conflict. For Vogler, 'rules' include both legally binding instruments and also those understandings and accepted practices that support them. If we take rules as having formally prescriptive and proscriptive duties for participants, we argue here that the informal or softer character of many practices is better understood in terms of abstract and concrete norms (see Chapter 3). Indeed, Vogler (2000: 36–8) recognizes the problems of studying these informal rules but does not conclusively deal with the question. Undoubtedly they are important, and we agree at the very least, as Vogler states, that they help us to understand how rules of distribution and compensation are flexibly applied in different situations. He does, however, provide us with a useful classificatory framework for understanding rules in terms of function.

1 *Standard-setting rules* promote desired outcomes and prohibit practices which result in environmental degradation.
2 *Distribution rules* allocate shares and rights to the commons as well as specify obligations to ensure renewability or equitable provision.
3 *Information rules* provide a mechanism whereby parties to an agreement can offer assurance of compliance (preventing some parties receiving the benefits of the regime without implementing it).
4 *Enforcement or compliance rules* aid states in securing the objectives of the regime (in the absence of a central world state as an enforcement agency), i.e. effectivity depends on the willingness of states to ensure compliance in their jurisdiction (and the willingness of citizens and corporations to bear the costs of compliance).

5 *Knowledge rules* have a slightly different role in that scientific decisions impact on the construction of new issues and regime formation as well as affecting development, monitoring and implementation (such as on maintaining sustainable fish stocks in the example developed above).

In effect, it is these rules which ensure that national governments: stay within agreed shares of greenhouse gas emissions; eliminate CFCs; regulate the catch quotas of fishermen, whalers and hunters to ensure the capacity of a species to survive; and manage the equitable distribution of rewards for the extraction of mineral resources. But rules work only through the concrete application of rights and duties and do so most effectively when all relevant constituencies are involved and all participants ground their entitlements and obligations within the terms of the environmental issue in question. In the intergovernmental context, this suggests that effectiveness demands much more than legally binding agreements but depends on a broader culture of duties and obligations that balances the preoccupation with rights and entitlements which features prominently in the discourses of governments.

Difficult cases in the search for international agreement: state regulation through the lens of self-regulation

We know that some international agreements have been relatively successful, such as the International Convention for the Prevention of Pollution by Ships (MARPOL), implemented by virtually all maritime nations, improving the safety record considerably – serious maritime accidents halved between 1994 and 2004, and total oil spills declined significantly at the same time as the aggregate maritime trade almost doubled. The development of international environmental negotiations on climate change has been problematic but fairly successful. The Framework Convention on Climate Change (UN-FCCC), concerned with mitigation of greenhouse gases, was signed at the Earth Summit and came into effect in 1994 in order to stimulate policy proposals at a series of annual 'Conferences of the Parties', resulting in the protocol at CoP3 at Kyoto in 1997. The measures (defined in terms of the baseline of emissions in 1990) varied from country to country, with some having to commit to significant greenhouse gas cuts (EU 7 per cent; USA 6 per cent), others standing still (Russia, 0 per cent), and some permitted increases (Australia, 8 per cent; Iceland, 10 per cent). While EU states ratified the Kyoto Protocol in 2002, it took longer to secure the same response from other major countries. According to Article 25, the protocol enters into force 'on the ninetieth day after the date on which not less than 55 Parties to the Convention, incorporating Parties included in Annex I which accounted in total for at least 55% of the total carbon dioxide emissions for 1990 of the Parties included in Annex I, have deposited their instruments of ratification, acceptance, approval or accession'. Of the two conditions, the fifty-five-parties stipulation was fulfilled on 23 May 2002, when Iceland ratified. The ratification by Russia provided the tipping point on 18 November 2004, satisfying the 55 per cent stipulation, and brought the treaty into force (effective 16 February 2005). The main stumbling blocks, however – the USA and Australia – have still not ratified the protocol. For Australia, the rapidly growing competitor economies in Asia – China and India – are not yet classed as developed countries and so are not subject to the mandatory limits on emissions. Implicit in the Kyoto Protocol is the idea of emissions trading, which has a longer history, dating back to John H. Dales's *Pollution, Property and Prices* (1968) and various emissions trading schemes in the USA that sought to place a monetary value on units of pollution that can be bought and sold in a market. Intergovernmental regulation works best when a blunt measure is needed and political consensus means that there is a high chance of implementation, whereas alternative 'soft power' approaches are more effective when sub-national and transnational actors are crucial to success. Climate change raises different kinds of issues because of the significance of the IPCC (considered in Chapter 1). Generalizing from this experience, we should also consider the crucial role of NGOs and multilateral environmental initiatives in trans-boundary issues such as the agreement for joint action to place limits on carbon emissions and collaboration on low carbon and renewable technologies between the State of California and the UK in 2006. The Republican governor of California, Arnold Schwarzenegger, secured legislative measures (the Global Warming Solutions Act) in a bipartisan initiative with the Democrat-led State Assembly, and it is anticipated that nine north-eastern states in the USA will initiate a carbon trading scheme in 2009.

We now turn to the climate change initiatives in the EU. The long-term legacy of Kyoto and subsequent CoPs has been the legitimization of emissions trading as an incentive scheme for reducing overall greenhouse gas levels while the workability of the mechanism has been established through EU quotas imposed, for example, on the manufacture of bricks, cement, glass, iron and steel, oil products, paper and cardboard, and the generation of energy. Collectively, over 11,500 installations are included in the Emissions Trading Scheme (ETS), which, according to the European Commission (EC), accounts for between 46 and 51 per cent of greenhouse emissions in the twenty-five member states of the EU. As part of Phase 2 of the implementation of Kyoto from 2008–12, the EC has considered refining the definition of 'combustion installations' to ensure that a wider range of activities and non-CO_2 greenhouse gases are included, for example methane emissions arising from landfill and agricultural practices. Practical obstacles exist here, since the installations would, in many cases, be much smaller, more difficult to monitor and costly to administer. In addition, the quotas applied to different EU members have generated their own issues:

1   the ETS deficits of countries that constituted the EU prior to enlargement have been offset by the surpluses of new members of the EU as a result of post-communist industrial restructuring;
2   some new EU members are unhappy with the quotas because they do not always take account of the precise energy source mix in individual countries (such as the reliance on oil shale, which generates higher CO_2 emissions, by Estonia, which has joined Poland, Hungary, the Czech Republic and Slovakia's legal challenge to the EC on the grounds that the caps do not account sufficiently for their need for economic development);
3   the EU cap and trade system is primarily internal and presents obstacles to emissions trading with developing countries outside the EU;
4   the implementation of ETS within the EU does not provide the same incentives to develop clean and energy-efficient alternatives for production processes that are difficult to regulate compared to those that are not.

Also, owing to scientific uncertainty, carbon sinks such as forests are not included in the ETS, in part because of the absence of evidence that the long-term effects of tree plantation will have the anticipated positive effects (it could possibly have negative effects), and the most efficient carbon sequestration projects through this route are fast-growing monocultural plantations (with implications for biodiversity), but also because of the pragmatic concern to drastically reduce industrial greenhouse gas emissions from large-scale installations between 2005 and 2015. The issues raised in Chapter 3, when considering the application of financial (dis)incentives for individual citizens, are applicable to some extent here as well. The ETS is primarily a market where the overall availability of a commodity is set politically – it is the EC in consultation with member-state governments which sets the overall level of emissions. Rather as in the case of household waste rationing, there is a financial cost for excess that some participants in the process will be willing to bear (in the case of some areas of industry, such as energy produced from oil shale, the costs of developing cleaner production techniques exceed the costs of buying the emissions surpluses of other installations). At the individual citizen level there has been a move to reduce landfill waste by alternating between weekly recyclable and non-recyclable collections, while another proposal is to reduce the size of non-recyclable household waste bins. Similarly, if the political will is present, then the caps could be made more stringent, but this is where the analogy with individual citizens and households ends.

We must be careful not to commit the 'fallacy of composition', assuming that what applies to the individual citizen is also applicable to an industrial sector, a country or a regional economic integration organization, a legacy of the neoliberal doctrines developed in the West as part of Thatcherism and Reaganomics. An ETS with very stringent caps could lead to certain forms of production becoming non-viable and, in the context of capital mobility, their relocation to developing countries, such as China and India, that have exemptions from Kyoto and impose less strict regulations on emissions, is a real possibility. Indeed, many of the sectors that Phase 1 of the ETS regulates have witnessed dramatic growth in China. For example, cement production in China is envisaged to at least double between 2005 and 2015, partly to address the demands of rapid domestic urbanization and development, but also for export. ETS may well make certain areas of production less viable in the EU, resulting in plant closures and the economic costs that follow from such industrial restructuring.

On the face of it, this may make greenhouse emission targets in the EU even easier to achieve, but targets for aggregate emissions on a global basis (the processes that matter for Kyoto to be effective) will still not have been met. In short, to return to the analogy with individual citizens, households and communities, which can have a more positive impact through 'understanding the reasons' for changing practices, there are limits to the effectiveness of (dis)incentive mechanisms unless the 'installations' (a word that connotes an object subject to instrumental control) and all the relevant constituencies (including the employees and communities) become stakeholders in the policy-making processes that affect their operation. So far, there is very limited evidence of the ETS scheme in the EU developing this degree of accountability and transparency. Without this, the scheme is in danger of undermining the goals of Kyoto while achieving targets through the exportation of environmental degradation.

This does not mean that intergovernmental action at the regional or global levels cannot achieve substantive results. In some areas, it has had a significant impact, as in the case of the Montreal Protocol, 1987, whereby, for each designated group of halogenated hydrocarbons such as CFCs, the treaty provided an explicit timetable for phasing them out (with HCFCs, which are weaker ozone-depleting compounds, anticipated to be phased out by 2030). In other areas, however, such as deforestation, it has not been so effective, despite significant developments such as the Forest Stewardship Council (FSC), a not-for-profit organization that combines corporate and NGO representatives as stakeholders. The FSC has a third-party certification and labelling process whereby members demonstrate that the timber is tracked from source to market and manage the forest resources in a sustainable way. This development also highlights how intergovernmental action can take second place to self-regulation when addressing issues such as forest degradation, community conflict, illegal logging and the rights of indigenous peoples.

Whether one see stakeholder innovations such as the FSC as a symptom of the failure of intergovernmental action or as an alternative route to achieving the same goals depends on one's own framework of analysis. In our case, we argue that there has been a shift from intergovernmental to self-regulation which mirrors a shift in focus on duties as formal requirements in legally binding agreements to a focus on obligations and duties where the informal and formal meet through citizenly obligations (whether citizens are defined as individuals, groups, organizations, movements, communities, corporations, political authorities of different kinds, or actors acting as proxies for non-human animals, forests, mountains, ecosystems or the biotic community) that can promote virtuous thinking and practices. At this point, building on the arguments presented in Chapter 3, we want to reiterate that obligations are inclusive of duties and both are inclusive of voluntarily inspired obedience (just as rights and rights claims are grounded in entitlements).

To illustrate the slow pace of change in some areas, and reflecting on the impact of the FSC, we will first concentrate on the forests. The World Commission on Forests and Sustainable Development (WCFSD), established in 1995, sought to bring about what has often been described as a global conversation on forests and, like previous commissions, was independent of other institutions, interests and states. Its problems were apparent in the planning stage – in particular, forest user groups in developing societies were not included as an integral part of the composition of the project. Consequently, developing-society governments saw the Intergovernmental Panel on Forests (IPF) as a better mechanism for representing their interests, while NGOs focused on the CSD. As Humphreys (2007) argues, ironically the WCFSD did initiate a process of consultation with relevant constituencies which has been wider than any other process, but these constituencies were not represented as stakeholders in the process of deciding what was in the global 'public interest'. The IPF was succeeded in 1997 by the Intergovernmental Forum on Forests (IFF), also created by the CSD. Although the CSD was committed to multi-stakeholder dialogues from 1997, however, they emerged only in the United Nations Forum on Forests (UNFF) in 2000, which was established by UN ECOSOC to implement the proposals of the IPF and the IFF, as well as in terms of Agenda 21 to develop dialogue between governments and international organizations and policy recommendations on forest-related issues.

Box 4.2 Thematic elements of Sustainable Forest Management

1. Extent of forest resources – the desire to have adequate forest cover and stocking, including trees outside forests, to support the social, economic and environmental dimensions of forestry. For example, the existence and extent of specific forest types are important as a basis for conservation efforts. The theme encompasses ambitions to reduce deforestation and to restore and rehabilitate degraded forest landscapes. It also includes the important function of forests and trees outside forests to store carbon and thereby contribute to moderating the global climate.

2. Biological diversity – concerns the conservation and management of biological diversity at ecosystem (landscape), species and genetic levels. Such conservation, including the protection of areas with fragile ecosystems, ensures that diversity of life is maintained, and provides opportunities to develop new products in the future, including medicines. Genetic improvement is also a means of increasing forest productivity, for example to ensure high wood production levels in intensively managed forests.

3. Forest health and vitality – effective management so that the risks and impacts of unwanted disturbances are minimized, including wildfires, airborne pollution, storm felling, invasive species, pests, diseases and insects. Such disturbances may impact on social and economic as well as environmental dimensions of forestry.

4. Productive functions of forest resources – expresses the ambition to maintain an ample and valuable supply of primary forest products, while at the same time ensuring that production and

harvesting are sustainable and do not compromise the management options of future generations.

5. Protective functions of forest resources – addressing the role of forests and trees outside forests in moderating soil, hydrological and aquatic systems, maintaining clean water (including healthy fish populations) and reducing the risks and impacts of floods, avalanches, erosion and drought. Protective functions of forest resources also contribute to ecosystem conservation efforts and have strong cross-sectoral aspects, because the benefits to agriculture and rural livelihoods are high.

6. Socio-economic functions – the contributions of forest resources to the overall economy, for example through employment, values generated through processing and marketing of forest products, and energy, trade and investment in the forest sector. Also addresses the important forest function of hosting and protecting sites and landscapes of high cultural, spiritual or recreational value, and thus includes aspects of land tenure, indigenous and community management systems, and traditional knowledge.

7. Legal, policy and institutional framework – to support the above six themes, including participatory decision-making, governance and law enforcement, and monitoring and assessment of progress. Also involves broader societal aspects, including fair and equitable use of forest resources, scientific research and education, infrastructure arrangements to support the forest sector, transfer of technology, capacity-building and public information and communication.

Source: Food and Agriculture Organization of the United Nations, <www.fao.org/forestry/24447/en>

A key part of the UNFF mission was to monitor, assess and report on progress and maintain the momentum established in promoting sustainable development in this area. Initially, the UNFF was established for five years, subsequently extended for ten years in 2005, resulting in a Non Legally Binding Instrument on all types of forests in April 2007, seeking to encourage political commitment towards Sustainable Forest Management (SFM; see Box 4.1) and provide a framework for action. The UNFF has also sought to enhance the role of member groups such as the Collaborative Partnership on Forests to harmonize voluntary monitoring, assessment and reporting so that the national reporting burden is reduced. Since attempts to develop a binding international forestry convention have so far fallen on the stony ground of national-interest politics, the UNFF has also focused on voluntary compliance with four objectives on forests set out in ECOSOC resolution 2006/49 (reversing forest cover loss, enhancing social, economic and environmental benefits, increasing protected areas and developing financial support for SFM in the wake of declining official development assistance). As with many other areas of international and transnational cooperation, this demonstrates a shift of focus from strictly intergovernmental environmental problem-solving towards developing strategies that include not only issue-specific coalitions such as the Collaborative Partnerships on Forests (CPF) but a range of transnational and sub-national organizations. Non-legally-binding projects also raise the importance of moving beyond formally binding duties towards considering a broader politics of obligation through which duties are solidified.

As with many other areas of international and transnational cooperation, this demonstrates a shift of focus from strictly intergovernmental environmental problem-solving towards developing strategies that include not only issue-specific coalitions such as CPF but a range of transnational and sub-national organizations. Non-legally-binding projects also raise the importance of moving beyond formally binding duties towards considering a broader politics of obligation through which duties are solidified.

Citizenship, movements and environmental governance from above/below

So far we have focused on formal political institutions at the international and regional level. In this and subsequent sections we consider the effects of top-down governance on self-organizing environmental movements, where movements and NGOs are incorporated and where they produce resistance from the communities affected. Besides considering the successes and failures of LA21 (to be considered in more detail later), this section will also draw attention to how citizen movements concerned with environmental issues prompt us to reconsider the assumptions of social movement and resource mobilization theory. At this point it is important to highlight how civic engagement strategies are becoming more diverse and innovative, but also that there are problems of accountability in environmental movements and NGOs. Later in this chapter, we consider how the ideas of environmental citizenship and responsibility have been deployed in policy communities and (building on the arguments of Chapter 3) how personal values and financial (dis) incentives can work together.

As we have seen, one of the most significant transnational actors in environmental governance is the EU (a Regional Economic Integration Organization through which states have pooled sovereignty to achieve collective outcomes and more effective coordination), although, as Weale et al. (2000) state, environmental policy initiatives have developed pace in periods of economic growth and slowed down in recession. Weale et al. (ibid.) go so far as to suggest that there now exists a 'system of European environmental governance' in that there are now rules that distribute political authority for making rules in the institutionalized system of policy formulation, development and implementation in a way that complements environmental policy at the national level. As with all areas of policy, pressure groups provide vital local and sectoral information without which policy-making is often arbitrary and ineffective. As a result, many environmental groups have achieved the position of insiders in policy-making similar to that held by trade unions in the 1950s. Much of this is a result of the distinctive character of EU institutional formation, following what has been described as the Monnet method, whereby institutional development follows well-established technical development in terms of policies and rules.

The EU is also an important actor in intergovernmental negotiations on environmental issues (having formal responsibilities or duties resulting from treaties), especially on issues such as climate change where it has acted as a standard-setter. We will, however, broaden the scope of issues coverage beyond the concerns of global environmental problems. In terms of top-down initiatives, legislation in the form of EU Directives has been developed to cover:

- Pollution control and air quality (specifying ambient air quality standards for specific pollutants as well as national emission limits for nitrogen oxides, sulphur dioxides and vehicle emissions) and water quality (bathing and drinking water standards).
- Solid waste management.
- Control of genetically modified organisms.
- Protection of landscape, wildlife and countryside (rural areas).
- Exchange of information among member states on environmental quality, data reporting and public access to environmental information.

These require that the EU regulates environmental administration, management, reporting and auditing. In the half-century after the Second

World War, something remarkable happened in the issues and concerns of groups and organizations involved in political representation in this context. New groups and movements characterized by informal networks, while also mobilizing considerable resources around single-issue campaigns, came to play a significant role. As a starting point, we will explore the emergence of social movements that cut across state boundaries and at the same time draw their vital support from particular communities aroused by local environmental concerns. We will examine why these movements are emerging, their significance, and whether they pose a challenge to and represent a departure from traditional politics. We will argue that they illustrate a change in how governance is conducted and that the EU has become a new site of struggle as communities, collectivities and organizations seek to construct or pursue their own identities, lifestyles and values; and at the same time, national governments, the EU and other public agencies seek to exert varying degrees of social control over them.

Social movements are different from conventional forms of political participation such as political parties, for they mobilize support outside established political institutions. Sometimes they promote interests or causes that have been marginalized or neglected by mainstream forms of political representation. Since they have oppositional origins, their organizational character is shaped through their struggles to ensure that their concerns are recognized. For example, they may bring together consumers against producers, local residents against a company responsible for some pollutant, disabled or ethnic communities against discrimination and prejudice, feminist movements against sexism, so they are as diverse as the citizens they mobilize. Since many such movements have operated outside the usual ways of exerting political influence, their strategies are more likely to include direct action, such as demonstrations, strikes and civil disobedience, and as a form of collective action they bring the concerns of everyday life into touch with the formal institutions of government, not only to make a difference in policy-making but also to change the cultural attitudes and values we hold. It used to be assumed that old and new social movements were of different types (see Table 4.1) but, as with all ideal-type constructs, the conditions have changed dramatically.

The period between the 1920s and the 1950s has often been described as the age of the labour movement, with the 1960s witnessing the birth of new social movements concerned with the operation of power both in the public domain and in private lives, which researchers had tended to ignore. In rehearsing these academic stereotypes, old social movements

TABLE 4.1 Old and new social movements

	Old social movements	New social movements
Location	Polity	Civil society
Ideology and aims	Political integration Economic rights	Autonomy in civil society New values/lifestyles
Organization	Formal and hierarchical	Informal network and grass roots
Medium of change	Participation in political institutions	Direct action and cultural politics

Source: Martell (1994: 112)

were concerned with influencing policy-making in political institutions predominantly through mainstream political parties. In central European countries, trade unions have strong historical ties with leftist parties such as the German Social Democratic Party, but have also built connections and alliances across the political spectrum with Christian Democratic parties. Moreover, trade unions have aimed to become insiders in the policy-making process of economic management. While formal hierarchical structures are a common feature of organizations with large numbers of members, for trade unions they were also necessary for securing members' compliance with successive government policies in exchange for influence. Their primary task is to defend their members' interests through whatever means are feasible and effective, from legal cases to industrial action, although in this context the latter is usually a defensive option when negotiations fail. Unions secured their economic rights through participation and integration within industrial relations networks. With large memberships and applying the 'iron law of oligarchy', a hierarchical organizational structure developed to coordinate members, and since most members cannot participate fully in the organizational activities, activists and officials have a disproportionate impact on the decisions made in the organized movement.

New social movements were portrayed as having a different set of concerns, values and organizational forms – in many cases, as informal associations with active participation by members and without a central leadership. They sought to promote different ways of life while also acting as advocates for groups of the population that were marginalized or the 'underdogs' of civil society, and against those who exercised power, defined broadly as any individual capable of making authoritative decisions over others in the criminal justice system, educational institutions and psychiatric care; they argued that power relations operated in private relationships (for example, the concern with domestic violence on the part of feminist movements) as well as in the public sphere. These movements addressed gay rights, disability rights, civil rights, prisoners' rights and the welfare of psychiatric patients, and the social change they wanted was likely to be delivered not by legislation but from a transformation in the cultural values of society, i.e. cultural politics.

The impetus for a social movement can be a threat to economic interest, concern about a particular environmental hazard, the promotion of a cause or ethical message and/or the desire to forge new identities or protect established identities, so each is distinctive, complex and subject to change. Consequently, the explanations for the emergence of social movements vary. In the case of the labour movement, they are the products of changes in the social and economic structure, such as the introduction of assembly-line factory production, as witnessed in the attempts at unionization in South-East Asia and China (Pangsapa 2007; Lee 2006, 2007; Koo 2001; Pun 2005; Soonok 2003), where common class identities are forged through the lived experience of long hours, low pay and poor working conditions. In European societies, collective action was most evident in those factories that had large-scale dissatisfied workforces engaged in monotonous semi-skilled labour. In the late twentieth century, the shift towards less organized forms of production, more mobile workforces and flexible working practices can be seen as being responsible for the fragmentation of class identity and the dispersion of the members of such working communities upon which collective action was based.

Social movements are also described as manifestations of post-materialism, growing affluence, improved education and social mobility in European societies shifting attention away from economic concerns and the quantitative measurement of human welfare towards new goals or values (see Table 4.2). This included a desire for greater accountability, transparency and participation in decision-making institutions. In more recent research, Alberto Melucci (1989) suggests that social movements are cultural laboratories for new lifestyles and values, often existing as latent currents in cultural relations and manifest only in visible outbursts at certain times. Melucci goes farther, to argue that the preoccupation with sexuality, gender and ethnic identity that features in the 'submerged networks' of social movements makes them cultural rather than political, i.e. it separates the political from private life, and concludes that social movements are both pre-political because they derive sustenance from everyday life and meta-political because while their interests can

TABLE 4.2 Materialist and post-materialist goals

Materialist goals	Post-materialist goals
Maintaining a high rate of economic growth	Giving people more say in important government decisions
Making sure that strong defences are maintained	Progress towards a less impersonal and more humanitarian social order
Maintaining a stable economy	People should have more say in the decisions made on their behalf
Fighting price inflation	Progress towards a society where ideas are more important than money

Source: Cotgrove and Duff (1981: 96)

be represented they can never be fully captured by parties. We should also highlight the fact that since ethics are culturally specific the ethico-political assumptions of each movement are context dependent.

Since the late 1970s a new explanation has developed, concerned with the specific contexts within which social movements emerge and the resources they can mobilize in support of their goals in a way reminiscent of that outlined in Table 4.1. This resource mobilization approach, developed by Charles Tilly (1994), is more focused on whether the movements are insiders (polity members) or challengers (fighting from the outside), so collective action is thus interpreted as an attempt to stay in or to join the polity. It also focuses on the opportunity structures that exist within political institutions for these different movements including:

- the capacity of the movement to mobilize support or resources from public opinion in order to be taken seriously;
- the willingness of political institutions to integrate their concerns;
- the willingness and capacity of the state to establish measures which address the movements' concerns.

For example, anti-nuclear protests in the UK and in France have faced the problem of public apathy (even when local communities have been subject to hazards), as well as the lack of will in the political apparatus to integrate their concerns. In Sweden and Germany, the problem is less one of public support and political openness, and more one of the implementation of effective policies. This approach also highlights how movements and counter-movements tend to emerge in waves; for example, libertarian movements concerned to make criminal justice more accountable tend to generate 'law and order' movements in response, thus making the rights of defendants an area of contestation. It also explores how political crises are relevant for success in achieving objectives. The primary focus here is the way in which people recognize the injustice involved in the issue with which they are concerned, organize themselves, raise funds and mobilize others for direct action, as well as how the organizational structure affects a movement's relationship with other movements, parties and institutions. So whether the movement is old or new is less relevant than what it seeks to achieve and how it acts. This redirects our attention to the interconnections between governing institutions and the self-organized forms of governance from below.

Explaining environmental movements and the links with Green party politics

Since the 1960s, various social movements have emerged which are grounded in debates over cultural differences, gender, human rights, peace and, our focus here, the environment. The rise of social movements as self-organized expressions of collective identities cannot be reduced simply to class location. This has prompted a rethink about the motivations for political action and why certain issues matter to citizens. It is useful to recap briefly on some of the key differences between old and new social movements. Whereas the unions tended to be characterized by formal and hierarchical structures, the new social movements are largely made up of informal networks and participative associations (which is why they have been linked to post-materialism; see Table 4.2). Such grassroots organizations have sought to change public opinion and transform relationships in civil society rather than concentrating their attention on being integrated into public policy-making bodies. Indeed, until the late 1980s such movements were often marginalized in conventional party politics and ridiculed in the media. Unions saw it as their primary duty to defend their own members' interests within political institutions; new social movements attempt to change attitudes and transform social relationships more generally. Environmental organizations are quite diverse. Some seek to change public opinion while others focus their attention on lobbying mainstream political parties oriented to the labour movement or the business community. Some attempt to construct broad platforms while others are fixated upon the hazard in their own backyard. Four main explanations have been developed to account for the rise of environmental movements, of which the first two are closely linked to the explanations for social movements considered earlier.

1 Changes in the class structure have seen the decline of the

traditional working class and the emergence of a new middle class employed in professions, middle management and public services.

2 Changes in values within developed Western societies: the values acquired during the depression and war years of the early twentieth century (when economic security and growth were the prevailing concerns) have been increasingly supplanted by an alternative post-materialism among the post-war generations (notably among the children of parents with material security).

3 Corporatism as an institutional arrangement focused exclusively on the relations between capital and labour among political regimes in Austria, Sweden and West Germany. This has been seen as partly responsible for environmental movements becoming oppositional challenging groups in these national contexts. The state becomes their main antagonist – a direct consequence of the exclusion of environmentalists from participation in policy-making (Scott 1990). Environmental movements have thus been consistently loud and prominent in the media, for the quiet mechanisms of influence have often been closed to them. Nevertheless, the transition from oppositional movement to potent political force depends more on the electoral system than the precise environmental issues raised. In politically open societies with proportional representation (such as Germany) and financial support for electioneering, Green political representatives can secure seats in the national assemblies. Electoral systems and political institutions are especially important in accounting for variation across Europe.

4 The visibility of environmental deterioration has had the effect of generating a greater environmental consciousness in post-war Europe. This would also explain the greater intensity of environmental action in southern Germany, northern France and the Netherlands, where direct experience of problems such as air and water pollution is more likely. In the UK, however, environmental concern is well integrated into the party political framework, with pressure groups such as the Campaign for the Protection of Rural England and the National Trust (sometimes referred to as the 'ecoestablishment') providing a moderate avenue for political influence. Direct action is usually limited to issues where extensive consultation with environmental groups has been inadequate, such as nuclear power and highway construction.

Each of these explanations, although all are relevant, offers a partial account of the reasons for the rise of environmental movements. Recent studies consider these movements as expressions of disaffection with the alienating conditions of urban life, impersonal social relations in twentieth-century culture and increased state intrusion into personal lives. These explanations similarly do not adequately account for the connections between environmental movements and political parties in some countries, a process that has produced innovative party politics. In the context of the EU, the environmental movements emerged and coalesced into the more formal political organizations that now make up the Green parties in national assemblies, regional assemblies and the European Parliament.

One of the most prominent environmental movements originated in Germany, which had a culture that harboured a widespread concern for environmental protection in local areas. From the 1960s to the 1980s, growing concern with the effects of industrial processes produced thousands of citizen action groups (*Burgerinitiativen*), which had sprung up in response to town planning issues (Boehmer-Christiansen and Skea 1991). These groups were radicalized by the experience of anti-nuclear protests and campaigns for nature conservation being ignored by established parties and political institutions. The formation of the Federation of Citizens Groups (BBU) provided a national platform for environmental politics and maintained the grassroots support of ordinary activists.

By 1980, an estimated 50,000 citizen action groups had been established throughout West Germany (about 1.6 million people – equivalent to the combined membership of political parties). These citizen action groups campaigned alongside the more traditional organizations for landscape and conservation, such as the BUND (the German Federation of Environment and Nature Protection). Since the BUND was established to defend the interests of landowners (unlike the broader defence of cultural heritage developed by the National Trust in the UK), it served as a conservative force when environmental issues were raised in mainstream politics. The BUND was especially strong where the German Christian Democrats were also the dominant political party, such as in Bavaria.

Although still very diverse, the BBU was also considerably more radical in its objectives. Its members were heavily involved in mass protests and direct action against nuclear power stations in Whyl (near Freiburg), Brokdorf (near Hamburg) and the Wackersdorf reprocessing plant (Bavaria), as well as against American military bases identified as holding cruise missiles directed at the Eastern Bloc prior to the end of the cold war. Both protesters and police came equipped for violent confrontation, and the notion that the environmental movement would serve as a means of social and political transformation provided a significant alternative to the union movement, which remained closely affiliated to the SPD, the Social Democratic Party of Germany (Mewes 1998).

The formation of Die Grünen (the German Green Party) in 1979 provided a new mechanism for environmental pressure to be brought to bear on mainstream politics. As a political organization it had a middle-class membership and a strong appeal for those born since the 1950s. Nevertheless, the membership (approximately forty thousand) is no reflection of the diversity of the 3.5 million voters it attracted in West Germany (and more so since the unification of Germany). As a political party Die Grünen has drawn support away from all the mainstream parties, although its association with leftist politics makes it a considerable threat to the Social Democrats. It draws support from BUND members who have become so dissatisfied with Christian Democratic responses to environmental issues that at key moments they have voted for Die Grünen (Mez 1998). In addition, the strong and organizationally effective eco-feminist strand in the Greens emphasized the links between the domination of women and the degradation of nature. This part of the environmental movement sees equal rights in the workplace as a distraction from the way in which the organization of work is itself part of the ecological problem. Eco-feminists celebrated the role of women in social reproduction and highlighted the inequity of unpaid domestic labour in order to draw upon the support of mothers with small children (Smith 1998a: 82–8). This also explains how the feminist ethics of care has resurfaced in recent debates on ecological citizenship. Furthermore, the transformist politics of the Greens provided younger voters with a natural place for protest. This alliance of diverse interests also presented its own difficulties in coordination and in listening to members' concerns.

Green political parties are often caught between two imperatives. They draw from models of democratic thinking which emphasize the importance of participating in the decisions that affect our lives. They also recognize, however, that making a difference to policy-making means that they have to redirect the demands of the broader environmental movement within the confines of existing political institutions. As a result, they could continue to act as a protest movement coordinating a fragile alliance of movements or they could try to build a party that could make a difference to policy-making. In order to achieve influence and secure voting support, Green parties throughout Europe and within the European Parliament decided to play by the rules of the political game. This enabled them to present a clear policy line which can be assimilated easily within media sound-bite presentation, as well as to recruit members and voters, raise money for campaigns and so on. According to the 'realists' in Die Grünen, all this could be achieved much more easily through a hierarchical party structure. 'Fundamentalists', however (including the eco-feminist wing of the party), were willing to risk being less effective in order to maintain their identity as transformative organizations. The internal divisions that led up to and followed the realists' victory over the 'fundis' on internal structure and organization also severely harmed the electoral performance of Die Grünen at state and federal levels (Roth and Murphy 1998). Similar divisions and consequences were evident in the British Green Party in the early 1990s as it transformed itself from a party of protest to a professional party with the same centralized leadership and formal, hierarchical organization as mainstream parties.

In both Germany and the UK the result was a fall in membership as many activists moved on into related movements focusing on direct action on single issues. These have included the eco-warrior strategies adopted in protests against airport extensions and new construction (such as the Camp for Climate Action at Heathrow airport, 2007), highway construction (such as mass trespasses at Twyford Down, 1993/94, and Newbury, 1996) and the 'The Land Is Ours' movement, another UK-based movement inspired by historical political experiments such as the Diggers, which also occupies and builds urban eco-villages on brown-field waste sites in protest at green belt developments (such as the Wandsworth campaign on derelict land for over five months in 1996). Environmental movements also tend to promote local initiatives, such as non-monetary exchange systems, self-sufficiency projects, producers' cooperatives, slow food networks and other citizens' initiatives. They are concerned with developing strategies for change in their private lives and are sceptical about the capacities of the state to find the right answers.

So, it is more accurate to acknowledge the variety of environmental movements in very different cultural locations and recognize the ad hoc and informal character of these kinds of social movements throughout Europe. They do not usually exist in a pure form that fits the definitions devised by social scientists; they draw from the lived experiences of complex communities with a mix of social classes and culturally specific groups, as illustrated in the Kalamas campaign, considered in more detail in the next section.

Mobilizing communities: the Kalamas campaign

Environmental movements often involve specific communities mobilizing and coordinating their activities against an environmental hazard or planned development. They present a sustained challenge to power-holders and state bodies through feisty demonstrations of 'commitment, unity and worthiness' (Tilly 1994: 7). In the Kalamas campaign, an alliance of Thesprotian communities and the island of Corfu in north-west Greece, we find an example of a challenging group. Such a campaign

demonstrates the interaction of opportunity structures and the mobilization of resources in specific circumstances. To understand any campaign
we need to consider the context in which a movement emerges. The
Kalamas campaign was a localized environmental movement against
the construction of a sewage treatment plant planned by the municipal
authorities in Ioannina. In this development project, treated effluent
would be discharged into the River Kalamas and so would alter the ecosystem upon which prevailing agricultural practices and growing tourism
were based.

This project was instigated by the Greek central government, which had
provided grants for technical and financial support from the EU as part
of a longer-term programme of urban development. Solving this problem
of urbanization, however, produced a massive backlash and extensive
community mobilization to challenge the project. This was due largely
to the perception that urban benefits would generate costs for the people
who lived in the surrounding rural areas and on the offshore island of
Corfu. This did not mean that the campaign was against development,
but it sought a strategy that worked with rather than disrupted existing relationships between local people and the ecosystem. In addition,
of special concern was the potential damage to fisheries and tourism.
A major study of the internal organization of the campaign by Maria
Kousis (1997) revealed a complex decentralized committee system that
emerged spontaneously and solely to press the case of Thesprotia and
Corfu at local, regional, state and international levels, including to the
World Health Organization. The various tactics used – from lobbying
and demonstrations to strikes, blockades and occupations – secured
extensive media coverage.

The campaign was grounded in local cultural knowledge and signalled
a distrust of technical experts (for backing the sewage project in the first
place). It also built links with broader environmental movements (including RIXI in Athens and Die Grünen). No formal membership list existed
and all participants were volunteers. Yet, through poster announcements
and a limited and loose committee structure, an extensive range of
actions was successfully initiated. The Kalamas committee (chaired in
rotation among its members) was more important in preventing splits
in the movement than in providing a central organizational focus – i.e. it
sought to coordinate activities under way rather than direct the campaign.
When necessary, mobilization of supporters was swift and very effective,
including a successful forty-one-day blockade of the provincial capital,
Igoumenitsa. The extent of cohesion was impressive:

In public referenda, all unions and associations and individual locals voted to cease all activities – even schools and hospitals were closed – and to block all routes of transportation to the city. The municipal town hall was chained and locked up by members of the Struggle Committee and public buildings were occupied by local citizens. On a number of occasions, farm tractors were used in these mobilizations though the actions were characterized by non-violence. These mobilization tactics were also used in Athens, in front of parliament and in front of the major TV stations, by internal migrants from Thesprotia and Corfu. (ibid.: 249)

The state of the local economy had produced high levels of migration from Thesprotia, so the campaign could rely on 'internal migrants' throughout Greece to act on its behalf and organize pressure from every possible direction. The Kalamas campaign was also not an isolated incident in this country but part of a pattern of action by environmental movements. It coincided with the active mobilization of communities on the island of Milos against a geothermal power-plant project and the successful Astakos campaign against the government granting a licence for a toxic waste storage and disposal project to a European waste company. Each campaign had distinctive qualities but they shared deep roots in the collective identities of their communities.

In such spontaneous self-organizing networks in defence of local interests, concerned with social as well as environmental justice, we can identify many features of environmental movements throughout Europe since the 1970s. These examples highlight how environmental movements have deep roots in both the collective identities of communities and a variety of interests. There are parallels between the forces mobilized in favour of environmental protection and the attempts to defend communities through trade unions.

All such development projects need to be considered in terms of the wider plans for modernization and development supported by the EU. On many occasions it will be the European regional development initiatives which will be challenged for their effects on the environment and communities. Governance involves both regulation from above and mobilization from below.

Building common causes: integrating movements across issues

As can be seen from the previous examples of the way such diverse groups are able to mobilize around a common cause, the differences between class identity, regional or national affiliation and environmental concerns are not especially clear cut. Networks of alliances often emerge between unions, environmental movements and other campaigning groups, but these can be unpredictable and changeable. For instance, during 1999 a wide variety of European groups took part in the demonstrations against the World Trade Organization (WTO) in Seattle. The promotion of global free trade by the WTO has been blamed for its negative impact on both the environment and those people employed in industries that were shielded from open competition by tariff barriers and other controls. Of the 1,448 non-governmental organizations from eighty-nine countries supporting the Friends of the Earth/ASEED (Action for Solidarity, Equality, Environment and Development) petition against the trade talks in Seattle, 575 were situated in European societies. In addition to political representatives from Green parties and international environmental and union organizations, a whole variety of locally based groups and organizations signed up, such as the Alternative Consumer Association and Fur for Animals (Netherlands), the Finnish Association for Nature Conservation and Grandmothers for Peace (Finland), HempLETS (a local exchange trading scheme) and the New Economics Foundation (UK), the Women's International League for Peace and Freedom (France), as well as the Norsk Okologisk Landbrukslag (Organic Farmers' Union) and Oljearbeidernes Fellessammenslutning (Federation of Oil Workers' Trade Unions) from Norway. The fact that many of these groups are small scale, are focused on specific issues or were formed to defend particular interests in a variety of cultural locations demonstrates the heterogeneity of groups within the environmental and associated movements.

Since this chapter has focused to some degree on Europe, it should be added that the history of environmental awareness throughout, in this context, has been closely connected to labour movements engaging in attempts to improve the urban environment or creating greater opportunities for urban populations to have access to the countryside. Public health improvements were always a feature of the reformist policy platforms of trade unions as well as the political parties with which they have been aligned. The impetus for town planning and the amelioration of environmental hazards from smog to cholera have been as much a feature of rightist political parties concerned with national efficiency as of leftist ones focused on social justice. Environmentalist initiatives such as organic farming (including permaculture) and forest conservation were also a feature of fascist regimes in the early twentieth century. So it should be stressed that environmental movements have links and influences across the political spectrum, including the far right neo-Nazi movement.

In addition, it should be emphasized that the effects of environmental movements are also patchy and uneven, even coming into conflict with the stated objective of 'sustainable development' within the EU (Baker 2001). Both unions and environmental movements are engaged in these kinds of struggles and both have experienced the dilemmas involved in choosing to oppose or become part of the process through which policies are formulated and implemented. Most notably, labour unions have often campaigned for government financial support for environmentally damaging heavy industry and manufacturing to preserve employment and communities, as well as supporting leftist economic growth strategies that can deliver higher wages and improved working conditions for their members. Similarly, as demonstrated by the connections between social democracy and environmental movements in Germany above, the UK Labour Party has a long history of seeking to develop environmental legislation to improve health and safety in industries using toxics and in regulating pollution affecting the surrounding communities that provide the workforce. As Ann Taylor argued years before she became a senior Labour politician:

> Health and safety in the workplace is a vital element of and in some ways the key to environmental protection for the simple reason that where industry pollutes, its workers will be the first to be exposed to risk. Clean, safe and healthy workplaces will, on the other hand, make for a cleaner, safer and healthier environment. Specific illnesses have always been associated with particular industries – pneumoconiosis in the mines, asbestosis among asbestos workers and, among textile workers, byssinosis, which despite hundreds of deaths and maimings was not recognized as an official disease or as an occupational illness until the 1970s. These occupational hazards usually have their counterparts in public health risks, as is the case for pulmonary disorders resulting from the burning of coal, and even more pointedly in public exposure to asbestos used in construction. Similarly, it is estimated that every year ... [in developing societies] 10,000 people die from and 400,000 suffer pesticide poisoning ... Most of the casualties are farm workers handling chemicals with inadequate training and precautions. (Taylor 1992: 25–6)

This statement highlights how both employees and communities have been and continue to be casualties of inadequate regulation of industrial production. In this socialist account of environmental quality, we face a problem of definition right from the start – the problem of defining socialism. There are very different views as to what socialism means, depending on one's own assumptions and values, and whether one is hostile, sympathetic or indifferent to the ideas involved. For some, especially conservatives, socialism is a form of idealism that is attached to rationalist projects for constructing new social and political orders wholesale and, as a result, wipes the historical slate clean (rather than maintaining tradition). This interpretation places all Taylor's account in the category of 'utopianism', an example of unrealistic and potentially dangerous social engineering. For liberals, however, socialism is often associated with collective wish-fulfilment – the projects based upon socialist principles imply severe consequences for individual freedom, whereby the interests of individuals are sacrificed for the greater good. The label of 'socialism' also conceals substantial variation, so some broad differences between social democracy, democratic socialism and Marxism are presented in Table 4.3.

Ecological politics has always been seen as fundamentally opposed to industrialism and its associated goals of perpetual progress and endless material growth. In practical terms, ecological activists have found a receptive audience on the political left among those social groups that have suffered as a result of the process of industrialization. Despite their different views as to the cause of the problems, these groups have a common concern with the effects of market-based or capitalist production on lower-social-class human communities as well as the natural world. In practice, environmental issues have sometimes been addressed at a grassroots level by the labour movement, as in the actions of the National Union of Seamen in preventing the dumping of dangerous wastes in the North Atlantic, an act that had some implications for employment in a declining industrial sector in the UK. Labour unions and environmental movements often find themselves opposed to the decisions of the same people, and often there is a common appeal for environmental action on the grounds of concern for the needs of future generations. For Taylor, it is the practical outcomes which matter (the ends) rather than the means through which they are delivered. Whether these goals are realized through market-based mechanisms or more directly through state regulation appears to be secondary. In this sense, at least, Taylor advocates a partnership of public and private means to achieve environmental ends. In addition, her understanding of the historic links between socialist and environmental practice draws on the advocacy of localized strategies for improving the quality of life and of the use of clean technology that would not be out of place in contemporary environmental politics on a global scale.

It has to be stated that in developed societies states regulate occupational health very strictly, but in the conditions of a global market, and considerable variation in regulative capacity by states, many of the processes that have been outlawed or are subject to close scrutiny for

TABLE 4.3 Socialist variations in Western societies

	Social democracy	Democratic socialism	Marxism
The 'good life' – human welfare/well-being	Human welfare (greatest good for the greatest number), specifically through the amelioration of want, idleness, squalor, disease and ignorance. This is often seen as closely related to 'welfare liberalism'.	Human well-being is identified and secured through greater participation in the political system – social democracy and Marxism impose simple answers on complex problems.	Human well-being shaped by the material relations and forces within a class-based social order, whereby one class extracts the surplus produced by another. In capitalism, the bourgeoisie exploits the proletariat.
The role of 'the state'	The state is viewed as the benevolent head of the family on a larger scale, i.e. it has a responsibility to act on behalf of those unable to help themselves and in so doing maintains the social fabric.	A mixture of state ownership and regulation to facilitate greater accountability of sectional interest to the collective wishes of the social system and the needs of local communities.	State as executive committee for managing the 'common' affairs of capital. The short-term amelioration of some forms of poverty is no substitute for recognizing the underlying interests of the working classes in social transformation.
The 'market economy' and regulation	Management and regulation of the market economy in a responsible way to ensure economic growth and long-term stability to facilitate the redistribution of income and the amelioration of social inequalities.	Democratization of all social and political institutions (businesses, military and trade unions) fosters a different kind of social structure where the organization of the economy and political regulation are oriented to the needs of communities.	The unregulated market economy is driven by a set of laws that produce periodic crises and present opportunities for change – the answer is to change the economy, not manage it. Regulation cannot overcome the harmful effects of capitalism in the long term.
The public/private distinction	Partnership of public and private spheres to achieve medium and long-term objectives. This involves the conciliation of the interests of capital and labour within an institutionalized negotiation system.	Public/private distinction and the role of politics as an expression of class power will become obsolete – with the state ultimately absorbed into civil society.	Capital and labour are in a relationship of irreconcilable antagonism which can only be subdued for short periods and which re-emerges in each crisis. The public/private distinction helps to mask the power relations in the economy.

occupational health protection in the West are still apparent in other parts of the world, such as outsourcing manufacturing and the recycling of scarce resources to China, India and South-East Asia. To highlight a personal story, one of the authors had the opportunity of joining an apprenticeship scheme for shoemaking in the UK at the age of sixteen, on the assumption that it would guarantee a 'job for life'. In later years, this major shoe manufacturer was asset-stripped by a larger company with production rationalized and relocated for a brief time in the UK. Shortly afterwards, the production was largely or wholly outsourced, in common with that of many other shoe manufacturers in Europe, to southern Asia. In South India, the regulations regarding chemicals used in leather hide softening are not in place and the growth of shoe component production (the components themselves are often assembled in Europe to ensure a 'made in ...' label to suggest they were produced within the EU) has had an adverse impact on agriculture around these rapidly developing towns. These environmental impacts have thus ensured that for local communities there are few agricultural alternatives to factory work.

Let us now move from toe to tip and consider the conjoined occupational and environmental impacts of the apparel trade alongside other areas of manufacture that are a key part of consumption in Western societies. One of the key countries in outsourced apparel and leather goods production is Thailand. In the manufacturing sector, it has been increasingly recognized that workers suffer from a variety of health problems related to poor working environments. There is a high prevalence of lead and other forms of metal poisoning among women workers in the electronics industry, as well as occupational lung disease, also known as byssinosis ('brown lung'), caused by inhaling cotton dust among garment workers in textile factories. According to Foek (1997), it is estimated that approximately 30 per cent of female workers in the Thai textile industry suffer from this respiratory disease as a result. Similarly, in 1997, it was reported that 75 per cent of the 4,500 workers who worked in the Dynamics toy factory in Bangkok suffered from respiratory infections (ibid.).

A key development in the last fifteen years, addressing compensation for workers and their families, alongside cases for unfair dismissal and non-payment of back wages, has been the use of the legal system. Karaket, a Thai woman employed to clean spinning machines, successfully claimed compensation from the state-managed Workers' Compensation Fund. She said that it was very dusty, hot and noisy in the factory, and after eighteen months on the job she fell severely ill. On consulting a specialist, she was diagnosed with byssinosis and told that it had destroyed 70 per cent of her lungs in this short period. Only in her twenties, and no longer able to work, in 1993 she successfully campaigned for compensation on occupational health grounds. Another garment worker, Ms Somboon, found herself suffering from the same occupational disease and, with help from several NGOs, and alongside other women suffering in the same way, founded WEPT (the Council of Work and Environment Related Patients' Network) in 1992 (Committee for Asian Women 1998). WEPT also became part of the Assembly of the Poor, a social movement that demanded that the Thai government address the severity of occupational health problems alongside land rights, rural poverty and compensation for environmental degradation. In April 1998, WEPT launched a campaign to collect 50,000 voters' signatures to push for the Occupational Health and Safety Protection Bill. Rawan worked in the soldering section of an electronics factory for eleven years, suffered from lead poisoning and reported that her daughter was very weak, constantly ill, had thinning hair and memory loss. Mayuree suffered from alumina poisoning, and reported that workers were given no protective gear, which caused their fingers to bleed or be burnt when handling the hot circuit boards. An investigation into the deaths and widespread illnesses at the Seagate Technology factory in Thailand (which had a workforce of 21,000) revealed that workers had high levels of lead poisoning in their blood (Foek 1997). According to the ILO, the high industrial accident rates in India prompted labour unions to become actively involved in occupational health and safety issues. The worker-initiated Occupational Health and Safety Centre was able to get the Employees' State Insurance Scheme to compensate mill workers suffering from occupational byssinosis in 1994 (Jose 2002: 328). Similarly in South Korea, women assembly workers in the MASAN free trade zone also suffer from occupational health hazards. In 1994, forty-five workers at the LG Corporation suffered from solvent poisoning. One LG worker reported that women were diagnosed with premature ovarian failure and bone marrow failure and had struggled for two years to make the company accountable for its negligence (Committee for Asian Women 1998). Like the Thai workers, the LG workers decided to open a centre for occupational health victims to pressurize the company to fulfil the terms of their collective settlement.

We selected these personal cases to highlight two things: that work-related environmental problems are common across developing societies in Asia and that progressive movements are seeking to address them as real and tragic consequences for workers, their families and communities, as the following examples also testify.

Occasionally, major fatal incidents take place. In May 1993, 188 workers lost their lives and 469 workers were injured in the Kader toy factory fire. Many of the workers died because of locked fire doors and escape exits, but also as a result of the poorly built factory structure, which collapsed in fifteen minutes (ibid.). Survivors reported that they landed on the bodies of their co-workers when they jumped from the building to escape the flames. One worker expressed anger upon learning that the employer had insurance for the toys they were making but no insurance for the workers. A workers' musical group, Paradorn, was formed after the Kader tragedy to build awareness about the poor work conditions in the manufacturing industry.

Similar events have taken place in South Asia. For example, in Bangladesh the rapid expansion of the garment industry has similarly resulted in hazardous working environments and poor building structures. Between 1993 and 2003, approximately fifty major and minor fire accidents took place in the garment sector, killing more than two hundred workers and injuring thousands (AMRC 2003: 18). In addition to factory fires, garment workers also suffered from a number of chronic diseases including typhoid, jaundice, dysentery and reproductive health problems. These highlight the combined effects of bad conditions, long hours, poor living environments and wages that barely allow for subsistence. Hearing loss is another common health problem among workers in the manufacturing sector, but it is not recognized as an occupational disease because noise-induced hearing loss cannot be easily observed or diagnosed (ibid.: 72). We could add more examples from all over Asia, but the significance of these brief cases is clear – workers' groups are organizing, sometimes with the help of NGOs and often in alliance with other social movements as the effects of rapid industrialization have dramatic effects on the health of the labour force and the communities in which they live.

Just as European and American unions sought to limit these hazards for their members, as the dirtier aspects of production have relocated, labour movements are beginning to address the environmental consequences of the global supply chain alongside their demands for improved pay and conditions. At this point, we should also factor in the effects on local environments of outsourced production. Rapid industrial growth and urbanization generate a variety of new hazards and environmental impacts, ranging from air pollution and contamination of water supplies to inadequate storage of toxic waste, and since most growing cities are in coastal regions or on major waterways, this means diminished access to fertile local marine ecosystems and a consequent loss of biodiversity. Population density poses a whole series of additional challenges, since waterways often take the brunt of household waste and partially treated or untreated sewage. So much attention is devoted to waste in the West and the despoliation in the global South that the growing effects of industrialization and urbanization in this context are sometimes ignored.

Rapid industrialization has produced a proliferation of city developments on the seaboard, where the unanticipated effects of these processes really become evident. In August 2006, Greenpeace, along with the Eco-Waste Coalition, conducted a waste survey documentation to monitor the extent of plastic pollution at Manila Bay, considered to be one of the most polluted bays in Asia. They collected approximately four cubic metres of plastic trash floating on the bay's surface, highlighting the urgency of implementing waste management laws concerning the use of disposable plastic packaging. According to Greenpeace, the bay, 'once considered one of the most beautiful in the world', is now full of 'the sludge, human sewage, industrial waste and, especially, plain garbage'. Much of the garbage consists of 'plastic from "single use" sources such as plastic bags, beverage bottles, cups and other items' that are carried along river deltas and estuaries and inflict great damage on mangrove trees and marine life. 'The immense volume of assorted plastic garbage littering its coasts and floating in its currents is symbolic of the trashing of Manila Bay, and serves as a visual reminder of the pollution that is slowly killing the seas,' a Greenpeace Southeast Asia campaigner stated. Manila Bay was declared a pollution hot spot in 1999 by the Partnerships in Environmental Management for the Seas in East Asia (PEMSEA), and the damage has not only directly affected the health and livelihoods of around ten million people but has also led to the destruction of the bay's mangrove, sea grass and coral ecosystems, and the death of birds and marine animals. Eco-Waste Coalition secretary Manny Calonzo stated that the government needs to prohibit environmentally unacceptable products, and that corporations need to make real efforts to 'phase out the manufacture and use of disposable plastic products and packaging to enable consumers to veer away from such disposable plastic products' (Greenpeace 2007).

Urban growth also transforms the rural areas by prompting a shift towards intensive agriculture in order to meet the food and resource demands of the urban and peri-urban environments. Cases of such effects are proliferating – for example, the Jing Quan rice-wine factory in north-east China, where the hydrofluoric acid used to etch bottles by hand (the only work protection was rubber gloves) was placed in an unlined pit and consequently contaminated local water supplies in Leifeng and Puxing from 2001, causing unexplained deaths in livestock, skin

Environmental governance, social movements and citizenship

125

rashes, stomach disorders and ultimately making at least five hundred people seriously ill. Tests of the water also revealed excessive levels of fluoride. In this case, an NGO specializing in legal advocacy through class actions in the context of environmental law, the China Centre for Legal Assistance to Pollution Victims, has initiated legal cases with mixed success. They identify a number of key problems: environmental impact assessment (EIA) is inadequate, resulting in industry being placed in high-population areas and close to waterways; pollution control technologies are often absent or unused, so waste disposal is often in its pure form or diluted by water; the public has a lack of awareness about the problems; Environmental Protection Bureaus in the locality have been reluctant to enforce regulations; pollution reporting by factories occurs only in seriously polluting industries, limiting available environmental information; and the Chinese legal system does not have clear compensation standards on pollution cases (plus current environmental laws lack specification and only some judges have environmental law training). Most cases have focused on water pollution since causal attribution here is easier to establish and explain in a legal context while air pollution is much more difficult. China is currently constructing a coal-fired power station each week and air pollution problems in its cities have become more apparent, especially when combined with dust storms resulting from desertification (a consequence of diverting water for irrigation and overgrazing). In 2007, a WHO report on the problems of air pollution in Beijing for the 2008 Olympic Games prompted a car-use rationing test to explore ways of reducing emissions from the 3 million vehicles in the city. In August 2007, political authorities in Beijing took 1.3 million automobiles off the streets in a four-day experimental scheme that, according to first reports, reduced air pollution by 15–20 per cent (BBC News, 21 August 2007).

Resource scarcity and higher commodity prices have also produced the growth of recycling businesses using cheap labour throughout Asia. Electronic waste recycling in India and China often takes place in residential areas and in the open rather than in enclosed factories. The recycled components include lead, gold, copper and tin, but besides the problems of lead, e-waste includes cadmium, brominated flame retardants (BRFs), polychlorinated biphenyls (PCBs) and mercury. The Basel Action Network (BAN) was founded after the 1989 Basel Convention on the movement and disposal of trans-boundary waste, which came into force in 1992 and which was amended in 1994 to secure a ban on the disposal of the effluent of the affluent in developing countries, which it sees as an act of environmental injustice that is tantamount to both environmental crime and a human rights violation. BAN has highlighted the growing trade in e-waste, with 80 per cent going to developing countries in Asia and most of this to China (although recycling and dumping are increasing in Africa).

Some cities in China have become specialists in e-waste recycling, such as Guiyu, in the Guangdong province in southern China. Of note is the proliferation of backyard recycling enterprises that lack the expertise to do this safely and efficiently, leading to significant lead pollution in workers and their families. Overall, recycling accounts for three-quarters of the local economy. The resource extraction process, most often completed by hand, involves using heat to melt the materials and hydrochloric acid, leading to air and water pollution. The inefficiency of the process ensures that a considerable proportion of the dangerous materials escapes into the environment, and since the non-recyclable components, such as the flame-retardant plastics, are bulky, a common practice is to burn them or deposit them in landfills. Besides inadequate protection of the labour force in this sector, the extent of recycling in these human waste hot spots is such that whole communities are affected by a range of pollutants that cause cancer, respiratory diseases, thyroid disruption and physical impairments for employees and their children.

Managing development in a more sustainable way: learning from European experience

For much of this chapter, we have focused on self-organizing governance from below as a direct response to immediate environmental hazards. As indicated earlier, however, at the intergovernmental and national levels NGOs, Green political parties, labour unions and environmental movements have become more progressively engaged in environmental policy-making. Just as the objectives of unionism were promoted through governance from above, so too can those of environmental movements. The difficulty in achieving this in developing countries lies is the fragility of the rule of law and accountable political institutions. In the instances we have described in previous sections, the fostering of ecological citizenship is more effective where forms of civil, political and social citizenship have already been established. To assess what needs to be in place in developing countries, it is useful to look again at the European experiment in governance which has been so effective in dealing with trans-boundary as well as more localized environmental issues. In 1972, the heads of government of the then EC developed a joint statement making a clear commitment to environmental protection in the following ways:

- pollution should be prevented at source and costs should be incurred by the polluter;
- project planning has to take environmental impacts into account;
- environmental policies must work in a fashion compatible with the broad objective of economic and social development.

Ever since then, environmental policy-makers have faced the difficult task of finding a balance between achieving environmental objectives and promoting open economic competition and development across the community. For instance, environmental protection legislation could be interpreted as a restriction on trade. The 1972 declaration coincided with one of the key landmarks in the rise of environmental awareness, the Club of Rome report (*The Limits to Growth*), which contained a direct challenge to the idea that growth and environmental protection can go hand in hand. This report highlighted the ecological limits on the processes of industrial development, both in terms of the finitude of natural resources and the capacity of existing ecosystems to act as a sink for pollution. This enormously influential report combined the expertise of industrialists, business advisers, civil servants and academics in order to develop simulated predictions of the effects of resource depletion, population growth and pollution. In the various scenarios of the computer simulation developed in the report, there were definite limits to the continuation of growth. It is now widely accepted that the report was too fatalistic and underestimated the potential of technological solutions. Nevertheless, the broad view that the solutions to the effects of growth will be social rather than technical and scientific remains a feature of environmental politics. These dilemmas between growth and environmental protection, and between finding social solutions or techno-fixes for problems such as resource depletion and pollution, are central to the emergence of environmental governance.

Especially important in assessing the role of the EU are the contradictory implications of the idea of sustainable development that predominates in European policy – development that 'meets the needs of the present without compromising the ability of future generations to meet their own needs' (WCED 1987: 43). The sustainable development approach assumes that we are adversely affecting our descendants and that we should find ways of organizing our own affairs in a more sustainable way by leaving the world for our immediate successors roughly in the same state in which we found it. Similarly Chinese political leaders are beginning to make vocal similar concerns about the dangers of borrowing the environment from future generations. This is one of the most frequent justifications deployed for environmental action, yet on the development side it also assumes that problems such as poverty and disease should be addressed.

The ongoing five-year environmental action plans that followed the 1972 declaration were primarily concerned with hazards such as chemicals, industrial accidents, agricultural practices, biotechnology and the protection of the natural heritage. Another significant step was the 1985 Directive on Environmental Impact Assessment, which required member states to assess the environmental consequences of major projects such as oil refineries, steel and cast-iron plants, power stations, airports, highways and facilities for the storage and disposal of nuclear, asbestos and chemical waste. This came into full force in 1989 and carries with it the requirement that the public must be involved in prior consultation (see Baker 2001).

The event that changed environmental policy-making and produced an important shift in public opinion on environmental issues (as well as in attitudes to environmental movements, which had often been seen as on the fringe and cranky) was the Chernobyl incident. During the night of 25/26 April 1986, following an energy experiment, the Chernobyl nuclear reactor near Kiev exploded, producing radioactive dust and gas which drifted across Europe for the next two weeks. The extent of the deposits of radioactive fallout largely depended on rainfall, but the most seriously affected areas were Poland, Scandinavia (especially Sweden), Germany, Austria and, finally, the UK and Eire. Alongside global awareness of the problems in terms of the supply of fresh water, pollution of riverways and the seas, ozone depletion and global warming, there was an increased recognition that environmental protection was needed against creeping and invisible problems which were not tied to local areas in the manner of traditional industrial pollution. Increasingly, questions were raised about the top-down approach of national governments and European political institutions in addressing such complex and uncertain threats, as well as the need to find appropriate solutions at the regional and local levels.

One legacy of the formation of the EC as an economic community has been the tendency of policy-making to be located within centralized bodies accountable to the national governments of respective member states; thus power has resided largely in the executive bodies, creating the democratic deficit ('decisions in the EU are in some ways insufficiently representative of, or accountable to, the nations and people of Europe'; Lord 2001: 165). Until the SEA (Single European Act, which, as part of its revision of the Treaty of Rome, included environmental policy as a function of the community), environmental policies required unanimous consent from all member states. As a result, the measures were often narrow and focused on specific problems (in order to meet the least possible resistance). The SEA identified DG XI (Directorate-General for Environment, Nuclear Safety and Civil Protection) of the Commission as the institutional vehicle for environmental protection. In addition, environmental legislation became subject to qualified majority voting, with the European Parliament given the power to amend but not to veto the legislative measures (Heffernan 2001). While still a top-down approach to policy-making with the executive in the driving seat, this at least enabled environmental policy to move from being concerned with remedial actions towards preventive measures (for example, regulating large combustion plants in 1988). Some of the obstacles to EU-wide regulation of the environment have been removed. The first four environmental action plans have produced a variety of concrete results leading to improvement in the quality of bathing water, limits on sulphur dioxide emissions, restrictions on lead in petrol and in air, as well as controls on industrial emissions and the disposal of waste. In the Fifth Environmental Action Programme (1992–2000), the emphasis on maintaining the quality of life, access to natural resources and avoidance of lasting environmental damage did not, at first sight, suggest a radical and ambitious campaign (see Baker 2001). Nevertheless, it introduced performance targets for the recycling of resources used in production and consumption. Of note is the attempt to reduce CO_2 emissions to 1990 levels by the year 2000 and plans to harmonize energy taxation throughout the community. The regulation of energy production has now moved to a crucial stage. With the 1996 Framework Directive on Integrated Pollution Prevention and Control (IPPC), the various forms of pollution are to be considered in terms of their impact on ecosystems rather than as forms of air or water pollution. This Directive targets the production of energy, metals and chemicals as well as the manufacture of products such as paper, ink and dyes as being of immediate concern. The legal instruments devised are not binding, however, for they depend on market forces, through the use of financial incentives and support (such as the provision of funds to cover investment expenses), to produce spontaneous changes in the behaviour of citizens and firms.

The most significant development in the 1990s was the ongoing effect of the resolutions of the United Nations Conference on Environment and Development (the Earth Summit in Rio de Janeiro, 1992). This international conference sought through an action plan, Agenda 21, to encourage local responses to ecological problems by mobilizing a range of groups and favouring the development of new forms of governance that could ensure their involvement as stakeholders in local decision-making processes. Environmental problems and political institutions in each locality or region were quite distinct and responses had to work at this level. Under Section 28 of Agenda 21, local authorities had to exchange information and coordinate plans with local stakeholders (representatives of municipal and environmental service providers, universities, trade unions, environmental movements, health agencies, industries, farmers and youth groups). Each area was to hold an environmental forum by 1994 and, following a consultative process, reach a consensus on a 'Local Agenda 21' by 1996, prioritizing the environmental issues in each case. The discretionary character of Agenda 21 means that implementation is enormously varied (Lafferty and Eckerberg 1998): some countries were 'pioneers' in initiating LA21 measures (Sweden, the UK and the Netherlands); some 'adapters', modifying existing environmental policies (Finland and Norway); and others 'latecomers' (Ireland, Austria and even Germany, where citizen action groups had lost momentum in the 1990s).

The activities associated with LA21 range from fiscal measures, policy integration, public–private partnerships and local business development to ethical investment and eco-auditing. The precise effects of this initiative have also varied with culture, institutions and groups involved. In Eire, branches of organizations such as Friends of the Earth and Greenpeace have concentrated their efforts on the national government to ensure its continued interest in global issues. An Taisce (the National Trust in Eire), however, with its own organizational history based on dialogue and informed discussion, has become heavily involved in the consultation process and the emerging partnership between local authorities and stakeholders (Mullally 1998). So it seems that some kinds of organizational cultures are also more likely to find a constructive place in this kind of consultation.

Susan Baker argues that two types of environmental policy have featured in the European context and each has definite implications for environmental movements. First, there is the traditional incremental process of European policy-making, whereby general policies of environmental management and quality control emerged in a slow step-by-step manner. This approach does not challenge the prevailing economic and social objectives and adapts environmental policy to ensure that it is implemented. Second, there are the radical policies, which are directed towards the reorganization of consumption patterns in order to produce low or zero growth in a steady-state economy (or by redistributing resources and reforming political and military structures along the lines suggested in the early days of Die Grünen). While the Green parties across Europe and many environmental groups seek to achieve the second policy option, this would not fit easily with policies in other areas (for instance, those directed towards fulfilling the Social Charter discussed earlier). In conclusion, Baker argues that a weak version of sustainable development is much more likely to be implemented in the EU (Baker 1997: 91–106; Baker 2001: 199–229). If the environmental movements are going to have an impact on European politics, they will have to challenge the economic and social priorities of the EU at some point.

The growing status and significance of the European Parliament have provided one way in which movements grounded in civil societies can have an impact. In the 1990s, since the Maastricht Treaty, policy-making has become more inclusive through the principles of openness and subsidiarity. It was increasingly recognized that policies should not be developed at EU level when they could be more effectively delivered through national governments (Liefferink and Anderson 1998). This creates opportunities not only for drawing in a wider range of environmental movements, but also for national governments to avoid the implementation and monitoring of environmental policy. As a result, there are greater opportunities for regional and local organizations as well as environmental NGOs to make their presence felt in formulating and implementing policy through policy review groups, dialogue groups and the general consultative forum (which brings together environmental NGOs with national and local authorities). Underpinning these developments is the belief that such policy-making will foster a new social partnership based on shared responsibilities. Whether this will produce a kind of eco-corporatism, with groups from civil society working within institutionalized mechanisms for collaboration on the formulation, implementation and monitoring of environmental policy, only time will tell. What is more likely is a continual interaction of environmental regulation with environmental movements emerging spontaneously from below in response to specific problems and unanticipated hazards. Ironically, the decline of the influence of unions in developed societies opened up new opportunities for broadening consultation with a wider variety of social movements, and much will depend on the relations between political institutions and private corporations. The strategies developed by environmental movements, with the emphasis on low growth and a reorganization of production towards the local level, were always unlikely to be warmly endorsed by business. There have been some moves towards Green consumerism, and recycling businesses have become better organized and more efficient. In addition, some companies, such as the Body Shop, have been careful to have their production processes audited periodically for their environmental impact. Inevitably for any company marketing goods with an ethical message, the Body Shop has been subject to close scrutiny and has been both praised and criticized for its environmentally friendly policies (i.e. the use of 100 per cent 'natural ingredients' in products that are tested on animals). Having built a reputation for representing 'Green business' practices, its founder, Anita Roddick, was recognized by the UNEP in 1997 as one of twenty-five female business leaders who have made outstanding contributions to the environment, and her company was voted the twenty-seventh most respected company in the world by the *Financial Times* the following year (Xiao 2000), despite the fact that they changed the labelling on their products from 'Not Tested on Animals' to 'Against Animal Testing' (Suzuki 1996). Controversy around the company surfaced in 1992 when a journalist commissioned to investigate the company discovered that its cosmetic products often contained synthetic ingredients that were tested on animals. In 2006, the Body Shop agreed to a £653 million takeover offer by the cosmetics giant L'Oréal, a company that still uses animal tests. More radical change along the lines suggested by eco-activists, however, would challenge the role of profit-making and the continual accumulation of capital through which businesses measure their success, an issue explored in more detail in the next chapter.

Considering these developments, the presumed difference between old and new social movements is now anachronistic and Eurocentric. Unions often occupy a less influential position within the policy process than some environmental NGOs, but that is very specific to each location. Unions now have less hierarchical or increasingly 'flat organizations' in order to effectively promote members' interests while environmental movements, which tended to be decentralized and with 'grassroots volunteerism' expressing lifestyle politics, have become (or are becoming) more institutionally embedded and more hierarchical as a result of participation in policy-making. For instance, Greenpeace now tends to focus on producing scientific reports and sustained lobbying rather than frequently engaging in media stunts. The door is now open in political institutions for many environmental movements. Most Green parties have compromised their ideals on participatory democracy in order to achieve some of their policy objectives; rotating spokespersons have become leaders and participatory conferences have become stage-managed events, as with other mainstream parties.

There remains the question of whether environmental movements are a product of the alienation from modern urban life, an underlying romanticism about the natural world within many Western cultures, the emergence of new environmental hazards, the willingness of local communities to defend their own space (NIMBY – not in my backyard), or part of a broader shift towards post-materialist values that reject growth and perpetual development (NIABY – not in anyone's backyard). It is probably a little of each. What is clear is that we are witnessing the emergence of new self-regulating forms of governance which are slowly drawing in environmental groups and organizations to provide advice and possibly act as transmission belts in the implementation of policy. New sites of struggle have arisen in communities seeking to defend their way of life, collective identities, lifestyles and values. To understand environmental movements we have to take account of the culturally specific practices that produce, regulate and organize the meanings communities use to represent the environment (their values, beliefs, customs, conventions, traditions and habits). The self-organizing networks, such as the Kalamas campaign, demonstrate how communities and collectivities can construct common interests, identities, ideologies and socio-political projects in order to challenge power-holders. At the same time, national governments, the EU and other public agencies seek to exert greater control to realize objectives agreed upon by political representatives and civil servants across Europe. The top-down governance mechanisms whereby environmental policies are devised at the centre may also be seen as intrusive, costly and likely to generate resistance. The emergence of environmental policy-making is also a product of broader global attempts to coordinate environmental policies in developed and developing societies. In this context, Agenda 21 offers an important step in identifying local and regional environmental concerns within a general framework that attempts to develop environmental policies in a cohesive way. The question remains as to whether environmental movements will become heavily involved and use the opportunity to make a difference.

What can be done in developing societies? Living with 9 billion people who deserve a good life and environmental quality

Returning to the environmental problems in Asia, it is not appropriate and could be disastrous to suggest that the political institutions specific to European societies can be transferred to other parts of the world, just as the decolonization process in the 1950s often left a legacy of bitterly divided plural societies with the wrong kinds of electoral and democratic processes. What we can conjecture is that there are certain kinds of mechanisms that are essential to ensuring an improvement in environmental quality (or at least avoiding some of the worst effects of industrial development) and the promotion of responsible actions by all relevant actors, including corporations, citizens and movements as well as political institutions. They have to be suited to purpose in that context. In summary, various mechanisms do tend to work in Western societies (although this often depends on the presence of certain political institutions) and these may help us identify the prospects for ecological citizenship in Asia.

In the Asian context, development projects are considered primarily in economic terms, in contrast to the EU, which considers development projects also in terms of their contribution to social development and environmental consequences. Moreover, Asian governments do not have the same long history of developing environmental legislation to improve health and safety in industries, since such protective legislation goes against foreign direct investment (FDI) incentives and export-oriented development policy. Environmental issues such as pollution from industries using toxic chemicals are treated as an expected side effect of industrial development. For the EU, governance involves both regulation from above and mobilization from below, but in Asia the impetus for regulation comes primarily from local grassroots organizing rather than from the state. This prompts us to ask how the state can become more involved in the regulation of environmental problems while also recognizing that the effectiveness of state action has diminished. The state is not a panacea but can be drawn into partnerships with broader movements located in civil society. Another problem is the limited transparency and accountability in political institutions in many developing-country governments. For example, in terms of regional policy in South-East Asia, the heads of government within the Association of South East Asian Nations (ASEAN) have only just started to consider environmental protection and still prioritize regional economic development and trade. When environmental issues are addressed, this is often linked to conserving resources or the promotion of tourism (one of the major contributors to GDP in many areas of the region). The failure to confront environmental issues is also replicated in other areas of policy, such that individual governments 'have either been unable or reluctant to confront human rights issues implicit in international labour migration in this region' while regional institutions such as ASEAN, the Pacific Economic Cooperation Council (PECC) and Asia-Pacific Economic Cooperation (APEC) have, until recently, 'been unwilling to deal with complex social issues' (Ball and Piper 2006: 229). It is unlikely that we will see initiatives such as the 1985 EU Directive on Environmental Impact Assessment come into play in the near future owing to the absence of regional integration, so national states provide the best basis for creating a precautionary attitude through stricter regulation and controls and partnership initiatives.

We can point to four important precursors to tackling the issues:

1 fostering an environmental law tradition in national contexts with clear compensation principles for pollution victims;
2 promoting more inclusive political processes linking human rights labour standards and sustainability, thus creating partnerships between political authorities and civil organizations;
3 establishing trans-boundary environmental agreements that are complementary to regional and national development strategies;
4 promoting precautionary approaches through environmental impact assessment.

Some environmental degradation is a necessary side effect of development and we must not pretend otherwise. Demographic shifts in the West, such as the growth of single-person households, have also increased aggregate impacts, even though population growth has lessened. In the West, it is largely a matter of mitigating impacts, the ecological restoration of damaged environments and finding ways of building cities that have a lighter footprint. The environments we seek to protect in the West are those formed after the processes of industrial development, so we must be careful not to adopt romantic assumptions that lead to the conclusion that developing countries are to blame for destroying pristine environments. In many parts of the developing world it is much too late for that, and in any case there would be precious little support from many citizens in those countries. We should also acknowledge that Western lifestyles are dependent on the environmental degradation in other parts of the world. One of the problems of the environmental movements and NGOs in the West (including those concerned with global environmental issues) is a failure to recognize that all citizens have entitlements to a better quality of life and that this will come with an environmental cost – the key is to find solutions that avoid the worst effects. If ecological citizenship is to be effective it has to be based on social as well as environmental justice. One of the inadvertent results of the climate change debate has been the focus on the aggregate processes rather than the particular conditions in specific countries, regions (both within and including countries) and localities. Consider the environmental problems in China outlined above. The most pressing issues here are addressing the effects of air and water pollution combined with the consequences of changing land use. A sustainable solution in this context and throughout

Asia has to prioritize specific issues. Intergovernmental agreements have not prevented the trade in waste nor addressed the energy solutions that have been part of rapid industrialization. Western citizens can be seen as directly benefiting from the cheap imported manufactured goods that are produced by sweatshop labour, in urban contexts, worsening health and environmental degradation.

We do not need universal solutions or blueprints; instead we need strategies that take account of the immediate issues in each situation, i.e. greenprints (Smith 1998a: 82). Some environmentalists are sceptical about the links between social and environmental justice (Dobson 2003b), and we place much of the blame for this on the ideology of the Green movements of the past that were nurtured in industrial societies, articulating a sense of loss and the same fears that struck John Ruskin when he contemplated the prospect of the English working class having access to the Lake District. Some deep ecologists have called for the completely impractical solution of a massive reduction in human souls to match the carrying capacity of the earth. The very fact that such suggestions, along with the advocacy of both voluntary and compulsory population control, originated in developed societies that are currently experiencing demographic stability speaks volumes. It implies that some lives are more valuable than others. It is these discourses of disposability which provide an undercurrent to legitimize the processes in the global supply chains that have engendered a host of environmental crises as well as violations of human rights and labour standards. To avoid this kind of environmental colonialism, we need to rethink what the environment means to us. Environments are urban and rural, they are in the global North and the global South, they are resources subject to different kinds of instrumental value, but also have intrinsic value. This may sound like a contradiction in terms until we realize that all forms of valuation arise from human judgement and values, a theme that will be developed in the conclusion. The environment is not a single-issue area of politics but central to all aspects of human fulfilment, and we need to avoid the politics of fear that stalks many environmental interventions, especially when considering issues of climate change. Similarly, we should avoid the stark choice of addressing environmental issues or alleviating poverty. Sensible solutions to environmental issues have to address social injustices as well, if only because the formulation of greenprints that address concrete situations demands it. Except for the preservation of wilderness areas with no human populations, environmental issues always have a social justice dimension, and since environmental impacts are driven by development then labour issues cannot be completely separated from environmental ones. Yes, workers have an entitlement and should have rights to safe and clean working conditions, but workers, their families and communities also have an entitlement to environmental quality free of the problems of air and water pollution identified above. Going farther, the peoples that migrate to urban centres not only have entitlements to be free of these environmental 'bads', they should also have access to environmental 'goods' such as clean air and water and green spaces, and financial support to reduce their own environmental impacts. Corresponding to these entitlements are a wide range of obligations. These obligations vary according to the role of the actors involved. States tend to view their obligations and, more formally, their legally binding duties as specific to citizens within their own territorial boundaries or to citizens of other states with which they are legally bound. Similarly, citizens often think in terms of reciprocal obligations between members of their own community – for example, in urban contexts, that they are bound by rules regulating litter, recycling and other forms of waste (including dog excrement) and the symbolic associations with other localized forms of social malaise such as crime (see Burningham and Thrush 2001). Some environmental issues are better thought of in terms of reciprocity while for others, such as trans-boundary and global environmental issues, non-reciprocal ties that bind provide a more useful starting point. Incidentally, the fact that Dobson (2003a) characterizes these ties in terms of globalizers and globalized already implies a close link between environmental and social justice that he considers to be questionable (Dobson 2003b). At this stage, we wish to make a practical case for the view that effective solutions to environmental problems will have a social justice dimension, but equally that the character of the link will depend on the nature of the environmental issue and the character of the social injustices associated with them. In the remaining, shorter chapters of this book, we will focus on how to establish these links and the precise qualities of the ties that bind.

5 | Corporate responsibility and environmental sustainability

Coordinating the two ends of the global supply chain: linking production to consumption

It is often said that state regulation is not an overriding factor in preventing environmental degradation, especially in developing societies, but as the previous chapter illustrated, there are environmental issues in which states and more localized political authorities can really make a difference. But before we revisit this issue there is one group of actors who are a key part of the picture at all levels, i.e. businesses, the linchpin in understanding the links between production and consumption in the global supply chain. These 'for-profit' civil organizations are immensely powerful actors and collectively implicated in all the environmental controversies highlighted so far in this book. We mention this at this stage because states do have less control over private corporations than in the past, and civil society actors or public–private partnerships are increasingly the preferred actors of intergovernmental institutions on many issues. So why not make a virtue out of a necessity? This is a deliberately provocative starting point from two authors influenced in profound ways by the New Left, and the immediate gut reaction from fellow travellers is to shout betrayal from the rooftops. But if we are really thinking about the capacity of marginalized groups, the working class, the disempowered and the disenfranchised making a difference in the global economy, we want to pose the question: what if these actually could have an impact on the decisions made by non-state for-profit actors in the global economy?

This chapter considers how private corporations have responded to the challenge of constructing, implementing and monitoring codes of responsible conduct in relation to the environment. The development of corporate responsibility and, more recently, corporate citizenship is central to effective actions for environmental sustainability. This chapter will also highlight how corporate social responsibility and corporate environmental responsibility are increasingly linked in the marketing of specific brands – companies are being prompted to rethink the sourcing of products and packaging in terms of environmental sustainability, fair trade and the protection of human rights and labour standards. The idea that corporations should have obligations towards those affected by their decisions is not new – it was embedded in state regulation before globalization became such a burning issue. As Korten (1995) and Richter (2001) demonstrate, however, the classification of companies as 'natural persons' entitled to protection within the terms of the US Bill of Rights already created scope for corporate citizens to take advantage of the entitlements of citizenship without necessarily having the responsibilities possessed by individual citizens.

It should be added that companies also have the strategic advantage of being singular actors or capable of effective organization through business associations when compared to affected constituencies such as employees and, especially, consumers. State regulatory policy held many companies to account until the long-term effects of the inter-nationalization of capital and the emergence of neoliberal policies reined in the ability of states to legitimately regulate their actions. In Western societies, this led to a dramatic depoliticization of many areas that had hitherto being subject to state intervention. From 'the environment' and labour relations to welfare, housing and education, the rationale for state regulation was weakened so that unemployment, industrial relocation, poverty, homelessness and so on were portrayed as personal difficulties and not social problems, never mind global ones. States re-sorted to offering to reduce the burdens of regulatory practices and handing out subsidies to attract increasingly mobile capital investment projects (including developing societies, which did not want to inhibit industrial growth). Subsequently, with transnational corporations as a fact of life, 'the impetus for industry regulation shifted from the UN to the business and NGO community' (ibid.: 8). As confirmation of this trend, the final attempt to develop more comprehensive international regulations on the environment (drafted by the United Nations Centre on Transnational Corporations, UNCTC) as part of the United Nations Conference on Environment and Development (UNCED) in Rio in 1992, with the aim of embedding these in Agenda 21, met effective opposi-tion from key UN members and private corporations. In its place, the World Business Council for Sustainable Development provided some non-binding guidelines or recommendations on the environmental re-sponsibilities of corporations. International regulation has been off the agenda, replaced by self-regulation within corporations or co-regulation with other civil society bodies.

Before we address the substantive issue of corporate social and en-vironmental responsibility, it is crucial to highlight the importance of private corporations in achieving or failing to achieve more sustainable outcomes in all the issues addressed so far. While state action in principle can secure environmentally responsible outcomes within a given territory, the shift towards facilitative policy and incentive schemes for institutions, communities, citizens and nationally based companies, and the problems of generating multilateral agreements and intergovernmental regimes, means that additional levers are necessary. If private corporations become more environmentally responsible they can affect outcomes in a variety of contexts that nation-states cannot reach. The tentacular character of global supply chains and the bargaining power of Western brand companies in relation to production, while making it notionally difficult to regulate and mobilize against, also presents a unique opportunity if these corporations internalize a culture of obligation. This would also ensure that they can respond to criticisms that corporate responsibility is more than window dressing. At this point, we want to highlight a couple of examples that will to many readers seem unlikely.

While Wal-Mart is often targeted as one the big beasts of corporate irresponsibility, using its leverage to squeeze the margins of suppliers, resulting in labour standard violations, there have been some effects that have had environmentally beneficial consequences – for example, a reduction in product packaging, with the savings distributed to both suppliers and Wal-Mart. In addition, as Box 5.1 illustrates, the growth strategy of the company (pile it high, sell it cheap) limits its capacity for responsibility initiatives compared to many other companies.

Box 5.1 Wal-Mart and responsibility

In January 2005, Wal-Mart CEO Lee Scott kicked off an aggressive nationwide campaign to correct what he says are the misimpressions Americans have of Wal-Mart. Tackling wages, for instance, Scott has said again and again, and with evident pride, that the average wage of hourly store employees is 'almost twice the federal minimum wage'. But it isn't clear that Scott has any idea what that means. The company says that, in its home state of Arkansas, it pays store employees an average of $9.18 an hour. For a single mother with two kids who opts to buy health insurance from Wal-Mart, that translates to take-home pay of $290 a week. If our single-mother Wal-Mart associate is living in an apartment that costs only $500 a month, she's got just $660 a *month* left for everything else: the electricity bill, car insurance, feeding and clothing her kids, saving for retirement. Even if she shops at Wal-Mart, that's lean living.

Wal-Mart has recently taken to explaining that retail jobs such as those it offers, although paying double the minimum wage, are nonetheless intended as supplemental income, not as support for a family. The problem with that is that for two-thirds of Americans, Wal-Mart is the largest employer in the state where they live. The misperceptions cut both ways. Critics often glibly describe Wal-Mart as just another big, greedy corporation. If you took the company's total profit for 2004 ($10.3 billion) and gave every dollar to Wal-Mart's employees (1.6 million), you would distribute about $6,400 per employee. Microsoft had an even larger 2005 profit of $12.3 billion. But Microsoft has just one twenty-sixth of the number of employees of Wal-Mart – its profits come to $200,000 per employee, or thirty times those at Wal-Mart. More to the point, perhaps, for its hourly employees, Wal-Mart's profit comes to $3 an hour over a typical year. So although there may be some dispute about whether the average Wal-Mart store associate earns $8 an hour or $9 an hour, Wal-Mart could not afford to pay those people $12 an hour. There isn't enough money – at least, not without raising prices.

Source: Fishman (2006: 14–15)

There are steps that can be taken, however, to reduce the distance that goods, especially food products, travel, which would require two sacrifices: slightly higher food prices, as this affects economies of scale, partly offset by smaller transport costs and reduced standardization in terms of the products. Similarly, imagine, if you can, that the local McDonald's, KFC and Burger King were not part of a global franchise but local businesses and cooperatives trading under a broader ethical franchise, and that in the local McDonald's in Chiang Mai, Mumbai or Manchester, the eponymous 'burger' uses meat from local sources and natural flavourings from the area rather than being manufactured to have the same consistent and often dull taste in all parts of the world – as George Ritzer (2008) suggests when analysing how Starbuckization is prompting McDonald's to shift its strategy from its uncomfortable and unwelcoming design to softer furnishings and more sociable spaces that encourage customers to linger. Just as standardization and scale have inevitably reduced the quality of Starbucks coffee, McDonald's and similar fast food chains are having to appeal more in terms of food quality. As global-brand chains reach the limits of the standardized expansion strategy, market growth can be achieved only through diversification and quality improvements, which can be facilitated by local suppliers and a trade-off between the competing pressures of higher prices and lower costs.

This does not mean that Starbuckization has been anything other than the McDonaldization (i.e. rationalization in the Weberian sense) of higher-quality coffee products; indeed, if Starbucks achieves its target of 40,000 shops worldwide (at the time of writing it has just under 14,000 owned, joint-venture and licensed shops in forty countries, expanding at a rate of six openings per day), then, as already demonstrated in the current expansion, then bulk-buying coffee will undermine opportunities to use high-quality beans. Starbucks has, however, maintained a high profile in corporate responsibility in terms of its products and packaging sourcing, energy use, waste reduction and recycling, as well as in promoting partnerships with source communities to encourage small-scale farmers who adopt environmentally sensitive and socially responsible practices. While the Starbucks mission is being diluted, it has prompted change elsewhere – for example, Dunkin' Donuts and McDonald's selling higher-quality coffee and other coffee chains such as Costa and Caffe Nero in the UK distinguishing their profile by placing a stronger emphasis on Fair Trade sourcing. All these are converging on the breakfast market currently dominated by McDonald's, which, considering the rapid expansion of coffee shop chains to a strict design model of coffee, cookies, cakes, pastries and cold snacks (i.e. with very limited kitchen space), is quite a transformation. Starbucks' solution in these 'breakfast wars' or 'egg-muffin wars' is to nitrogen-freeze the breakfast range and instal high-speed, high-heat ovens, preserving their preference for highly automated customer service (see ibid.: 211–31). Nevertheless, the market pressure on companies like McDonald's will force them to compete within the terms of the company's intangible assets, such as ethical reputation.

Hence at the consumption end of these global supply chains there needs to be a two-pronged approach – seeking social and environmental responsibility in proportion to the capacity of private corporations to deliver and, rather than castigating the companies for their sins, seeking active engagement to ensure that the sales and marketing strategies of these companies address a wider range of markets than the cut-price basement. Other areas such as cheap sports clothing sold through sports fashion retailer companies are more difficult, especially for parents purchasing the latest Nike, Adidas and Reebok apparel for their rapidly growing children (reducing the product life of the purchase). In the UK, for instance, companies such as JD Sports have expanded rapidly through more cheaply produced and more cheaply sold brand-name sports clothing that has rapidly become a uniform for many British teenagers. Persuading parents that they should spend more on clothes that are barely worn before they have to be discarded is an almost impossible task.

In other areas, companies see a strategic market advantage in adopting ethical standards, appreciating that the investment can be recouped by encouraging regulative regimes in national states that drive out competition from other companies that have not adopted initiatives couched in terms of responsibility. For example, in 2006 Vodafone, Unilever, BAA, the John Lewis Partnership, Tesco, Shell and eight other leading companies lobbied the UK government to institute stricter regulations on climate change through the adoption of low-carbon technologies. These companies see themselves as 'first movers' and wish to take advantage of market-share growth in the context of the cap and trade systems being developed in the EU (see Chapter 4). The inevitable effect of this would be an industrial shake-out of companies that are not able to invest on the same scale or accommodate the costs of excess emissions.

This event coincided with the formation of a distinctive lobby organization, the Aldersgate group (a public–private partnership bringing together government agencies, think tanks, industry and environmental NGOs), which, contrary to CBI lobbying activity against regulations on emissions, recognizes that sustainability is compatible with competitiveness and profitability when combined with 'smart regulation' to ensure that eco-efficient industry benefits through lower costs and creating new markets. Volkswagen's business strategy is to reduce fuel consumption and emission levels as a response to rising oil prices. Combining products with services also has the potential to benefit the environment among companies such as Xerox (photocopiers) and IBM (computers) marketing themselves as service producers, or in the wireless service sector, where cell phones are sold to consumers along with a calling plan. Similarly, in the cable television industry 'set-top' boxes enable conversion from analogue to digital reception without charge to subscribers in the UK (Cooper and Evans 2000). Some companies have focused much more on environmental than social responsibility. One company at the forefront of Green business is Fuji-Xerox, as illustrated in Box 5.2.

As with the Fuji Corporation, the method of reducing environmental impact throughout the product life cycle has become increasingly popular among companies with an expressed commitment to environmental responsibility. Clean Production Action is an NGO that works with environmental and public health advocates, trade unions, progressive companies

Box 5.2 A case study in greening business

Fuji-Xerox and its affiliates release annual environmental progress and sustainability reports that document the company's activities in relation to the environment in the Asia-Pacific. The company states that it is committed to 'the realization of a sustainable earth environment'. Fuji-Xerox established its Basic Environmental Strategy in 2001, introducing eco-efficiency as a corporate performance indicator, and set the targets to be achieved by 2010. Its objective is to transform the company into a fully recycling-oriented company that offers environment-conscious products and environmental solutions to customers. Some examples of its environmentally friendly activities include: the elimination of all greenhouse gases except for CO_2 from all its production processes at one of its affiliate companies in Japan; being granted certification by the State Environmental Protection Administration of China (SEPA) for its affiliate company in Shenzhen; developing an eco-conscious copy/printer paper by blending woodchips from the companies' own plantation in New Zealand; implementing a campaign to save energy in all its main and domestic affiliate offices; producing media resources for its annual Sustainability Report and corporate citizenship; improving its image by running booths at annual eco-product exhibitions and fairs. Fuji-Xerox already has a track record in environmental responsibility. In June 2000, the Australian subsidiary was elected to the Global 500 Roll of Honour for outstanding contributions to the protection of the environment by UNEP for developing high-quality and cost-effective recycled copy paper for digital and high-speed applications, reducing pressure on forests and landfill disposal, with 20 cents per ream of paper donated to local land-care environment groups in the region where the paper is made. In 2004, Fuji-Xerox issued a new set of environmental, health and safety requirements, adding to 'Reduce, Reuse, Recycle' (the 3Rs) the term 'Refuse', which has been applied to all subsequent supplier contracts that do not match their expectations.

Xerox leases 75 per cent of the equipment it produces, and often accepts trade-ins on products that are not leased. To increase the economic value of end-of-life materials and parts, Xerox implemented the Asset Recycling Management Program (ARMP) to identify design plans that optimize the use of materials that can be safely recycled into new products. By focusing on materials

145

that are beneficial throughout the life cycle, Xerox is working to have waste-free products and waste-free production facilities. The company has also taken steps to design out hazardous materials such as brominated flame retardants, lead and mercury. In addition to reducing the use of raw materials, Xerox has also worked to reduce energy consumption by requiring most of its products to be certified by the EPA's Energy Star programme, which indicates that a product goes above and beyond federal energy use regulations. Xerox estimates that its efforts to design environmentally friendly products have saved the company more than $2 billion, in addition to keeping 1.2 billion pounds of electronic waste out of landfill.

Source: adapted from <http://www.fujixerox.co.jp/eng/ecology/index.html>

and governments to promote the use of safer and cleaner products across their life cycle. Market-driven Extended Producer Responsibility (EPR) mechanisms, whereby a company finds it profitable to retain ownership and responsibility for a product throughout its life cycle through leasing it to consumers, not only produce customer loyalty but also secure environmental objectives. Avoiding the reputation of being an unsafe company is a key issue for many corporations. Greiner et al. (2006) profiled six chemically conscious companies – cosmetic manufacturer Avalon, Dell Electronics, clothing retailer H&M, furnishings company Herman Miller, carpet and fabrics manufacturer Interface, and healthcare provider Kaiser Permanente. They argued that the motivations for action beyond compliance range from business rationale to deeply held values such as customer, community and worker health and well-being.

Like all businesses, our six case study companies want to avoid 'toxic scares' and gain the long-term confidence of their customers. In all six cases, their work to reduce chemical hazards enhanced their brand reputation with investors, customers and environmental advocates. Some companies achieved considerable savings in the process. Others launched new product lines that differentiated them from their competitors. In several cases, their innovations led to the creation of new submarkets. Taken together, they exemplify the journey companies must embark on if they are serious about creating a healthy chemical economy. (ibid.)

Similarly, when considering the dynamics of environmental compliance in India's leather industry, Tewari and Pillai (2005) show how a small-firm-dominated sector responded effectively to two trade-related environmental regulations imposed on it by Germany. They found that India's relatively effective compliance with two German bans on Azo dyes and PCPs was due largely to state intervention and a broad support base from public and private institutions in the leather industry. The authors discovered that the Indian government 'became involved in a way that engendered a process of "negotiated" collective action among many public and private actors', which resulted in 'repeated and ongoing negotiations around various aspects of policy and implementation' and collaboration between the state and regulated groups. The Indian government targeted a more visible segment of the supply chain – the leather chemical input industry that produced the banned chemicals. By passing a law to ban the import and production of PCPs and Azo dyes in India, the government effectively turned the leather chemical companies

> into de facto diffusers of environmental compliance among a sprawling network of small-scale endusers of their products. Forced to shift to safer dyes, the chemical companies, who initially vigorously opposed the government's ban, began experimenting with the development of substitutes and then launched efforts to market them broadly to their primary clients – the small leather tanning and textile processing firms ... This targeting of an input industry indirectly shifted the burden of enforcement from government agencies to private industry. (ibid.: 248–9)

The race to the bottom has been a major feature of consumption in the global supply chain as well as production, but it does not have to be this way. As the previous examples indicate, we need to think of global supply chains as linking processes and practices between the production and consumption of goods where there are a number of leverage points to effect change. Some levers are best pulled within industry (such as in the last example) and others from outside, as in consumer awareness campaigns (occasionally boycotts) and coordinated activism through transnational networks. Interestingly, the metaphor of a 'chain' is not particularly helpful for it connotes solidity and a one-way process from production to consumption without allowing for the reconstitution of global supply, reallocation of capital and shifting practices of outsourcing as well as feedback mechanisms.

As with the earlier discussion of governance relations in Chapter 4, there are a number of different areas to consider but one overriding argument. The transformation of the global supply chain has created new problems in terms of holding companies accountable but has also generated a new awareness of the environmental issues and prompted the formation of a variety of NGOs and transnational activist networks specifically concerned with monitoring the broad- and narrow-scope effects on the environment. The separation of ownership and control of the production process between transnational brand companies, outsourced manufacturers and subcontractors also creates a point of pressure for coordinated action between NGOs and environmental movements. At the intergovernmental level, the Organization for Economic Cooperation and Development (OECD), World Bank and United Nations (including the Global Compact initiative) have sought to bring together private corporations, environmental and other NGOs and national governments to encourage self-regulating corporate responsibility and better environmental performance (through environmental management systems, auditing tools, performance indicators and environmental reports).

This has been more effective where the reputations and efficiency of companies are at stake (intangible assets are also important), or where corporations perceive a strategic market advantage. There is also evidence that corporations are beginning to use the guidelines to connect environmental protection to social issues such as human rights. Current concerns include the effectiveness of top-down initiatives, which can generate problems farther down the organizational hierarchy, as well as difficulties in coordination across different corporate sectors and between corporations, and the role of small or medium-sized enterprises (where proximity to environmental problems is an important factor for success).

The emergence of corporate citizenship has also led some companies to include affected constituencies in stakeholder deliberation with company structures becoming arenas for conflicts and negotiation, providing strategic opportunities for NGOs and environmental movements. There are two issues here: that the kinds of standards established in codes of responsible conduct may be too limited to close the gap between legal requirements (or actual practice) and justice; and the problems involved in ensuring that the obligations of corporate responsibility and citizenship stick. For this reason we now focus on the links between the different issue areas in codes of conduct and how environmental responsibility can become more embedded in corporate culture so that obligations are taken seriously.

Taking corporate obligations seriously: building on ecological modernization

Prior to the 1980s, most companies saw waste management, recycling and issues of social and environmental responsibility as an inhibitor on profitability and beyond their responsibility (which at the time was narrowly defined in terms of shareholders). Without incentives and a sense that this was the company's responsibility, very little was done to mitigate the externalities of pollution or to transform internal processes. In the waste control sector the approach is best summed up through the acronym CATNAP (cheapest available technology, narrowly avoiding prosecution). When change did occur it was more likely the result of a crisis (a pollution incident or the result of a company failing to implement new regulations), the fear of liabilities and class action lawsuits (especially in the USA) or economic imperatives to reduce costs in the face of increased competition. This began to change as environmental issues moved up the national and intergovernmental policy agenda in the six or seven years leading up to the 1992 Earth Summit. In addition, the development of post-Fordist production in many sectors (combining flexible specialization of labour with flexible automation) ensured that there was greater product variety and that production could be achieved in smaller batches just in time for the marketplace to address Green consumer concerns.

In the last fifteen years, a new phenomenon has emerged as a significant influence on business activity, highlighting a whole range of opportunities for combining economic and environmental reasons for altering production. Ecological modernization was first proposed in the 1980s by Joseph Huber (1982) and Martin Jänicke (1985) and achieved initial prominence through its consideration by the OECD conference on environmental economics in 1984. Maarten Hajer's account (1995, 1996) demonstrates that there are three kinds, with different implications in each case.

1 *Institutional learning*: organizations adapting to ensure that the scale and structure of social organizations can facilitate more effective responses to environmental issues. In the context of state regulation to facilitate institutional redesign in a way that benefits the organizations concerned and meets both the economic and environmental objectives of the regulators, less pollution equals more efficient resource use. As a collective pay-off, environmental conditions improve (the workforce is healthier) and, theoretically, more material growth can be achieved with the same or a reduced environmental impact. So ecological modernization can be packaged not only as a good strategy for achieving environmental objectives, it also makes good business sense – pollution prevention pays through a significant reduction in costs or by the avoidance of pollution taxes. Examples considered earlier include Fuji and the Indian leather industry.

2 *Technocratic project*: links faith in technological solutions with broader passions for consumerism and material growth, making connections between social and environmental objectives, seeing impacts on the environment as manageable and generating initiatives that have the support of private corporations, the World Bank and the IMF. Critics within environmental movements tend to characterize it as the latest version of technocentrism, as 'a discourse for engineers and accountants' (Dryzek 1997: 147), pointing to the limits of institutional inventiveness and highlighting the dangers of placing too much trust in 'techno-fixes' for environmental problems. Examples include Fuji, Xerox and Volkswagen.

3 *Cultural politics*: as an environmental discourse (a form of storytelling) that regulates the production of meaning in specific institutional situations such as the United Nations. The rules of conduct through which environmental discourses evolve are complex and unpredictable but they are stabilized through the 'truth claims' articulated within the discourse in question. For example, they can be stabilized through the scientific claims that global warming or ozone depletion are 'real' problems that deserve a policy response. This is an arena where environmental NGOs and movements have had some impact.

There are similarities between ecological modernization and 'sustainable development', particularly the emphasis on the close connections between social and environmental objectives. John Dryzek (ibid.) suggests that the appeal of both reflects the way in which they pose *no* difficult choices for policy-makers between economic growth and environmental protection. Ecological modernization is often contrasted with Ulrich Beck's account of the 'risk society'. Beck argues that there is a qualitative difference between the kinds of difficulties associated with industrialization and those we face now, that there are mismatches between the character of the environmental hazards and the way environmental problems are defined and resolved in the political and legal institutions through which responsibility is defined. Blowers presents a useful outline of the problems of both idealized models and highlights an absence of empirical awareness. The ecological modernization model offers a technical and economic account without acknowledging the dangers of risky technologies such as the genetic manipulation of foodstuffs. The risk society model focuses so much on the potentially explosive risks created through human activity that it neglects the many small institutional steps taken to monitor and regulate the hazards we generate. In response, Blowers begins to outline the ways in which governance has developed (from international and national responses to transnational and sub-state initiatives) in order to regulate environmental impacts and cope with the unanticipated consequences of human activities. For Blowers, the presence of environmental movements at a transnational and regional level is an important indication of an underlying shift in the strategic opportunities for ecological activists to make a difference. He also indicates, however, where the opportunities are less likely to be favourable; in particular, the shift of environmental regulation to 'regulatory bodies appointed by central government' or through self-regulation (Blowers 1997).

Much is made of ecopreneurialism, CEO-generated initiatives in CSR and environmental leadership, drawing upon a mix of skills (communication, dispute resolution, team building, as well as tact and discretion) in providing direction and exploiting opportunities that promote profitability and/or market share, at the same time ensuring compliance with regulations established by political authorities, avoiding liabilities and consulting stakeholders. The practical measures developed through environmental management of companies by reviewing procedures and processes include replacing old processes with new ones to achieve a reduced environmental impact and promote a sea-change in corporate culture to take account of responsibilities as well as potential liabilities and regulations. The discovery that lower emissions could often mean less efficient manufacturing and higher energy costs also prompted a consideration of the whole production process, i.e. the life-cycle of the product in each case, such as that developed by the Xerox company. Besides identifying more efficient use of resources and energy, life-cycle thinking also prompts consideration of processes prior to and after the company's involvement (i.e. sourcing and waste) and the ways in which consumers (including other companies) use the products and services provided. When stakeholders are involved in environmental management systems, this adds dialogue to reviewing the process.

One of the most challenging ideas developed in the corporate sector is the 'polluter pays principle', i.e. that the costs of measures necessary to address the impact of a company on the environment should be borne by the company – that they should be reflected in the price of the goods and services. For some environmentalists, this involves passing on the costs of environmental protection to the consumers, but in a global market there are additional incentives for companies to change their manufacturing and packaging processes to maintain price competitiveness and reduce impacts. While the polluter pays principle internalizes environmental externalities in the production process or can be addressed through environmental taxes, addressing the precautionary principle demands a more robust response from corporations. This idea highlights the importance of forward thinking when production processes are being planned by seeking to avoid pollution, searching for alternatives and less degrading forms of activity and considering whether a particular production process whose impacts will be substantive is actually needed.

The idea of stakeholder capitalism arose as an attempt to combine social responsibility with market concerns in the context of developing sustainable business enterprises, but needs to be extended in a more deliberate way towards addressing environmental issues. Interestingly, some of the criticisms of corporate activity (internal to companies as well) involve their inability to separate environmental and social issues (particularly environmental protection from health and safety), while the literature in management studies has consistently moved towards consideration of a triple bottom line – economic success, social accountability and environmental sustainability. It is arguable that in many cases environmental issues managed to push CSR concerns to a tipping point, so that when addressing eco-efficiency corporations took a wider variety of concerns under their belt. Similarly, companies subjected to concerted consumer-based campaigns on the outsourced sweatshop factories that provided their products found that when developing codes of conduct they had to take sustainability and human rights issues on board as well, especially since the UN Global Compact. There is a lesson for the disparate activist movements and NGOs here – hit a corporation so hard that they have to address one issue, then there is a door waiting to be pushed open on the others. In situations where civil society and good governance are weak, as in many developing societies, then this is an opportunity that should not be missed.

Environmental management systems remain one of the key components of sustainability promotion since tangible effects can be demonstrated, especially in the context of developing societies. In some countries, such as the USA and the UK, these systems can be augmented by a 'duty of care' established through environmental legislation, i.e. failure to observe this means that companies can be subject to fines or penalties. For example, following the release of a chemical cloud of sulphuric acid in Wurtland, eastern Kentucky, by EI DuPont in 1995, the US Justice Department and the Environmental Protection Agency initiated legal action under the Clean Air Act. This case highlighted inadequate checks and maintenance and so resulted in a settlement in 2000 whereby the company paid a penalty of $850,000 and invested $650,000 in an early warning emergency notification system across ten counties in the state. The US Assistant Attorney General, Lois J. Schiffer, made the rationale very clear in a signal for companies that 'We will hold companies accountable when they neglect this responsibility' (United States Department of Justice 2000).

In England and Wales, the duty of care principle was incorporated into the 1990 Environmental Protection Act concerned with the transfer, treatment and disposal of controlled waste materials, including the requirement that waste can be handled only by a legal entity that possesses a waste management agreement licence. In addition, documentation must be provided to the Waste Regulation Authority and the business or other institutions such as hospitals have a corresponding duty to identify where the waste is taken by registered carriers and visit the disposal sites to ensure compliance. In response to problems generated by illegal tipping (fly-tipping), under the 2005 Waste (Household Waste) Duty of Care regulations in England and Wales, householders have a duty to ensure that they take all reasonable steps to ascertain that their waste is passed to an authorized person. In addition, in 2006 the EU established new chemicals regulations (Registration, Evaluation and Authorization of Chemicals – REACH) for 30,000 substances whereby companies transporting controlled waste in excess of one tonne are required to register the process with a new body, the Chemicals Agency. This came into effect in June 2007. In the case of the 3,000 hazardous materials where no alternatives exist, producers have to submit a research plan demonstrating their search for less hazardous alternatives. All this points not only to the extension of the duty of care to individual citizens but also points to a convergence between the duty of care and the precautionary principle. In other words, what was once a matter of obligation is increasingly becoming a matter of duty.

Turning back to the global supply chain, as many private corporations moved from owning and controlling productive processes in developing societies towards outsourcing manufacturing to developing-country and intra-regional client companies, the initial response of companies was to claim that the conditions and effects were beyond their control. Companies such as Mars, Nestlé and Hershey's have only just started to accept that they have responsibility for child slave labour conditions on cacao plantations in West African countries, particularly Côte d'Ivoire. UNICEF and the ILO have both highlighted how, as in so many forced labour situations, the young male slaves are migrants from neighbouring countries such as Mali, Burkina Faso and Togo. The scientific name for the genus that includes the cacao tree is *Theobroma* (food of the gods), so it is doubly ironic that forced child labour is used to produce the base components of confectionery consumed by children in Western societies. In 2005, when the deadline for establishing a certification process for eradicating child labour in cacao production passed without fulfilment (a promise made by the world cacao industry in accepting the 2001 Harkin-Engel protocol), the International Labour Rights Fund (a Washington-based NGO) filed a federal lawsuit on behalf of three Malian children who were trafficked to plantations in Côte d'Ivoire, against Nestlé and two commodity traders, Archer Daniel Midland and Cargill. The legal response on behalf of the companies was that US Customs should not ban the imports as goods made by forced child under existing legal provisions but await self-certification processes to be developed. The loophole in federal law that allows the importation of such goods from outside the USA where domestic demand exists is now subject to a congressional amendment campaign led by Senator Tom Harkin alongside a public–private partnership with the cacao industry.

The problem in this case is that responsibility is distributed between actors, and while oligopolistic concentration is evident in the shipping and manufacturing, the suppliers are diverse and often small-scale developing-country companies and family plantations. In other cases, the positive efforts of one company can make a big difference. Rio Tinto is a resource extraction specialist (whose interests include gold, coal, copper, iron ore, diamonds and uranium) that has been considered a sustainability leader. Its importance is evident because these materials are part of the global supply chain of a wide range of companies. The primary extraction process, mining, has had severe localized effects on the health of the workforce and the immediate environment, owing to water use (affecting both water quality and quantity), pollution and slag materials. If Rio Tinto and other companies such as Newmont Mining Corporation did not focus so much on corporate environmental responsibility, then the environmental impacts would follow right down the chain to the consumer. Life-cycle analysis is often much easier when a company is providing a specific kind of product and the links in the chain are easily identifiable and the information on sourcing more transparent. Global trading of bulk products, however, generates additional problems for corporate responsibility. In addition, it should be highlighted that while companies such as Rio Tinto are developing a stronger reputation on environmental protection, and in a few cases community projects (such as diverting water courses around the mining sites to address the needs of local people), they continue to encounter well-organized campaigns attempting to hold them to account on labour standards. The International Federation of Chemical, Energy, Mine and General Workers' Union (ICEM), a global union federation representing 389 unions in 119 countries, has run a hard-hitting campaign for global union recognition across the activities of Rio Tinto since the mid-1990s. The Rio Tinto Global Union Network has coordinated union activities, sought wage increases, health and safety and collective bargaining rights as well as taking up unfair dismissal cases, especially in countries with poor governance records, such as Namibia. Some success has also been achieved through labour campaigns involving shareholder activism, resulting in pressure to improve human rights performance.

In another context involving poor governance, Rio Tinto's investment with Freeport McMoran in gold and copper excavation around Lake Wanagon in the province of Papua in Indonesia has also caused concern. In 1997, the Grasberg mine was permitted to increase production to 300,000 tonnes per day, provoking a number of incidents that have linked workers' issues to community and environmental activism. In 1998 and 2000, waste rock disposal collapses resulted in workers' deaths but also produced tidal waves of waste down the Wanagon river towards Banti village. A landslide in Lake Wanagon in October 2003, besides burying workers, also rang alarm bells for the Indonesian Environment Forum (WAHLI) because of the impacts of mining in a context of steep hillsides, heavy rainfall and seismic activity. The lake is also a sacred site for the Amungme people, but copper pollution has had severe ecological effects, to the point where Freeport may even filter copper from the water at some point in the future. The main environmental impacts in rivers and wetlands downstream appear to be increased acidification from the waste.

There has been a history of military action in the province since the 1970s, and questions were raised about the links between the company and both the military and police. A *New York Times* special report (27 December 2005) indicated that Freeman had paid at least US$20 million between 1998 and 2004 for police and military services to secure the site. In addition, monitoring groups such as the Mineral Research Institute have raised concern that the military forces in the province have used facilities owned by the company during actions that violated human rights. Local campaign groups have urged the cessation of mining and have pressed claims that the resources belong to the Papuans. Since the mine generates the largest single source of tax revenue in Indonesia, however, cessation is unlikely. The groups do have a more realistic option in pressing the case for suspension of activities until breaches of environmental law are addressed, and renegotiating agreements on the distribution of taxes and royalties.

From these illustrations, we can see how the last decade has witnessed the extension of discourses of corporate social and environmental responsibility throughout intergovernmental arenas, regional economic integration organizations (such as the EU as the prototype but potentially regional initiatives such as ASEAN), governments, private corporations and a variety of NGOs. In some cases, it has been suggested that private corporations and civil society organizations are crucial for providing the necessary information and capacities to make a difference in achieving environmental and social objectives, as we stated at the start of Chapter 4. There has also been a shift in the character of these discourses, with an increased concern with responsibilities and, within that, obligations and duties rather than the traditional focus on entitlements and rights in relation to environmental and social equity. Together, these developments have resulted in the advocacy of a culture of obligation in the decision-making processes of organizations combined with stakeholder deliberation to ensure greater accountability. The structural changes in the global economy, with nation-states seen as weakened out and therefore less capable of regulating the behaviour of corporations and the effects of capital mobility, mean that other ways of influencing the activities of international capital are seen as more effective. The rise in the West of NGOs concerned with sweatshops, human rights abuses, labour standards violations and unsustainable environmental impacts (in terms of both resource extraction and pollution) has prompted a new academic literature on how to hold corporations to account.

The harmonization of international trade (alongside trade dispute resolution) through the mechanisms of the WTO has also raised concerns that the long-term goal is to remove or reduce regulatory powers. In addition, the anti-globalization movement has highlighted the excessive influence of private corporations on the decisions made over the last ten years, especially through the deployment of trade sanctions. Similar concerns were raised about the proposed OECD Multilateral Agreement on Investment, which would have granted powers to transnational corporations to initiate legal proceedings against states for obstructions to free trade. In this context, the destabilization of the global economy in the late 1990s generated increased pressure for social accountability, including among those within the corporate sector itself who were concerned about unpredictable market conditions. This resulted in the UN/International Chamber of Commerce initiative for shared core values on human rights, labour standards and environmental sustainability, as well as the UNDP Human Development Report in 1999 calling for more democratic and effective global governance (including but going beyond voluntary codes of responsible conduct). Nevertheless, the pressure remains largely for public–private and civil society partnerships rather than international regulation. For some, such as Harris Gleckman and Riva Krut (1998) and

Peter Utting (2002), self-regulation needs to be reinforced by third-party verification of code compliance, as well as transparent reporting of the audit processes involved and stakeholder involvement throughout the process. Richter's hope for a new debate on intergovernmental regulation appears to be a much less likely option and (with the Global Compact in place) there is little prospect of the re-establishment of the UN Center on Transnational Corporations. Regulation is unrealistic and self-regulation does not guarantee objectives and enforcement. As a result, co-regulation strategies have emerged, including the partnerships that Richter portrays as inadequate.

The reinvention of 'the citizen': from constituencies to stake-holders in the global corporate sector

As we discussed earlier, the idea of 'citizenship' has been marked by two defining characteristics. First, it was associated with membership of a particular political community within a given territorial space. Second, it was assumed that citizenship was for the most part concerned with 'rights'. Even when distinctions between civil, political and social citizenship were made, it was primarily concerned with the expression of entitlements to private property, voting, free association and speech, education, healthcare and welfare (Marshall 1950; Saunders 1993, 1995). The other side of rights, that is responsibility, obligations and duties (such as respecting someone's right to free speech or dutiful payment of taxation to fund welfare), was always present but it was overshadowed. Both of these assumptions have been challenged as a result of the declining importance of nation-states in the face of global flows, transnational networks and the shift towards a politics of responsibility and obligation. There is also a growing awareness of and a sense of urgency in responding to simultaneous multiple injustices which exist side by side.

The reasons include the recognition of asymmetrical power relations between globalizers and globalized (see Chapter 3), post-materialist values, the problems of causal attribution for trans-boundary pollution (Beck 1992, 1995), the importance of global reach, making distant peoples and generations more proximate (described by Giddens 1990 as time–space compression), the informational technology revolution, and the emergence of the 'new economy' (Castells 2000) or some subtle underlying process promoting empathy and solidarity. In a neoliberal global economy, social citizenship (and the political networks that sustained it) has become less important as neoliberal projects have reined in entitlements. These projects, however, are not just an attempt to restore the primacy of civil and political citizenship (Hayek 1960); they provide a crucial punctuation point in seeing the relationship between entitlements and obligations as simply based on reciprocal relations between members of the same community. With reciprocity in doubt, ecological citizenship has been able to highlight obligations to other species, their habitats, trees, mountains and the biotic community (see Leopold 1949).

With the state no longer the primary agency and delivery vehicle of justice, the emergence of 'corporate responsibility' makes sense – the state is now just a player (and on many issues not a particularly important one) while other agencies of justice have become more important. NGOs, corporations and intergovernmental forums have become the route by which to mitigate environmental and social impacts. Corporate responsibility has had some concrete effects but much depends on the willingness of companies to develop robust codes of conduct and monitor their own activities and those of subsidiaries as well as contracted outsourced manufacturers and suppliers (as demonstrated by the Fuji Corporation). It is a stepping stone towards a more accountable corporate sector. If we assume that citizenship brings justice and responsibility together through civic engagement and is expressed in concrete political activity (from the most unorthodox and informal forms of participation to the more conventional involvements in political parties, elections and established pressure groups), then corporate citizenship should ensure that those groups (some acting as guardians or stewards for the environment) affected by corporate decisions are consulted and that injustices are avoided, resolved or mitigated within a precautionary framework. Such developments also create the potential for transforming corporate culture.

While corporate marketers promote brands through speaking the language of desire, the agents of justice seek to ensure that this includes an internalized set of obligations – that a politics of obligation exists whereby people understand the reasons for acting responsibly (as the right, good or virtuous thing to do). Zadek (2001) suggests that these NGOs, as 'not-for-profit' private organizations, create the possibility for civil regulation of 'for-profit' private organizations (such as corporations and public–private partnerships) by developing intimacy and knowledge of the production process, seeking to influence corporate and state decisions through audits and management systems as well as through personal relations and media-savvy campaigns. He also highlights the fact that there are limits to corporate responsibility in terms of events and states of affairs beyond the control of corporate executives, nor can companies can be blamed for seeking to take on board social and environmental responsibility only when it is commercially advantageous and/

or viable. Zadek provides an outline of how corporate citizenship emerged and assesses the willingness and ability of private corporations to behave responsibly. Concerned primarily with sustainable development, he offers guidance on making corporations accountable in the context of the 'New Economy', which has also contributed to the redefinition of the idea of being a citizen.

While research is becoming increasingly detailed in different areas of social and environmental responsibility, it is usually focused on one issue rather than considering the linkages between them. The research literature has explored some of these areas of concern, for example the environment (Ledgerwood and Broadhurst 1999; Hay et al. 2005; Steiger 2004), labour issues (Jenkins et al. 2002) and human rights (Rees and Wright 2000; Addo 1999), as well as business and international studies (Rosenthal 1999; Paine 2003; McIntosh et al. 2004; Tulder and Zwart 2006) and materials designed for corporate executives (Willmott 2001; Sadler 2002; Leipziger 2003; Damon 2004). These studies highlight the shifts in transnational corporate responsibility to forms of citizenship rather than considering the more complex mixes of corporations and counteracting movements in developing countries, where the need to address corporate responsibility is a more serious matter. Much of the research, and, indeed, the campaign activity, is ethnocentric, concerned with consumers, union members and corporate activity at the brand end of the global supply chain in developed countries, rather than the other locations where production and sourcing take place. Critical studies of corporate responsibility, such as Mitchell (2004), Richter (2001) and, more constructively, Zadek (2001), highlight the growing evidence of the capacity of corporations to accept responsibility for the impacts of business activities alongside the reluctance to accept the full costs involved. There is also an emerging literature developing the idea of corporate citizenship, ecological modernization and risk society approaches, including work by Zadek (2001), McIntosh et al. (2004) and Schwartz and Gibb (1999). In addition, Litvin (2003) provides historical context on these issues. Zadek highlights how 'business is increasingly moulding societal values and norms, and defining public policy and practice, as well as being the dominant route through which economic and financial wealth is created' (Zadek 2001: 1). It is clear that private corporate networks do have an important part to play in the formation and well-being of communities.

Companies have often sought to secure their longevity and brand security through acts of charity and public work and are seen as increasingly accountable for the social and environmental impacts of their activities. Corporate citizenship opens up a range of new conceptual and practical possibilities. For Zadek, it involves a recognition of social and environmental footprints but also acknowledges that the constituencies affected by corporate decisions (workers, communities, consumers, the unemployed and the environment, as well as shareholders, clients and corporate executives) should all be seen as stakeholders in the decision-making processes affecting them. Moreover, it is possible to develop shared values and common purposes to ameliorate the combined effects of social and environmental injustice. For example, labour standard violations in the Special Economic Zones (SEZs) along Thailand's borders are intimately connected to human rights violations and the environmental degradation in neighbouring countries such as Burma and Laos. In this case, the forced relocations and displacement of ethnic groups from Burma generates the 'disposable people' (Bales 2004) who provide low-cost and highly productive employees – stateless migrant labourers – to work in the sweatshop conditions of outsourced manufacturing factories in Thailand. At the same time, power generation and water redirection projects in Burma and Laos are commissioned, often with the aid of the World Bank and the Asian Development Bank (ADB), to provide the necessary conditions for economic development within Thailand, where the resources for rapid economic development are becoming scarce.

One of the striking features of corporate responsibility in the context of developing societies is the lack of willingness by corporations to engage in the monitoring and enforcement of codes of conduct unless forced to do so by activist campaigns. Rodriguez-Garavito (2005) highlights the key problems in monitoring codes of conduct on the responsibility and accountability of companies. First, whether the codes are unambiguous in providing a guarantee of free association and recognition of organized labour in collective bargaining. Second, the independence of the monitors, i.e. whether monitoring considers the supply chain as well as specific factories, as well as whether it is sustained over time and is activated without prior notice. Third, access to all members of the labour force and the communities affected. Finally, transparency, both in terms of the supply chain and in the dissemination of the results of the monitoring process, with penalties for non-compliance.

It should be stated that the divisions of ownership and control of the global supply chains place the subcontracting companies in a difficult position unless the transnational companies commit to accepting higher costs, highlighting one of the asymmetries of power between companies in the chain. Subcontracting companies operate in a competitive marketplace, and the implementation of codes of conduct could place them in a disadvantageous position in their regional, national or local market.

Transnational brand-based companies define the terms of their own codes of conduct on corporate responsibility but have limited scope for observing them except in terms of seeking out suppliers that broadly comply with the codes. The key question is whether outsourced manufacturers are willing to bear the increased costs or whether the subcontractors to outsourced manufacturers can implement these codes without squeezing the profit margins at the very bottom of the supply chain. In addition, intra-regional subcontracting companies often have more capital mobility compared to local firms, passing on the risks to subcontractors in a particular region, leading to industrial relocation by subcontractors and having adverse affects on responsible enterprises, which go bankrupt. If the culture of corporate responsibility is not to be a façade or a spurious public relations exercise, then the obligations and responsibilities have to be backed up by a willingness to accept lower profit margins and/or higher consumer prices.

New and emergent visions of corporate responsibility

Corporate responsibility as a form of self-regulation provides the basis for setting standards for private corporations so that their conduct meets ethical and political standards. There are two issues here: the kinds of standards that are established in codes of conduct may be too limited to close the gap between legal requirements or actual practice and justice; and the problems of ensuring that the obligations of corporate responsibility and citizenship stick. This is a realistic rather than a pessimistic assessment – corporations may produce better outcomes through self-regulation than can be achieved through incentive-driven schemes imposed through stricter legal regulation at the national level. For example, even in the USA civil fines imposed as part of enforcing safety and health regulations in the mining industry don't always achieve the desired objective of less dangerous mines. The largest MSHA (Mine Safety and Health Administration) fine of $605,400 for an incident resulting in thirteen fatalities in 2001 pales into insignificance when compared to the Federal Communications Commission (FCC) ruling of a $3.5 million fine on CBS as a result of the offence caused by the partial exposure of Janet Jackson's breast at the Superbowl half-time performance.

The objectives that labour unions and environmental movements wish to achieve will be more effectively realized if transnational corporations internalize their responsibilities and incorporate a wider range of constituencies as stakeholders. While laws impose specific duties, the spirit of corporate responsibility goes beyond making the necessary commitments to meet legal requirements, for it must embody a notion of good practice that can prompt ethically informed decisions as situations change. The situation is made more difficult as a result of two combined tendencies – international economic governance institutions (the World Bank, the WTO, the IMF) push for further deregulation of production and trade at the same time as the expansion of world trade is accelerating (Bromley and Smith 2004). The existence of almost 600,000 transnational corporations and subsidiary companies forming networks across national boundaries indicates that economic space is global. Unfortunately, social and political space is more fragmented, and intergovernmental cooperation to counteract the activities of private corporations is patchy and uneven. When considering whether transnational corporations can be prompted to change their behaviour, social scientists have monitored the gaps between attitudes and behaviour (or more recently between the values espoused in corporate PR campaigns and the actual decisions taken by corporations). Given the increased concern with environmental and ecological citizenship, the focus has shifted to finding ways in which corporate citizens understand why certain actions are virtuous, right or good so that desired changes in behaviour become more stable.

In 2003, the World Economic Forum's report on 'Responding to the Leadership Challenge' stated that private corporations face a series of new economic pressures, political uncertainties and social expectations that they are beginning to acknowledge, if not always address: 'Regardless of their industry sector, country of origin, or corporate ownership structure, they are under growing pressure to demonstrate outstanding performance not only in terms of competitiveness and market growth, but also in their corporate governance and their corporate citizenship' (WEF 2003: 2).

Grahame Thompson (2005) highlights how these kinds of developments, in part as a result of wider discussions on globalization but owing also to corporate scandals (Enron and Worldcom), involve a shift from corporate social responsibility to corporate citizenship. Companies such as Nike have been increasingly derogated for being irresponsible (so much so that many marketing departments in corporations use the buzzword 'NIKEmare' as a worst-case scenario). Transnational private corporations have increasingly sought an appropriate balance between the interests of investment and market share strategy, shareholders and market value and environmental concerns and social obligations. In short, corporations have sought growth strategies that depend on securing the increased value of *intangible assets* such as reputations, confidence of stakeholders (investors, customers, regulators and employees), brand identities, talent, capacity for innovation, intellectual property, networks and relationships with clients. Company structures are thus arenas for conflicts and tensions between competing imperatives – and, as such, we should regard these as strategic domains in which there are advantages to be gained for the workforce and the demands of environmental movements (that is, if they develop stronger links and coordinate their activities). It is also useful to consider what constitutes a sound basis for environmental responsibility in a corporate context.

1 The construction of a corporate policy on the environment that coordinates all the activities of the company, with measurable benchmarks or targets against which success can be identified.
2 Coordinated responsiveness to the task throughout the company, including adequate environmental leadership, open deliberative and integrative mechanisms within all parts of the company and transparent dissemination when a policy is achieved.
3 Flexibility to allow for innovation in all parts of the company and adequate resources to aid implementation (a key indicator that the company board and CEO are taking the issue seriously).
4 Understanding of the implementation of policy as a process rather than a static plan to accommodate improvements to internal corporate and external markets and environmental knowledge.

In addition, the prerequisites for achieving these include adequately trained and qualified staff, clear lines of authority, effective programme and project management arrangements, the opportunity for audits to review effectiveness and address problems (ensuring that mechanisms for corrective action are integrated into company procedures) and financial autonomy in the company's environment department so that expenditure is planned and least-cost solutions are avoided. In any ongoing process, there needs to be effective communication within the company from top to bottom and with external stakeholders, as well as analysis of the external regulatory frameworks and examples of good practice in the corporate sector so that the company can anticipate legal and market change. Certification of the company's production process is often secured through the generic ISO14001. Although this has few requirements beyond clear and measurable benchmarks and the search for continuous improvement, it retains the strength of being applicable to all firms. In addition, there are additional standards series focusing on environmental labelling and communication (ISO 14020-5), environmental assessment and performance (ISO 14030-1) and life-cycle assessment (ISO 14040-4).

These have also enabled corporations to reposition themselves as part of industrial restructuring while at the same time demonstrating a willingness to match the corporate strategy to environmental objectives by adaptation – for example, Shell and BPAmoco acquired the identity of energy producers rather than oil producers to address the transition to a low-carbon world. This does not require responsiveness to all constituencies, and for some companies the priority is to focus on improvements in specific areas of responsibility, as in the case of fashion brand companies being heavily concerned with labour standards to avoid being accused of sweatshop practices. Partial responsiveness to NGO and movement campaigns leads to one-sided responsibility in the corporate sector when the issues often demand a two-sided or multi-sided response. Similarly, companies that address environmental concerns do not address labour issues with the same rigorousness. In other words, although codes of conduct address a variety of issues, the character of their *visions of responsibility* has been shaped according to the unique production processes that pertain to each supply chain and the activist pressures that different companies have experienced. This is developed in more detail elsewhere (Pangsapa and Smith 2008b), but suffice to say here that there are significant opportunities for environmental NGOs and movements to highlight partial responsiveness as an additional lever and to link environmental standards to labour struggles, community campaigns and movements responding to human rights violations and political corruption. The main weakness of the ISO 14000 series of standards is the neglect of the issue of participation by relevant constituencies.

In a useful expansion of the stakeholder concept that adds value to the idea of corporate citizenship, Jean and Ed Stead argue that stakeholders should not only be seen as those affected by corporate decisions but also as those that affect corporations, i.e. anyone with an interest in the company concerned (Stead and Stead 1992: 150–51). Technically, if a company is engaged in overseas expansion, these could include the environment, communities and labour unions that could be affected in the future, so introducing a stronger precautionary element into corporate responsibility. Accepting this assumption would have enormous implications for thinking about responsibility for companies planning to extend their global reach.

Taking the intangible seriously: the basis of the UN Global Compact

The internationalization of the economy has affected all stakeholding or potential stakeholding constituencies – shareholders, suppliers, consumers, the workforce, etc. – although the existing transnational institutions through which their interests are given voice have an effect on company decisions, to ensure that some have greater weight than others. In any case, the final decision lies with the corporation, which is not yet obliged to take wider constituencies into account. In June 2004 the OECD brought together members of unions, NGOs and corporations for a round-table discussion of corporate responsibility focused on Chapter V of the OECD Guidelines for MNCs (multinational corporations) on environmental performance. Some broad points were: corporations were taking environmental management systems and auditing tools as well as performance indicators and environmental reports seriously where their reputations and efficiency were at stake; corporations were beginning to use the guidelines to connect environmental protection to social issues such as human rights; and top-down initiatives were more problematic lower down the organizational hierarchy.

Coordination across different sectors of a corporation and between corporations and small or medium-sized enterprises was recognized as a significant problem (although the latter's proximity to environmental problems meant that they were often more willing and able to take action). While the OECD and the World Bank have encouraged legal recognition of stakeholder interests (such as the Global Corporate Governance Forum in 1999), perhaps the most significant development is the UN Global Compact (2000), bringing together the ILO, international NGOs and UN agencies with a human rights mandate. The NGOs, including the Coalition for Environmentally Responsible Economies, the International Union for the Conservation of Nature, Global Witness, Amnesty International and Oxfam, represent a variety of constituencies that have the potential to become stakeholders.

Indeed, global corporate citizenship not only raises the internationalization of stakeholders and accountability of companies across national boundaries, it points to accepting a wider range of constituencies as stakeholders, many of which are still not regarded as integral. Thompson (2005) argues that 'the environment' currently stands in a similar situation to 'the unemployed', in that even though they are affected by company decisions the companies see responsibility as lying with the state authorities. (The OECD round-table on environmental performance also identified corporate uncertainty and confusion about where to place responsibility for environmental protection; also, NGO and union representatives were concerned that corporate involvement in politics was not always genuinely concerned with the environment.) Similarly, local communities may benefit from the voluntary altruistic measures of companies but they can only influence local state authorities that regulate the companies concerned (such as through local or regional planning).

Jonathan Porritt similarly argues that measures to reduce pollution and conserve natural resources can only realistically be achieved if companies see tangible material benefits in committing themselves to the process (the logic of ecological modernization, where cleaning up the production process and firms taking responsibility for recycling the products they sell to clients cuts costs and/or increases revenues). Thompson also highlights the potential in social activist models of corporate citizenship for changing the ground upon which these relationships work – since companies have the capacity to harm or benefit immediate stakeholders, wider constituencies and society in general (or perhaps a variety of communities in different nations), then they should acknowledge their moral obligations and take ethical considerations into account when making decisions (ibid.).

It is of course easy to be cynical when faced with the activities and decisions of some companies. The CEO of Nestlé, Peter Brabeck, has promised to investigate personally any hints of his company violating the World Health Organization corporate marketing guidelines (a concession to the history of baby milk products sold in developing societies). UNICEF has had a long-standing concern to sustain breastfeeding (attributing an estimated 1.5 million infant deaths annually to the decline in breast-feeding). Nestlé's expansion into the Chinese market with the use of inducements such as vouchers and stationing doctors in supermarkets in Beijing to address the concerns of consumers (i.e. the parents of young children) suggests that the commitment of the company to its own public relations on responsible conduct is still questionable. In addition, Nestlé resisted the withdrawal of some baby food products for having excessive iodine levels (CEM 2005). Opening up potentially lucrative new markets is of course the inevitable response of a transnational corporation experiencing stagnant share values.

It has long been acknowledged that international agreements on global and regional environmental problems have succeeded or failed on the quality of the monitoring and implementation process, and this is especially underdeveloped in corporate citizenship initiatives to date. Indeed, NGOs and unions seeking expertise on monitoring compliance with labour standards can draw much from the experience of environmental regulation, in particular, where the monitoring was flawed and compliance difficult to achieve (Vogler and Imber 1996). Of course, where companies have a vested interest in achieving objectives, in areas like security and civil liberties in conflict zones, for example, considerable achievements have been made (Snell 2007). We should not forget also that the success of some international treaties on the environment has been, in some significant measure, due to corporations being engaged in the formation and implementation of policy – most notably the Montreal Protocol and, to some extent, recent measures on climate change. Where corporations do not acknowledge their obligations, however, the progress is painfully slow, although higher normative standards on corporate behaviour combined with NGO and union monitoring are clearly making corporations more cautious.

Making the Global Compact effective

The Global Compact is often described as a 'historic experiment' in developing partnerships between nation-states, intergovernmental forums, private corporations, NGOs and local campaigns for social and environmental justice. By encouraging companies to move from a sole concern with profit maximization towards recognizing that they are integral to society as a whole, the Global Compact is likely to become Kofi Annan's main legacy as secretary-general of the United Nations. The spread of UN networks into the private sector (sometimes described as the privatization of the UN) was in large part a result of the financial crisis of the UN and the difficulties of reconciling US interests with those of the global South. In the face of these, this initiative is an attempt to develop a progressive response to global inequality. For Annan, when addressing the World Economic Forum in Davos, the issue was clear:

> We have to choose between a global market driven only by calculations of short-term profit, and one which has a human face; between a world which condemns a quarter of the human race to starvation and squalor, and one which offers everyone at least a chance of prosperity, in a healthy environment, between a selfish free-for-all in which we ignore the fate of the losers, and a future in which the strong and successful accept their responsibilities, showing global vision and leadership. I am sure you will make the right choice. (Annan 1999)

In addition, separating the discussion of corporate social responsibility and citizenship prevented it from being bogged down in trade and protection disputes in the arena of the WTO and other multi-/bilateral negotiations. Recognizing the existence of a global economic space is the first step in dealing with questions of social and environmental injustice. One of the distinguishing features is the role of inter-organizational networks, whereby corporations and civil society organizations seek to agree. In addition, the UN provides mechanisms for coordinating the participants (including the provision of the good auspices of the authority of the institution) and offers guidance on realizing a shared vision.

Such projects, by the nature of the novelty and challenges they face, inevitably have to be innovative, adaptable and flexible. Making the UN Global Compact more effective depends upon corporations changing their cultures and recognizing the penalties of not responding (rather than offering vague commitment to respecting codes of conduct). Given that it is a voluntary effort, the UN has no provision for an effective system of monitoring and enforcement. One possible prototype for assuring stakeholder involvement in corporate decision-making is AA1000 (launched by the corporate responsibility NGO AccountAbility in 1999 and followed by the AA1000 Assurance Standard in 2003).

AA1000 was designed as a road map (through planning, accounting, auditing, reporting and embedding) for private corporations to work towards best practice in corporate responsibility, while at the same time promoting effective stakeholder engagement through the whole process. It can be used in conjunction with other standards frameworks, such as the Global Reporting Initiative and ISO 14001 (AA1000 was also designed to highlight the quality of existing standards), or on its own. It has been regarded as a cumbersome and costly process, but rather than focusing on compliance and maintaining good public relations it was developed to encourage innovation and capacity-building within corporate decision-making. Also, it made positive steps in providing clear guidelines for working concepts of accountability and transparency and the process of defining values, issues and targets.

One of the difficulties arises from different ways of thinking about 'ethical' and 'social' – for some, ethics covers both the organizational system and individual behaviour, whereas for others ethics solely concerns the behaviour of members of the organization and is not relevant to the total impact of the organization's activities, including impacts on stakeholders and relevant constituencies. The latter provides a weaker basis for generating cultures of obligation. A key factor in ensuring accountability is the selection of appropriate performance indicators that match the objectives of the organization (i.e. in terms of its legally defined status and objectives) and the collection and analysis of relevant information while at the same time incorporating the aspirations of stakeholders (in part to ensure opportunities for revising both objectives and targets) by making sure that the methods are transparent, by measuring the scope of the audit, by providing quality assurance through specific auditors, and by communicating this information to all relevant parties. The AA1000 audit process involves the delivery of a social and ethical report that takes account of the objectives and targets while at the same time ensuring transparency to and seeking feedback from all stakeholders. The responsibility for this process is held by the governing body or committee of the organization in question, which may or may not include the stakeholders. In addition, stakeholders (including owners, trustees, employees, suppliers, partners or even customers, NGOs and public bodies) may have formal representation on the publicly recognized audit panel and/or be actually involved in the auditing process itself.

Another issue is that the relationship between the organization and each stakeholder group may vary, and the expectations of obligations and degree of consultation may be affected by whether the stakeholder relationship is internal or external, primary or secondary, local or international, as well as direct, representative or intermediary. Stakeholders are crucial in identifying the issues relevant to the organization (as well as how the organization is guided by the principles of inclusivity, completeness and materiality within the current cycle), but in some cases the issues may be more relevant to the organization and in others to the stakeholders. As a result, the issues may include the values, governance and operational practices of the organization, the way it is regulated or made accountable, the supply chain, and its impacts in terms of human rights, labour standards or environmental sustainability.

Materiality is also especially important, since organizations, once they have subscribed to a particular code of responsible conduct, have a responsibility to deliver their objectives in all geographic locations and in all their operating units. Targets are devised in line with the principle of continuous improvement of performance (as part of the process cycle), based on stakeholder commentaries. In this situation, failure to be accountable to relevant stakeholders matters, despite remedial measures to include the excluded later, and especially when the audit report creates opportunities for stakeholders to challenge the objectives and the process.

The AA1000 process presumes it is legitimate to demand higher standards from the organization. Selecting performance indicators that are appropriate to both the mission statement and codes of the organization, as well as the values and aspirations of stakeholders and wider society, depends on quality of information that is comparable, reliable, relevant and understandable. Information collection can draw on various research methods (indicators can include the use of qualitative or quantitative data) suited to the scale of the organization, using representative samples that take account of stakeholders (as well as diversity issues). This matches the description of Mode 2 knowledge production outlined in

Chapter 3 (i.e. research should be conducted in the context of applica-tion), which asserts that social 'robustness' is as important a criterion for practically adequate knowledge as reliability.

Despite the fact that the UN Global Compact lacks the resources and also the political will to effectively monitor and verify corporate responsibility – after all, it is an initiative for promoting learning through discussion – one of the startling effects has been that companies from the global South have often been more proactive than those from the global North (see Figure 5.1). As Senator John Warner stated when cross-examining Vice-President Al Gore during the Senate Environment Com-mittee investigation of climate change (drawing an analogy with arms control initiatives), 'we need to trust but verify', in both the public and private spheres. Similarly, corporate responsibility and citizenship initia-tives demand accountable and transparent forms of verification. Deborah Leipziger highlights the importance of the role of the office of the UN secretary-general as a 'moral authority' (Leipziger 2003: 73) in driving this initiative. Moreover, sharing knowledge and solutions to problems has long been a key part of strategies promoting social change, for: 'The Global Compact is not about sinners and saints. There will always be companies that lead and companies that follow. We want to keep the door open' (Georg Kell, in United Nations 2003: 8).

Leipziger suggests that unlike other initiatives that provide closer specification of outcomes, the UN Global Compact provides a flexible framework that encourages involvement – that a general approach has the virtue of generating critical mass behind a coordination of plans by many actors at state and intergovernmental levels as well as within what is often described as civil society. While it lacks the assurance mechanisms that would deliver specific results, it still provides the flexible learning curve needed to bring in companies and NGOs that otherwise would be reluctant or more cautious. Presently, there is considerable momentum behind the movement for corporate responsibility and the role of busi-ness leadership. Donald Evans (US Secretary of State for Commerce) stresses that it represents 'not just leadership but ethical leadership' in the corporate sector, focusing especially on the need for integrity in corporate decision-making.

Michael Novak (American Enterprise Institute for Public Policy Re-search) also highlights the importance of obligations and the need for trust and honesty (in particular, avoiding the destructive consequences of lies, illusions and duplicity). Novak follows J. S. Mill's perspective that economics should be seen as derived from ethics and suggests that 'The business corporation is the strategically central institution of

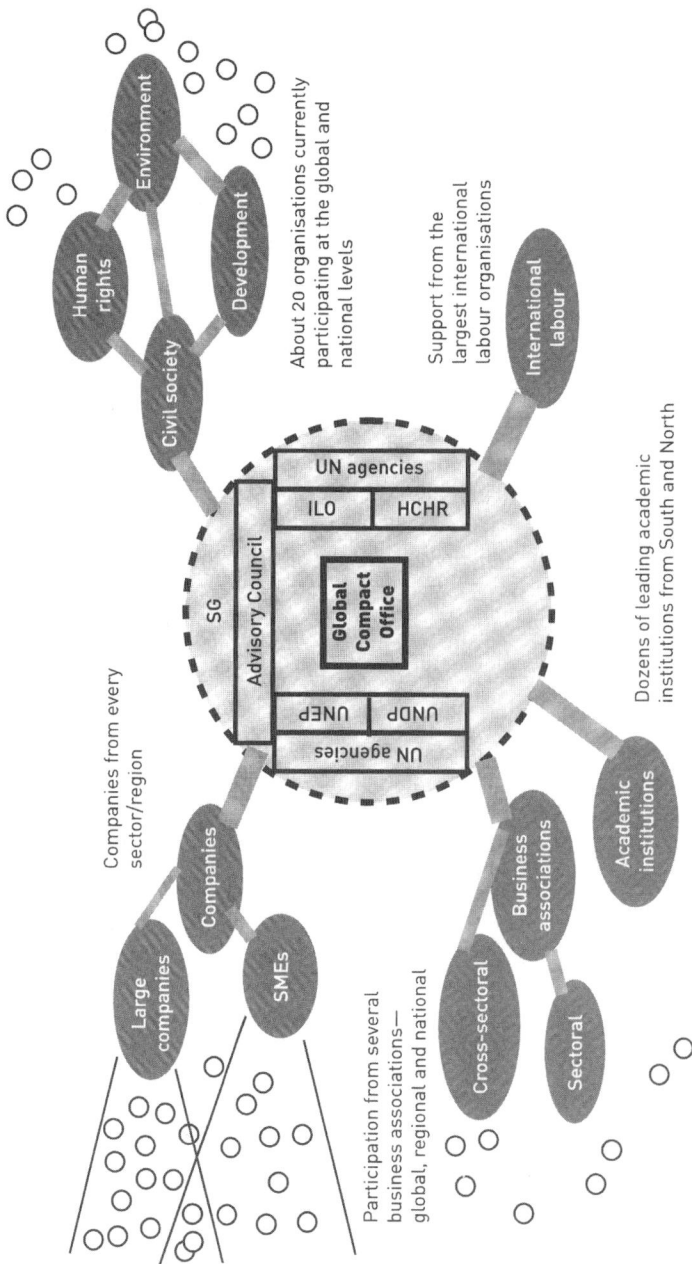

Figure 5.1 The UN Global Compact constellation
Source: Leipziger (2003: 74)

social justice; if the business corporation fails to meet its moral responsibilities, the odds against the rest of society [are] going to shrink to next to nothing' (Novak 2002). At the World Economic Forum in Davos, Switzerland, in February 2004, Matthew Bishop of *The Economist* said that CSR proponents have terrified the CEOs of the world. Nestlé CEO Peter Brabeck was the only chief executive willing to say for the record that the primary role of the company is long- or medium-term profit maximization to benefit shareholders: 'All of the other chief executives with whom I spoke said they thought he was completely mad to get up and say that in a public forum,' although Nestlé is a recent signatory of the UN Global Compact.

In ensuring responsibility, some targets are easier than others. The social entrepreneur Oded Grajew, founder of the ABRINQ Foundation (1990) focusing on child labour, initially helped move the Brazilian toy industry away from the use of child labour. Since then he has fostered a wider sense of ethical responsibility in business through the Instituto Ethos de Empresas e Responsabilidade (1998), as well as the World Social Forum (2001), a citizen sector alternative to the World Economic Forum. In this respect, the consolidation of Brazilian industry (100 companies constitute a third of Brazil's GDP) meant that action could be swift. For example, a child-friendly business programme led to a 40 per cent reduction in child labour in Brazil – through a child-friendly seal as an information tool for consumers.

With regard to labour standard violations, Social Accountability International (SAI) attempted to plug the holes that existed between the aspirations of intergovernmental organizations, such as the UN, ILO and OECD, to establish baseline standards on global labour practices and the inability of political authorities at the nation-state level to provide regulations that match these aspirations and/or enforce them effectively. The SAI process and performance standard SA8000 is based on the certification of all parts of the supply chain (rather than random checks), uses third-party monitoring for verification, offers inclusive processes for a variety of stakeholders (including NGOs and academic researchers), and provides for public reporting. The aim is to provide a transparent, participatory and accountable basis for ensuring more effective compliance. Neil Kearney (general secretary, International Textile, Garment and Leather Workers Federation) described SA8000 as the 'best management tool available to ensure accountability' (SAI 2001), especially since most previous standards focused on either process or performance. In addition, outsource manufacturers in developing societies have often opted for this standard even when not compelled to by brand companies (even though they usually bear the costs of training themselves), although there are incentives if companies award longer-term contracts to certificated manufacturers (Leipziger and Kaufman 2003). Because any participant can raise problems and highlight non-compliance on issues as diverse as forced labour (including bonded labour), collective bargaining rights, discrimination, child labour, health and safety, then the costs of potentially losing certification ensure that SA8000 also generates corrective action. This does not mean that there are no problems with standard-setting systems – all standards systems are expensive, require extensive training of all participants, and indeed small and medium-sized enterprises bear higher relative costs compared to larger transnational companies with more developed management organizations. This is a rapidly developing area, but concerted actions (pulling all the levers at once) are vital to success.

Conclusion: going beyond social and environmental responsibility towards corporate citizenship

While business-to-business associations (such as the World Business Council for Sustainable Development, WBCSD, and the International Business Leaders Forum, IBLF) and socially responsible investment strategies are taking positive steps forward, they often remain confined to narrow-focus deliberations between a limited range of organizations and, as a result, the aspirations and expectations reflect specific interests rather than those of all the groups affected. More promising are the strategies for partnerships (sometimes referred to as 'pairing') between NGOs and transnational brand as well as outsource corporations and stakeholder deliberation on code-making combined with rigorous and comprehensive third-party monitoring and verification processes. Without these kinds of checks and balances through civil organizations and/ or political authorities, social and environmental responsibility reports (such as through the Global Reporting Initiative) will remain publicity exercises to avoid the dangers of adverse publicity rather than genuine attempts to organize corporate conduct in a way that acknowledges obligations to all constituencies as well as bringing them into the process of deliberation as stakeholders.

The ideological character of the debate on corporate responsibility and citizenship tends to polarize the two options of the corporate sector regulating itself voluntarily and the need for the state to regulate in a mandatory way. Each has positive and negative qualities. Self-regulation will work when it is genuine in both the operational and participatory sense, but suffers from flaws when the company objectives produce

Five

decisions that bypass responsible actions. State regulation would work in situations where the political authorities have leverage over a company's decision-making processes but, in a global economy, if companies decide that regulations are onerous, then capital flight leads to the redeployment of problems in other political as well as social and environmental spaces. Initiatives such as SA8000 and AA1000 are interesting developments, for they offer practical ways to address these difficulties in the global supply chain and the externalities that result from the production, distribution and exchange of commodities. As a result, future research should focus on the intersections between intergovernmental, state and civil society initiatives, as well as highlighting the potentialities for effective verification and more inclusive stakeholder consultations.

6 | Environmental borderlands

Introduction: territory, responsibility and borders

This shorter chapter focuses on a particular problem, the role of territorial borders in developing effective strategies for preventing environmental degradation and promoting sustainability. So far, we have seen how national and regional territorial sovereignty can be an obstacle to the formation of intergovernmental agreements, can undermine the effectiveness of existing legally binding agreements or delay their implementation, and create conditions where those on one side of a border can abdicate responsibility for their environmental impacts that affect people on the other side. When we talk about borders, then, responsibility and its demarcation are immediately invoked. In the case of trans-boundary environmental problems, nations have often pooled their sovereignty, as the examples developed in the previous chapters illustrate – most notably where the EU has attempted to conserve fisheries, manage agriculture in more sustainable ways, regulate chemical waste disposal, address sulphur dioxide emissions or promote renewable energy sources. One of the most interesting side effects of these initiatives is the challenge to preconceived notions of citizens as tied exclusively to national states, and we would like to argue that if we began to see peoples in other countries as citizens in a common global community then that would radically alter the basis of how we see our entitlements and obligations. We have emphasized the importance of accountable political systems and established environmental law in developing societies. In these cases, the rationale is simply one that provides a quicker route to preventing environmental degradation while also addressing social issues, but in societies where these are more or less in place, it is possible to move beyond this in a way that will encourage positive developments elsewhere.

By way of a start, we will focus on a border that has impacts on both human and non-human animals – the border fence under construction between Mexico and the USA. This construction is designed to keep people from passing through while allowing lizards to scale it, but for larger wildlife, according to Christine Hass (assistant director of the Audubon Appleton-Whittell Research Ranch in Arizona), it is a barrier that 'has the potential to have more impact than anything we've ever seen' (Nijhuis 2007: 67). The border fence was approved in 2006 by the US Congress under the Secure Fence Act, which provides for 700 miles of double-layer fencing along the border. In addition, Michael Chertoff (homeland security secretary) waived the federal requirement for an environmental review, even though local range managers did not ask for a fence (they preferred traffic obstruction devices). So while species such as the flat-tailed horned lizard can move across the border, the large mammals that used to range between countries, such as the jaguar, ocelot, Sonaran pronghorn, 'gray ghost' Coates (a subspecies of the white-tailed deer) and two species of skunk, as well as some bird species, such as the pygmy owl, which can fly only up to a height of 12 feet, will all suffer from the absence of genetic diversity on both sides of the human-made border, and this despite the fact that some species on the US side are in danger of extinction. Since southern Arizona is a bleak environment, few species depending on wider migration and predation paths, already endangered in the USA, will be able to survive (ibid.: 64–70).

It is also increasingly difficult to delineate where a border actually is because it can have an important symbolic dimension. In these security-ridden times, borders can be in airports, cities, on the French side of the English Channel (for the UK) and in supermarkets, following recent business concerns highlighting extreme shoppers as potential terrorists (excessive purchases of fertilizer). Moreover, borders symbolically come into being through the construction of membership criteria for cultural communities. Those defined as members ('the same') in a given territorial or cultural space, usually associated with classification of a particular culture or peoples as 'the dominant', are opposed to those who are constructed as 'the other' (see Isin 2002). Similarly, with political communities, agenda formation and decision-making are inextricably linked to particular notions of national identity – i.e. that the responsibilities of the state (and other political authorities) should be primarily devoted to the needs and aspirations of its citizens alone. This is also a key premise of civil, political and social citizenship and the embedded assumptions of reciprocity within them. Sometimes this symbolic dimension of otherness is expressed through the metaphors of illness and disease – from the Spanish pox through to the 'gay plague' (Sontag 1989). For example, even though many of the Burmese migrants in northern Thailand suffer from ill health as a result of localized factors such as overcrowded camps, inadequate sanitation, poor working conditions and highly polluting local industries, many media reports treat the migrants as a threat to Thai health and focus on the conditions of state healthcare.

We should also add that the absence of borders, or even the presence of disputed borders, can be a problem, as we saw when considering the grab for seabed with the promise of significant oil reserves under the

Arctic, or the competing claims on landlocked seas such as the Dead Sea or oilfields that straddle a national border (the cause of the Iraqi invasion of Kuwait in 1990). In these situations, diplomatic and military conflict are a frequent possibility, and even more so as resource scarcity increases in the context of twenty-first-century development. In this chapter we will consider the effects of different kinds of borders, in particular porous borders, locked borders and borders where responsibility is contested.

It should also be stated at the start that borders do not always have negative effects or pose obstacles in all environmental problems. Much depends on the issue under consideration. Consider the global trade in endangered species, their skins and furs, animal body parts that are reputed to have medical properties and bush meats, as well as illegal logging and other organized criminal activities, such as smuggling classical antiquities, as well as the perennial issues of disease management and human and drug trafficking. Border checks have repeatedly prevented some of the worst aspects of species smuggling and the problem of invasive flora and fauna, as well as aiding conservation strategies.

Liquid politics on land and at sea: mobilities, flows and connections

The most significant international agreement in this respect is the Convention on International Trade in Endangered Species of Wild Fauna and Flora (CITES), agreed in 1973 by eighty countries. This agreement, which now has 172 signatories, seeks to ensure that the international trade in animals and plants (whether as living specimens or some derived product for medical, food, clothing, ornamental, timber or artefact uses, or even just for curiosity value) does not threaten their existence. We must bear in mind that the trade itself may not be the primary cause of endangerment but part of a mix of factors such as habitat loss, so the Convention may just provide an important additional safeguard. The 800 most endangered species, as a direct result of trade, are listed in CITES Appendix 1, and include primates (gorillas and chimpanzees) and big cats (tigers and jaguars). In addition, a non-detrimental finding and export permit is required for trade in over 32,000 other species. Of course, not all border controls work. In a recent case on the Thai–Cambodian border, following several successful cases and the 'repatriation' of orang-utans (an Appendix 1 species) from Thailand to Indonesia, a CITES investigation team discovered a number of juvenile orang-utans that had been smuggled from Indonesia (Sumatra) or Malaysia (Borneo) via Thailand. The safari park in question, linked to a casino resort, ran a duty-free shop on the border, and thus its vehicles were not subject to the usual border inspection processes. In addition to the likely slaughter of the young primates' parents, some of the orang-utans are rejected as a result of injury, health problems or for being too young before their sale at a price of US$1,000 (locally equivalent to eight months' wages) and transportation into Cambodia for a performance life of between four and ten years. Once males reach sexual maturity, they are often difficult to handle, so they become a long-term financial burden on the proprietors.

For longer-distance migrating species, territorially based responsibilities are directly relevant, whether on the 1,800-mile round trip by wildebeest, gazelle and zebra through the Serengeti and Masai Mara region that crosses the border of Tanzania and Kenya, or the routes of migrating birds or insects, which in some cases can cover a range of national territories (including that of the Arctic tern, which migrates between Antarctica and the Arctic, or the Monarch butterfly, which migrates between central Mexico and the US–Canadian border). Responsibilities regarding fish and sea mammal migration are complicated by the 200-nautical-mile jurisdictional limit of national states (established under the United Nations Convention on the Law of the Sea, in force since 1994) and partial knowledge of the migration routes. In some cases, fisheries conservation has been fairly successful when located primarily in a single territorial space. For example, the willingness of the Icelandic government to militarily enforce an exclusion zone to ensure sustainable management around Iceland in the North Atlantic (an action known as the Cod War) provides one of the first examples of the notion of environmental security leading to state action, but as we'll see below, this is also a rationale for actions that have received much criticism from environmental NGOs. In the open seas, which are a global commons, the most significant example is, of course, whaling, which managed to overexploit whales (great whales are CITES Appendix 1 species) until the 1980s, when only the minke, of seventy-nine species of cetaceans, was left with a population that could be harvested commercially, leading to a moratorium. As John Vogler states, the collapse of the whale population had been on the cards for a significant length of time, and was temporarily postponed only as a result of the redeployment of merchant marine vessels in the two world wars (2000: 48–51).

The International Whaling Commission (IWC) meeting in Anchorage in 2007 revisited the proposals from Japan and Iceland for resuming the commercial whaling of some species for the fifteenth time. The former has a special permit licence for scientific whaling primarily in the South Pacific, while the latter restarted commercial whaling of minke and fin whales in the North Atlantic. While Iceland is considering ending whaling permits (quotas will not be issued in 2008) on the grounds of the lack of a market, stimulated in part by health concerns about PCBs and mercury in whale products, the geopolitical response of the government after joining CITES in 2000 (and the IWC in 2002) was to indicate reservations on the Appendix 1 listing for blue, humpback, minke, fin, sei and sperm whales, which allows Iceland to trade in whale products with countries with the same reservations (i.e. Norway and Japan). In addition, small cetaceans are excluded from wildlife protection measures. Norway also maintains commercial whaling, and in 2006 had an annual quota of 745, which, with the unused quotas of the previous two years, means that the total was 1,052 minke whales. With consumer groups in Japan pushing for an end to North Atlantic whale imports, however (another illustration of borders at work), the Institute of Cetacean Research in Japan indicated after the Anchorage meeting that scientific whaling in the South Pacific would be extended to fifty endangered humpback whales as well as 850 minke and ten fin whales. South Pacific countries have reacted negatively to the damage that this will cause to the growing and increasingly lucrative whale-watching tourism industry (a vital new ecotourist source of income for Pacific island states).

Coordinated activities between the countries that share responsibility for migrating species are essential. On land, the wildebeest migration has been secured by the construction of a national park in Serengeti and a national reserve on the Kenyan side of the border, with funded anti-poaching units. With this in place, all species in the area benefit indirectly and biodiversity has been maintained. To provide an example of where a migrating species has not had such protection across national borders, the saiga antelope once spanned the central Asian plains, but with the break-up of the former Soviet Union into separate post-communist states and subsequent economic collapse, the saiga became a source of food across the steppes in Russia and Kazakhstan. In addition, with the opening of the border to China, a profitable trade in saiga horn developed for medical purposes (like the rhino horn, it is reputed to counteract fevers and now retails in the illegal economy for around US$6,500 per kilogram). Today, rather than the million saiga that migrated in the 1980s (twice that in the 1950s), only about 50,000 are left in the wild. According to Fred Pearce in a *New Scientist* report, this was partly the result of UNEP appointing WWF ecologist Esmond Bradley Martin to prompt pharmacists in Asia to substitute rhino horn with saiga horn as a result of the rhino becoming an endangered species (Pearce 2003). Examples such as this highlight a shift in conservation thinking, from focusing on a few key species towards seeking to conserve biodiversity, especially in ecological hot spots (although the funds for achieving this may often be secured by emphasizing higher-order animals such as elephants and leopards), and the increasing prospects of a mass extinction phase.

These examples highlight some of the ways in which territorial borders matter and how the character of the border, for example its porosity, can have a detrimental effect on environmental issues. On the one hand, sovereignty can limit environmental degradation on one side of the border, as in the case of Thailand considered below and in part of the following chapter. We will argue that environmental movements have been very effective in this context, but this has been achieved at a price – the exportation of environmental impacts to neighbouring countries. In the case of the saiga antelope, Chinese demands for particular medicinal products (the saiga became extinct in China before these developments) and a porous border almost led to the extinction of the species outside China. Market forces can also result in the inhibition of overexploitation of resources, however, as witnessed by Iceland's difficulties in regenerating the commercial whaling sector. Borders, like nation-states, are a mixed blessing, for they offer regulative potential but have an increasingly limited scope when addressing global issues.

It is not only species which are on the move but, as we have seen in previous chapters, capital and labour as well. Heavy transnational migration by people (as in rural-to-urban migration) can also place severe stresses on the ecological sustainability of their destinations. This is probably more the case in relation to capital than labour. These are symptoms of living in a world of increased and more frenetic mobilities in terms of trade, wealth, people and environmental impacts. Goods can be transported very cheaply from developing to developed societies with waste sent out in return. Capital can close down production in one location and find cheaper costs elsewhere, though not as quickly as Western brand companies that can change their outsourced manufacturers. Rodriguez-Garavito (2007) suggests that we need to think of a post-Westphalian world where national state borders are less important, but that does not rule out national and transnational factors both having continuing relevance. As many of the previous chapters have demonstrated, national politics and legal systems are key arenas for addressing environmental issues on the ground, and it is important to remember that many 'global environmental problems' are the aggregate effects of localized and regional problems. Similarly, while much of the literature focuses on trans-boundary impacts, transnational activism and intergovernmental cooperation, there is another side to this problem.

Borders still matter for more immediate and localized problems and conflicts over jurisdiction can be used to undermine environmental responsibility. This chapter uses three case studies to highlight the range of problems generated by borders and the continued importance of national state politics.

Case 1: responsibility, Love Canal and the US–Canada border

The history and long-term effects of the Love Canal incident in Niagara County were addressed in some detail in Chapter 1. In this case study, the long-term impact of the Love Canal incident is assessed in the context of debates over environmental responsibility for the Great Lakes region. In particular, we highlighted the role of Love Canal in generating the political will to create the EPA Superfund to clear up toxic waste sites. You will remember that Love Canal, which is situated close to the border with Canada and the Niagara river, has experienced waste problems on both sides. In 1991, the International Joint Commission that resulted from the Boundary Waters Treaty, agreed by the USA, Canada, the UK and the Great Lakes states in 1909, halted all discharges into the Niagara river on the grounds that the organic compounds and heavy metals in Lake Ontario required assessment. At the time, it was estimated that PCB discharges amounted to 1,200 pounds per annum.

Unlike the Love Canal Homeowners Association (LCHA), which largely disbanded after federal intervention on resettlement, the interfaith campaign on Love Canal, the Ecumenical Task Force (ETF), while not a grassroots organization like the LCHA, continued to build on the movement. In particular, it developed links with other citizen groups concerned with environmental problems in Buffalo and Niagara (Hyde Park Boulevard, 102nd Street and the 'S'-Area landfill on Buffalo Avenue, all used by Hooker Chemicals for waste disposal), as well as coordinating campaign work with similar movements in Canada. The 15-acre Hyde Park landfill had received 80,000 tonnes of chemical wastes (including the deadliest dioxin, tetrachlorodibenzodioxin), some of which had leached into Bloody Run Creek and then into the Niagara river gorge, contaminating the Devils Hole State Park. Occidental and the EPA agreed the terms of the clear-up of twenty-three sites where rock and soil had been affected by dioxins in 1986 and replaced the material in the landfill. Despite these emergent links on the Niagara frontier, Canadian NGOs and state regulators were more concerned with environmental damage to marine environments from US corporate activity, while the ETF for Niagara and associated campaign groups, as well as political actors in New York State, were more concerned with responding to the specific problems of toxic

Six

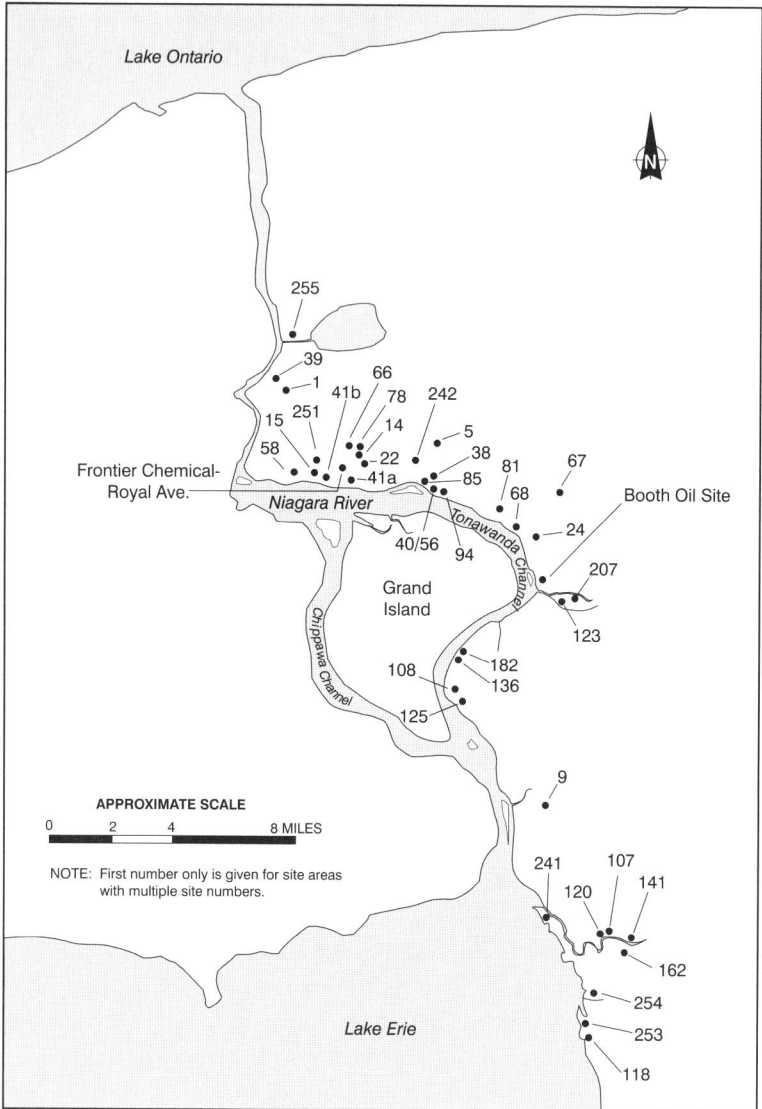

Figure 6.1 Location of significant Niagara river waste sites in the USA

waste storage and disposal. This is in part the result of the distribution of industry generating waste along the frontier, but also because the toxic dumps in Niagara were servicing New York State.

While we have focused on just a few of the major waste problems in Niagara, Figure 6.1 highlights the range of remediation efforts that are

USGS site nos	Site name
41b–49	Occidental Chemical (OCC) – Buffalo Avenue
81	Niagara County Refuse Disposal
14	DuPont Necco Park
78a, b	CECOS International/Niagara Recycling
39	Occidental Chemical (OCC) – Hyde Park
40, 56, 85, 94	102nd Street
5	Bell Aerospace Textron
66	OCC – Durez, Niagara Falls (formerly BTL)
41a	Occidental Chemical (OCC), S-Area
255	Stauffer Plant (PASNY)
251	Solvent Chemical
1	Vanadium Corp. (formerly SKW Alloys)
58, 59, 248	Olin – Buffalo Avenue
15–19, 250	DuPont – Buffalo Avenue Plant
254	Buffalo Harbor Containment
120–122	Buffalo Color, including Area D
118	Bethlehem Steel
136	River Road (INS Equipment)
67	Frontier Chemical – Pendleton
24–37	OCC – Durez, North Tonawanda
253	Small Boat Harbor Containment
68	Gratwick Riverside Park
141	Mobil Oil
162	Alltift Realty
242	Charles Gibson
22	Great Lakes Carbon
182	Huntley Power Station
241	Times Beach Containment
108	Tonawanda Coke
107	Allied Chemical
207	Tonawanda Landfill
125–127	Dunlop Tire and Rubber
123	Columbus-McKinnon
38	Love Canal
9, 15, 141	Iroquois Gas/Westwood Pharmaceutical

Source: Reduction of Toxic Loadings to the Niagara River from Hazardous Waste Sites in the United States. Niagara River Toxics Management Plan (NRTMP) Report, June 2004, <www. epa.gov/glnpo/lakeont/nrtmp/hwsreport2004.pdf>

under way in the Buffalo and Niagara areas. In many cases, the problems are not as severe, but they are still areas of significant concern for local populations. The majority of the sites have a close proximity to local populations, even though the 'S'-Area Landfill, next to Love Canal, contains a wider range of waste (63,000 tons of organic and non-organic materials, including building waste from chemicals plants, organic phosphates and tars, as well as acid and chloride compounds). The site is also located very close to the local water treatment plant serving 77,000 people in Niagara Falls. The focus on these waste facilities helps to explain an important dislocation between discourses concerned with preserving wilderness areas and environmental commons such as the Great Lakes on the one hand and campaigns linking environmental problems with social injustice in the USA on the other. The political discourses that have been very important in the environmental justice movements in the USA used established civil rights approaches to achieve environmental objectives. For citizens' organizations in Buffalo and Niagara, the concern is with local community effects, such as localized air pollution, drinking water and the potential direct effects of the dumps on blue-collar housing developments. Lois Gibbs emphasized the blue-collar working class as the grassroots base of the LCHA, and the US Census in 2000 indicates that the Niagara Falls community as a whole is 80 per cent white. Recent analysis of the shifting racial composition and residential segregation of the Niagara and Buffalo population, however, highlights the fact that despite the trend towards minority group suburbanization, populations in areas with a higher concentration of waste facilities and older closed landfills are likely to be populated by minority groups, although these include not just African-Americans but also Hispanic and Asian American minorities.

In some respects, the Canadian government has adopted similar environmental legislation and regulation to the USA, because, as Fletcher suggests, they wanted to avoid becoming a 'waste haven for the US'. Unlike in Europe, landfill space is ample in Canada, which can inhibit recycling initiatives. Nevertheless, Canadian waste management tends to be provided by crown corporations (public utilities), such as the OWMC in Ontario, while private sector waste transportation and disposal are preferred in the USA. Attempts to develop public sector decisions in New York State have failed owing to community opposition (Fletcher 2003: 17, 215–17). It should be added, however, that both governments strictly regulate industrial waste regardless of public or private sector management. Fletcher argues that while the legal context is very similar, the style of policy-making is not. In the USA, the driver is federal regulation, with states expected to develop their own equally strict regulations, while Canadian federal regulations are more general and accept some state autonomy regarding the operating permits for waste facilities. In addition, Canadian public–private partnerships in cities such as Toronto, which encourage environmental responsibility on the part of citizens, are more developed than on the other side of the US border, especially where personal decisions are involved, such as in recycling. If we compare this to Buffalo in New York State, where only 6.5 per cent of household waste is recycled and the largest tote available for household waste for each apartment can have a 95-gallon capacity, there is a significant shortfall in citizen-based responsible action compounded by inadequate waste service provision and waste education.

There were a number of Niagara waste issues after Love Canal, but this time the citizens' action groups formed from that experience were ready (even though the LCHA had faded away) to form broader alliances. One particular issue was the Hooker Chemical dump in Hyde Park. As a result, ETF changed its name to the ETF of the Niagara Frontier, establishing links with Great Lakes United (concerned with water, air and environmental remediation throughout the region), as well as more localized citizens' organizations such as the Campaign to Save Niagara, LaSalle and Niagara Demand (LAND), the Society to Oppose Pollution in Towns, and the Evershed Restoration Association (Edelstein 1989; Fletcher 2003: 160–61).

Nevertheless, what happens in Niagara has effects on two countries and compounds deeper problems that reside in the Great Lakes region (which accounts for almost one-fifth of global fresh water). Environmental responsibility in the region is also a matter of concern for various bodies with overlapping jurisdictions, including Environment Canada (which oversees the Great Lakes Water Quality Agreement, GLWQA), the International Joint Commission (established to prevent and resolve disputes within the terms of the Boundary Waters Treaty, 1909), the Commission for Environmental Cooperation (established in 1993 to coordinate activities in Canada, USA and Mexico), and the agencies involved in the Canada-Ontario Agreement Respecting the Great Lakes Basin Ecosystem (CAO), agreed in 1971 to implement phosphorous discharges from the GLWQA but amended to focus on persistent bio-accumulative and toxic chemical pollution and various urban and rural run-offs in order to promote the restoration and protection of the Great Lakes. Subsequently, the CAO has extended its reach to cover significant areas of concern, broaden the range of human impacts on the Great Lakes that deserve monitoring and remediation, and also encourage citizen participation in all these matters. In Canada, the federal government has responsibility for conservation and protection of water resources (the Great Lakes are implicated in 45 per cent of industrial activity), fisheries, navigation and international agreements, while the provinces and local authorities are responsible for water management, water and quality treatment processes

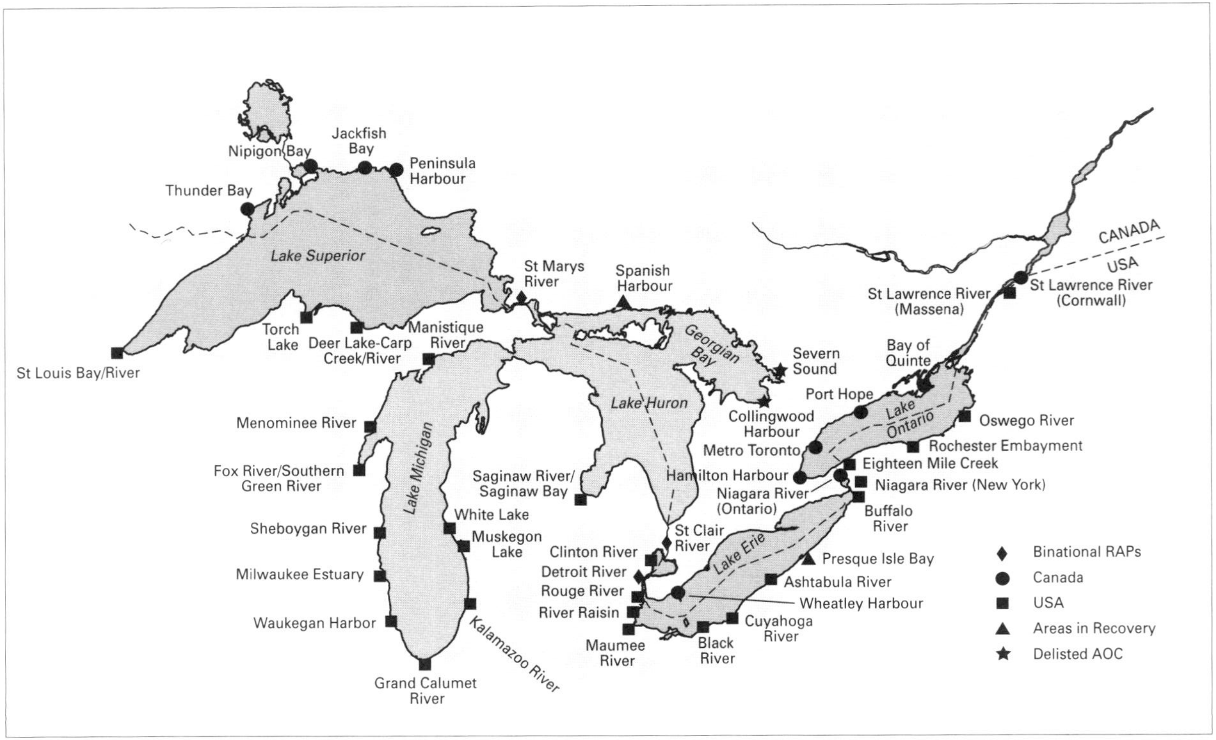

Figure 6.2 Areas of concern in the Great Lakes–St Lawrence River Basin

Source: Canadian Remedial Action Plans, <www.ec.gc.ca/raps-pas/default.asp?=En&n=96A7D1F1-1>
© Her Majesty the Queen in Right of Canada, Environment Canada, 2003. Reproduced with the
permission of the Minister of Public Works and Government Services Canada

and waste disposal, with responsibility shared between these levels of governance for agriculture, national water issues and health.

While the levels of heavy metals and PCBs in the Great Lakes remain a cause for concern, invasive species shed from maritime ballast tanks such as the zebra mussel, an invertebrate species originating in the Caspian Sea and spreading throughout European waterways in the twentieth century, and further spread by transoceanic shipping, were identified in the Great Lakes region in 1988. Zebra mussels are very efficient at filter feeding, reducing food sources for other species in the food chain (especially for larval fish) but also colonizing slow-moving species and man-made structures, adding significant economic costs to the water supply industry. In Lake Erie, with population densities that have even reached 1 million per square metre, they have significantly changed the water clarity, and in so doing also accrete persistent toxic materials. They have also been implicated in increased oxygen depletion and the emergence of dead zones in the central areas of the lake. More recently, since 1997, invasive zooplankton, also originating from the Caspian Sea, has displaced indigenous plankton species. Similarly, other invasive species, such as round goby and Eurasian ruffe, have caused problems for indigenous bottom feeders such as darters, logperch and mottled sculpin. The next major threat is from Asian carp migrating from the Illinois river, hopefully kept at bay by an electric barrier in the Chicago Sanitary and Shipping Canal. The Asian carp species (especially silver carp and big-head carp) that have infested the Mississippi, Missouri and Illinois river systems are prolific breeders that consume 40–60 per cent of their own body weight in plankton (the key part of the food chain for many other species) daily and can reach a size of 60–100 pounds. They prefer cold-water environments and so have migrated north, having the capacity to jump over small dams to enter the tributary systems. In some areas, they now constitute 90 per cent of the fish stocks. If they reach the Great Lakes system they will probably take over the river systems in Canada as far north as Alaska and Hudson Bay, driving out indigenous fish species and severely damaging commercial sports fisheries. Besides stricter regulation of ballast on vessels, a key issue has been drawing fishing organizations into the remediation measures to encourage the use of responsible baits (i.e. preventing the use of young carp as bait). In addition, academic research units such as the Sea Grant Institute (University of Wisconsin) have developed outreach programmes on invasive aquatic species.

The Love Canal incident and subsequent cases also highlighted the existence of two toxic waste hot spots in the border region – Niagara and

Detroit. In particular, Niagara had the only two toxic waste dumps in the state and was taking some waste out of state. On the Canadian side, toxic waste density is less, but it should be pointed out that Ontario's only commercial hazardous waste incinerator in Sarnia is close to Detroit. Fletcher adds that in the ten cases that served as a focus for his study, Canadian sites were likely to be in rural areas, while on the US side suburban and urban communities were usually the hosts for hazardous waste facilities (Fletcher 2003: 123–6). Canadian spills in the Saint Clair river near the industrial town of Sarnia have also had a disproportionate effect on the Ojibwa First Nation community that straddles the border in terms of fishing and hunting, resulting in the community buying in food and bottled water.

Given the complex mix of environmental issues in the Great Lakes region, environmental NGOs have been stepping up their activities to promote cross-border regional cooperation and a full reassessment of the GLWQA. These groups include citizens' campaigns on community health and toxic waste, branches of the Audubon Society or other environmental advocacy groups such as Environmental Defence, the Sierra Club, chapters of labour unions (Canadian Auto Workers), local campaigns focused on rivers and fishery stocks, and so on. These NGOs, totalling sixty-four on both sides of the border and addressing social and environmental justice, have developed a common platform to transform responsiveness to citizens' knowledge and action in the Great Lakes. In particular, these moves call for full public consultation where relevant experts, citizens' organizations, commercial interests and citizens from each country concerned with the activities of both Environment Canada and the EPA, as well as other government bodies, can come together. This would include a citizens' advisory board for the International Joint Commission (IJC), citizen participation on all IJC boards and in all government initiatives relating to the region, as well as opportunities for citizens' petitions as new issues arise. Concern has been raised regarding the grievances of First Nation peoples that have not been adequately addressed. In addition, there have been calls for a full public hearing on the proposals for changes to the GLWQA.

While the issue can often only be addressed in a regional way and with regard to the complex connections between waste issues, ecosystem balance, commercial interests in exploiting the lakes, and water quality issues, the territorial jurisdictions of each body often generate policy coordination problems, especially if each government is concerned with different kinds of environmental issues. The environmental NGOs also suggested that there should be independent and ongoing professional and detailed third-party monitoring as part of the assessment of progress and performance that requires government institutions to make all information available through regular reports (especially since the last similar review was conducted by the National Research Council in the USA and the Royal Society of Canada prior to amendments to the GLWQA in 1987). A particular concern was the scope of the existing agreement, and the belief that it should consider a wider range of stressors on environmental quality than hitherto (including air pollution from beyond the basin, fish farm by-products, new invasive species, and recent pollutants such as endocrine disrupters, neuro-developmental toxic substances and flame retardants) and be extended to include the Saint Lawrence Seaway (i.e. the ecosystem beyond the US–Canada border is also relevant). Finally, there was a demand that a more proactive approach to the development of ongoing scientific monitoring be instituted to address funding cuts in this area. All these suggestions focus on making the GLWQA process more accountable and transparent, integrating affected constituencies as stakeholders in any future policy-making and clarifying the roles of the various bodies that have obligations in the region. What this shows is that in the absence of a sense of responsibility on the part of many citizens on both sides of a border, NGOs have a crucial role to play in coordinating policy with state and international bodies where these borders cut through an ecosystem.

Case 2: the Bay of Gibraltar and transnational answers to political deadlock

The Bay of Gibraltar case study is also one with a long history, a function of the blockade of Gibraltar by the Spanish government under General Franco in 1969 (after years of territorial tensions between the UK and Spain) until the newly democratic Spain brought this to a close in 1982. Nevertheless, the long-term animosity between the respective governments over the sovereignty of Gibraltar still makes intergovernmental negotiations on environmental problems in the region very difficult to resolve. Before and during the blockade, the proto-fascist authoritarian Spanish state created a series of major industrial projects (an oil refinery, steel manufacture and for part of the time nuclear waste storage, which is a 'shock horror' story in itself) in the Bay of Gibraltar, in part to compensate for the unemployment problems in southern Spain following the blockade. The long-term effects on public health on both sides of the border, and the recent attempts to forge alliances between environmental and labour campaigns across the border, are considered here, as well as the significance of Gibraltar as a military and naval base.

For those unfamiliar with the significance of Gibraltar, formally a UK overseas territory since the Treaty of Utrecht in 1713, it has been a strategic military base in many conflicts from before the Napoleonic wars and through the world wars of the twentieth century. As Minister of the Environment Jaime Netto explained to us as we explored the Rock, as a result of the base there are more roads inside the mountain than in the city that inhabits it. Deep historic resonances linger in political discourse regarding this tiny but geopolitically important space, using metaphors of siege and attrition, a war of position punctuated with occasional wars of manoeuvre. Its geopolitical significance was in providing a naval base that effected considerable control of the Strait of Gibraltar – the entry and exit point of the Mediterranean Sea to the Atlantic Ocean.

Until the 1990s, the economy of Gibraltar was dependent on the military and navy and the Rock served as a ship repair yard for the British fleet. The economic driving force now, however, is a combination of finance and tourism, with high annual rates of growth in the last few years, exceeding 10 per cent in 2006/07. As a result, the population has expanded to over 27,000 residents and significant land reclamation has resulted in luxury apartments and a marina that sports expensive pleasure boats, establishing the location as a cosmopolitan playground for the wealthy in the Mediterranean. The influx of new wealth has had some negative effects, such as producing property speculation and driving up house prices to the point where residents on low incomes have difficulties securing a mortgage. By virtue of its geographical form, Gibraltar has few resources and is dependent on imports for many basic products, although the end of the blockade has allowed for both resources and employees to cross the three-quarter-mile border with Spain.

Periodically, in this highly charged political atmosphere fuelled by the testosterone of national difference, disputes that have environmental significance regularly break out. In 1999, following the seizure of a Spanish fishing boat, 300 fisherman blockaded the border as part of a dispute on fishing rights in what should rightly be regarded as a commons, responsibility for which rests on all parties. During 2000/01, the British navy nuclear-powered submarine HMS *Tireless* was docked in Gibraltar for repairs, which eventually lasted almost twelve months. The Gibraltarian government agreed, despite protests from its own citizens, after it had employed its own safety experts to assess environmental security, while Spain made a diplomatic protest on the grounds of safety for 250,000 Spanish citizens and reactivated the sovereignty dispute. Spanish protests were also evident when the submarine briefly docked again in April 2004. Other disputes relate to telecommunications (despite agreement on both sides on this) and Gibraltar's small airport, although direct flights from Madrid were permitted for the first time after the Cordoba Agreement in 2006. Spanish authorities have also repeatedly accused Gibraltar of being a haven for tax evasion, money laundering and smuggling.

In 2007, the partial sinking of the *New Flame* off Europa Point produced another spate of interventions by the mayors of La Linea and Algeciras over potential spillage of tanker fuel in the bay. The vessel she collided with, *Torm Getrude*, a petrol tanker, was heading into Algeciras, while the *New Flame* left Gibraltar without securing clearance first. While the political opposition in Gibraltar adopted the line that cooperation with Spain on the collision would suggest that Gibraltar was not in control, local Spanish politicians called for the UK to intervene. Meanwhile, amid the acrimony, local environmental groups have focused on potential hazards to the environment. Campaign groups, as well as the government in Gibraltar, have long expressed concern about water and air pollution from the industrial sites in the bay on the Spanish side, in particular the effects of the oil refinery and steelworks on the local people on both sides of the border. In situations like this, where local economic interests are under threat and national boundaries are not always clear (especially in terms of water boundaries), there is a tendency to blame all negative impacts on the inadequate regulations and enforcement of the other side.

The continuing existence of Gibraltar as an overseas territory has been politically secured by appeals to the principle of self-determination for all peoples through the UN and the International Court of Justice, consolidated by two referenda in 1967 and 2002 which produced an overwhelming majority in favour of not becoming part of Spain. Diplomatic relations between Spain and Gibraltar can sometimes be tense, but the election of the Social Democratic Party in 1996 facilitated dialogue and communication with Spanish authorities in Madrid and in the region and secured trilateral negotiations with the UK and Spain, with Gibraltar as an equal partner. The new constitution, endorsed by the 2006 referendum (60 per cent in favour), established the Gibraltar parliament as a fully elected legislative body for the first time. Since all parties have been members of the EU since Spain joined in 1986, the same EU Directives, explored in Chapter 4, apply in all cases on both sides of the border. As far as the local communities are concerned, the industrial sites in the bay originated under the authoritarian regime of General Franco, ensuring that environmental impacts were not an issue with workers and their families occupying housing in close proximity to the facilities. In a suggestive public health study, Benach et al. (2004) have highlighted

191

how southern Spain is associated with high mortality risks, raising questions of environmental justice and calling for more detailed research on regional clustering of these risks – particularly environmental factors such as air pollution and heavy-metal water contamination, occupational factors such as asbestos, and social factors such as overcrowded housing, poverty and unemployment.

While environmental issues led to mobilization in either Gibraltar or southern Spain individually, the impetus for the environmental movements addressing both sides of the frontier was a response to the increased political opportunities created as relations between the respective governments relaxed in the 1990s. While the Environmental Safety Group (ESG) was originally formed to stop repairs to a British nuclear-propelled submarine, this led to the launch of a core group of activists and scientists still active and involved today. In particular, the ESG encourages cross-border action by citizens and environmental education. Some activities have been focused purely on Gibraltar, such as the 'Cleaning up the Rock' campaign to deal with a particularly bad litter and waste problem. Groups such as Friends of the Earth in Gibraltar tend to have a similar focus. Friends of the Earth Gibraltar focuses mainly on parent-driven global campaigns (although locally they lend support to Green campaigns). The ESG has initiated civil organization activities and partnerships, however, as well as developing a membership campaign to recruit both Spanish and Gibraltarian citizens.

As with all citizens' organizations, the strategy and tactics unfolded as they moved from one issue to the next. In 2003, the ESG introduced the Bay Bucket Brigades, promoted by community campaigners such as Denny Larson. The buckets are relatively cheap air pollution monitoring devices developed by campaigners in northern California in the mid-1990s. Edward Masry (the head of Erin Brockovich's legal firm) was representing citizens from Rodeo in eastern San Francisco Bay, and in order to accumulate evidence quickly asked an engineering company to find an affordable alternative to Summa canisters using cheaper components – hence a 5-gallon plastic bucket device that can collect air samples for laboratory tests. While this kind of evidence is open to legal challenge, the very activity of gathering community air samples can prompt the corporate management of a facility to settle on pollution victim compensation claims. In the Rodeo case, Unocal reduced its discharges of 'catacarb' and Masry secured a settlement from the company of US$80 million for 6,000 residents.

Subsequently, these monitoring devices have been used in Texas and Louisiana in the USA, as well as in Mexico, South Africa, Thailand and the Philippines. In the Bay Bucket Brigade case, which brought ESG members into closer contact with members of Spanish NGOs, the air samples were compared with a range of toxic substances, highlighting where the substances exceeded legal limits, and thus added weight to the case calling for a full public health analysis by all political authorities in the bay. One of the lessons of cases like Love Canal is that epidemiological studies add a considerable time lag to the promotion of greater responsibility on the part of corporations, but can also prevent problems arising in subsequent years. As highlighted in Chapter 1, LCHA research and activism did prompt remediation measures, but the failure there to broaden the campaign for full public health assessment has meant that focused site remediation at the core of the contamination area often leaves local communities on the periphery vulnerable. The DIY Bucket Brigade method can clearly generate considerable pressure, but as one of the spokespersons for ESG highlighted in addressing border issues, it should be pursued in a trans-boundary way to encourage a regional solution based on comprehensive evidence.

What has sustained the ESG campaigns in particular has been the support and guidance of deeply committed and knowledgeable advisers from around the world. 'Protesting alone is outdated, what is needed now is increased corporate responsibility and compliance with various environmental regulations ... we are community watchdogs, pressing several pressure points and maintaining this pressure which we believe yields results in "encouraging" companies to clean up their act. We have seen this with the Refinery but much, much more needs to be done,' says Janet Howitt (ESG spokesperson). Even though the bay is being described as a 'public health crisis' by adviser and WHO specialist Professor Benach, and an 'environmental hotspot' by marine biologist and IUCN environmental consultant Sandra Kloff (who is also an ESG committee adviser), the political situation is relaxed and the broader economic interests are still the main priority for governing authorities. Visiting MEP Neil Parish was shocked when he saw the impact the petrochemical plant was having on the surrounding environment, claiming he could see, feel and even taste the pollution.

One of the obstacles to cross-border action in the bay by civil society organizations in the past has been the reluctance of local unions on the Spanish side of the border to be involved with environmental NGOs. Nevertheless, despite the continuing importance of the refinery in terms of employment, the union leaders are increasingly recognizing that the health problems of workers and their families, particularly respiratory diseases and cancer, are likely to be related to the facilities in the bay.

This led in March 2006 to the ESG joining a coalition of fourteen political and civil organizations, La Plataforma por el Estudio Epidemiológico – AGADEN (Asociación Gaditana para la Defensa y Estudio), including Asociaciones de Vecinos de Algeciras, Ayuntamiento de la Línea, Colegio de Médicos, CGT, CCoo, Derechos Humanos, Izquierda Unida, Partido Popular, Partido Andalucista, Partido San Roqueno Independiente, and UGT 14 Verdemar – and participating in the first joint protest by unions and environmental activists on bay pollution in Algeciras on 3 June 2006. Another avenue for the ESG has been to lobby the EU for action on the refinery's air pollution (an ESG legal complaint against CEPSO for illegal discharges had already been lodged with the European Commission) and secure the support of MEP Neil Parish, as well as highlighting the need for a cross-border epidemiological study (since at present the Spanish authorities would have no powers to conduct one in Gibraltar and vice versa). The La Plataforma coalition has also submitted a petition with 13,500 signatures demanding exactly this in 2007. Obviously Denny Larson's empowering campaign on sampling neighbourhood air quality strengthens existing campaigns with scientific proof of the chemicals present. The ESG has forged links with Spanish environmentalists from Agaden and Verdemar, who themselves have maintained a sustained campaign for a better environment. The bond is strong and has seen the coalition through situations which, at times, have been politically sensitive and may have driven apart less committed citizens' organizations.

As with the Great Lakes Region, the complications of a variety of political authorities having overlapping and separate environmental responsibilities for the ecosystem inhabited by the bay communities have been compounded by the presence of a national border. In this case, however, civil society organizations have been able to press for a regional solution by linking environmental justice to social justice, particularly by drawing in union support. In the next section, we consider the case of porous borders in South-East Asia (an issue raised earlier regarding endangered species, but linking environmental to labour and human rights campaigns is also a necessary part of the solution in this situation too).

Case 3: exporting environmental degradation in South-East Asia

In this third and final case study, we examine borderland issues on the South-East Asian mainland where Thailand has recently been a driving force in economic development, following the success of regional tiger economies such as those of Singapore and Hong Kong (Bello and Rosenfeld 1990; Phongpaichit and Baker 1998). Unlike the highly regulated border zones of the Great Lakes region and southern Spain, the borders of South-East Asia and Asia generally are less of an obstacle to flows of people and resources. By way of illustration, in 2006 the Thai authorities discovered 175 North Korean migrants (men, women and children) in Bangkok, many of whom had travelled by foot over vast distances. The significance of porous borders has become more evident owing to the effects of internal depletion or use of resources within Thailand since the mid-1980s, when the economic boom gathered pace. In terms of politics, the uneasy balance between business, state bureaucracy and the military led to a phase sometimes described as 'money politics' (Phongpaichit and Baker 2004), wherein business interests were represented by regional factions within political parties and sought influence by realignments in coalition governments. Thai politics changed considerably after the 1996/97 Asian crisis, for those economic interests hit hard by global financial markets shifted track and sought to exercise more control over the state in order to protect Thai companies from the vagaries of world markets, eventually siding with Thaksin Shinawatra's Thai Rak Thai (TRT) project (which was closer to the developmentalist model adopted in the Singaporean modernization strategy).

In Thailand, environmental movements have become a major obstacle to development projects, especially in the areas of deforestation and electricity generation. As a result, given also increasingly limited forest reserves and fewer suitable locations for large-scale hydroelectric dams, since the 1990s the government has encouraged the exportation of environmentally degrading projects into neighbouring countries. This has caused population displacement of members of indigenous peoples within neighbouring countries (Soh, Thai Bor, Kaleung and Luam peoples in Laos) but also into Thai border areas (for example, the Karen, Shan, Karenni, Bamar, Mon from Burma into towns such as Mae Sot). In the case of Burma, flows of migrants without citizen status resulting from forced dislocation, human rights violations and environmentally damaging energy projects provide low-wage labour for the sweatshop economy in outsourced manufacturing in Special Economic Zones. Environmental and labour issues in these borderlands are intimately connected.

Environmental resources in Thailand are managed by organizations such as the Royal Irrigation Department (RID), the Royal Forest Department (RFD) and the Electricity Generating Authority of Thailand (EGAT), which do not have a strong track record in consulting the communities affected. Policy debate tends to occur within these organizations to varying degrees, with more open dialogue within the RFD and as regards discourses concerned with tourism. Current developments suggest that despite the unsettling events of the coup of 19 September 2006 and the consequent restrictions on political activities by civil organizations, the adoption of a sufficiency economy framework by the military government in Bangkok still creates opportunities for influence – perhaps more so than in many other non-democratic contexts. When we started our fieldwork and conducted our analysis in 2005, Thai Rak Thai had secured a landslide election victory, and despite some concerns about TRT control of the mass media, civil organizations could still have an impact – as demonstrated by the People's Alliance for Democracy protests that were stimulated by the Shin Corporation share sale scandal in January 2006. The political impasse that this generated, marked by anti-Thaksin demonstrations and pro-Thaksin counter-demonstrations, the Muslim insurgency in the south, election boycotts and the invalidation of the election drowned environmental and labour issues in 2006, especially outside Bangkok.

Land in Thailand designated as forest and woodlands is now at 30 per cent (14 million hectares), which is half the level it was in 1960, although official figures may be inaccurate (Fahn suggests that land is at 20 per cent). As a result, Thailand is an importer of wood (50 billion Thai baht, THB, per annum or US$1.2 billion), hence the pressure to identify timber resources in neighbouring countries. Fahn (2003) argues that the RFD is torn between two imperatives – commercial exploitation of forests through concessions and, as a result of government-sponsored scholarships, conservation values based on the US model (for the 'greatest good for the greatest number for the longest time' – Pinchot 1901). The RFD is the guardian for national parks (nature education and recreation), wildlife sanctuaries (biodiversity conservation and research) and non-hunting zones (allowing for some resource extraction). The 1989 logging ban in state-owned forestry, following flooding and mudslide disasters, has resulted in a proliferating illegal logging trade within Thailand, creeping but often unmonitored settlement patterns in woodland and forested areas, and both legal and illegal logging in surrounding countries. To counter this, successive Thai governments have secured logging, fishery and gem mining concessions in neighbouring countries for nationally based companies.

With restrictions in place within Thailand, legal logging concessions in Burma were politically facilitated by the Thai government, in particular by General Chavalit Yongchaiyudh, as early as 1988 – with border access to Cambodian timber starting in 1995, when Chavalit became prime minister. The relationship between military commanders in the border regions with Burma, Laos and Cambodia and the logging companies has always been an intimate one, with national borders being open to flows of both natural resources and people, so much so that Chavalit is often referred to as 'Mr Timber' in the Thai press. The impact of illegal logging and active sawmills is harder to measure (certainly no customs duties are reported) and complicated by organized crime syndicates in Thailand linking up with insurgent groups in neighbouring countries seeking to finance weapons in the borderlands of both Burma and Cambodia. The Salween logging scandal in 1997 (after the Asian crisis and the collapse of the Chavalit government) also revealed that Thai timber was being illegally felled, shipped to Burma and then exported back into Thailand stamped as Burmese timber.

Before we return to the current situation we will highlight some of the background trends. State-sponsored projects increasingly generated village resistance, as demonstrated by the problems faced by RID when constructing the Kaeng Sua Ten (rapids of the dancing tiger) dam on the Yom river or EGAT over the Pak Mun dam in the north-east of Thailand. Burma, Yunnan province (China) and Laos have agreed to a memorandum of understanding committing them to providing power supplies essential for the economic growth of Thailand and linking the power grids in these countries as a step towards an integrated ASEAN power grid. As part of this vision, Laos has signed contracts for twenty-three dam construction projects, primarily for export on the Mekong river system (ibid.: 102). Despite a long-term commitment to market liberalization, there are still considerable barriers to market entry, i.e. 'state sanctioned electricity monopolies and laws that have made wasteful large-scale power production the norm' (Ryder 2003: 17). EGAT is the sole buyer in this uncompetitive market and also controls the power transmission network. Environmentally damaging projects are effectively subsidized through projects that in times of drought can lead to power cuts as well as diverting investment capital from more sustainable, localized alternatives (such as solar power, wind generators and small-scale hydroelectric turbines) that do not depend on long-distance transmission networks.

The impacts of dam projects on the environment and on communities are seen as a political and legal matter, limited to civil compensation disputes rather than integrated into the cost–benefit analysis that underpins project planning and environmental impact assessment. As with earlier dam projects inside Thailand, the estimates of displaced households often understate the likely impacts. For the Pak Mun dam, the original EGAT estimate was that 262 families would be affected, but the final figure was 1,821 families in thirty-one villages, and over six thousand families received compensation for the decline in fisheries.

Box 6.1 Dams, displaced peoples and environmental degradation

Corporate activity on environmentally sensitive issues in the region has focused on large-scale dam construction projects in neighbouring countries. Consequently, the role previously played by EGAT and RID in Thailand has been enacted by transnational corporations, intraregional companies and developing country firms. We also need to bear in mind that corporate investment in these energy projects dwarfs the national income of countries such as Laos. The Nam Theun 2 consortium signed an exclusive supply deal with EGAT (for 995 MW of competitively priced energy), and invested US$1.5 billion in the dam and reservoir project. This project will flood about a quarter of the Nakai-Nam Theun plateau, a biodiversity site with 17 endangered species and newly discovered species such as the Saola. The deal also includes a plan to make the remaining area of the plateau a conservation zone. The consortium will run the dam for 25 years after which it and all subsequent revenues will be returned to the ownership of the Lao Government (which currently holds 25% of the equity). Laos will receive 75 MW of electricity and US$80 million per annum in the form of taxes, royalty charges, and dividends over the duration of the agreement. This is the largest single source of foreign exchange income and contributor to GDP

Besides the fact that the project produced 21 MW of power rather than 136 MW and cost 6.6 billion THB (of which 17 per cent was spent on resettlement and compensation rather than the original estimate of 3.9 billion THB), the Mun river activist networks and protests from 1991 to 1997 played a substantial part in the emergence of a new broader grouping, 'The Assembly of the Poor', the activities of which ensured that subsequent Thai governments now know that they will pay a high political price for initiating similar projects in the future.

With large-scale environmentally damaging projects seen as politically risky inside Thailand, Box 6.1 illustrates the kind of alternative to secure power supplies that have been developed in recent years. The kind of project described in Box 6.1 is subject to the World Commission on Dams' (WCD) recommendations that project design and negotiation of outcomes should be subject to participation from relevant stakeholders. FOCUS on the Global South (Guttal 2000; Guttal and Shoemaker 2004) has identified considerable problems with the 1995–97 consultation in Laos which already exports 75% of its electricity to Thailand and anticipates becoming the "battery of Asia" and does not take account of future energy needs - average energy use is Laos is currently 55 KWH compared to 1296 KWH in Thailand (Pangsapa and Smith 2008a).

The increased costs of the project led to corporate restructuring with EDF International (subsidiary of Electricité de France) taking the lead role in the consortium and Thai companies (Merrill Lynch Phatra Securities and Jasmine International) selling their stakes to EGCO (partly owned by EGAT). In addition, the size of the dam wall was increased so additional capacity could offset the costs (Pangsapa and Smith 2008a). Within Thailand, EGCO has diversified energy production from gas to water and coal and purchased shares in other Thai energy companies including the planned Bo Nok power plant in Prachuab Khiri Khan province. In Laos, it has sought other hydro-electric projects but has faced competition from transnational companies such as Daewoo Engineering and Construction, Loxley PLC and Tractebel. The presence of small private power companies such as HPower, and new aggressive market entries such as Tractebel created limited competition between companies using different energy sources, have also enabled EGAT to secure lower prices.

processes, which were focused on resettlement options and mitigation measures, meaning that the viability of the project and the information presented by officials and representatives were not subject to effective scrutiny. As with many other dam projects, there was a knowledge gap between local people and foreign experts. The implications of the project, many of which are irreversible and cannot be mitigated, were not fully appreciated and NGO participants concluded that they had become part of a public relations exercise to legitimize the World Bank's involvement as guarantor rather than being part of a genuine effort to ensure stakeholder consultation (Shoemaker 1999). In Laos, the absence of independent NGOs, independent media and an impartial judiciary, alongside violations of human rights, means that WCD conditions of a fair and transparent decision-making process to ensure that the outcomes are legitimate, positive and lasting have not been in place. As with Pak Mun, public disclosure of documentation by the consortium, delays in producing implementation plans and the fact that an effective and transparent monitoring process was absent meant that the construction programme took priority over local impacts.

While the Government of Laos has agreed to fulfil social and environmental obligations to secure loan disbursements and guarantees provided by the World Bank (underpinning the first WB-approved dam for ten years at US$1.2 billion), evidence of compliance is limited. Within a context of poor governance, a legal system for ensuring compliance does not exist, pro-poor public expenditure has not been managed effectively and transparently in the past, and baseline data were inadequate. Moreover, the project had already violated World Bank approval criteria owing to the systematic and large-scale logging and involuntary resettlement that had already taken place on the plateau. It should be noted that Bolisat Pattana Khet Phudoi (a Lao timber company owned by the military) logged a million cubic metres of forests, including hardwoods, in the affected area, 27 per cent of the official 1997/98 log supply (Thongleua and Castren 1999). Rather than the 4,000 estimated displaced people, Imhof and Lawrence (2005) suggest that 6,200 indigenous people will be displaced, 1,500 families engaged in fishing downstream of the dam will lose livelihoods, and 100,000 people living alongside Xe Bang Fai will be adversely affected by the water levels and declines in migrating fish stocks (most of whom are unaware of the environmental changes in store). The International Rivers Network and Environmental Defence reported in February 2006 that detailed resettlement plans for the Nam Theung plateau and project lands and environmental management monitoring (along with environmental, habitat and wildlife species conservation plans and scientific research on stream morphology and fisheries) were still not available (Imhof and Lawrence 2006). This is a crucial flaw, for detailed plans on these matters are a necessary precursor to effective monitoring.

Despite intensive lobbying by 153 NGOs and from forty-two countries, and internal concern within the World Bank, the financial agreement with the Asian Development Bank (ADB), European Investment Bank, Nordic Investment Bank, export credit agencies in Canada, France, Norway and Sweden and French development finance institutions, plus long-term loans from international banks (ANZ, BNP Paribas, Calyon, Fortis Bank, ING, Société Générale and Standard Chartered) and seven Thai banks, including Bangkok Bank, Bank of Ayudhya, Kasikornbank, Krung Thai Bank and Siam Commercial Bank (World Bank 2005), went ahead. This model for corporate and investment activity is likely to be adopted in other neighbouring countries such as Burma, with four substantial projects planned on the Salween river system which will have a much greater environmental impact than the Yadana gas pipeline (a classic case of a Western company investing in a project that devastated habitats while at the same time employing forced and child labour; see Pangsapa and Smith 2008b). The Salween river, the last large river system to be undammed in the region, runs through lands occupied by the Karen, Karenni, Mon and Shan indigenous peoples. In addition to hydroelectric dams and reservoirs providing 1,500 MW for EGAT by 2010 at a cost of US$4–7 billion, it is envisaged that these projects will divert water into the Bhumiphol and Sirikit reservoirs within Thailand. Besides the World Bank considering US$1 billion of financial guarantees, the Japanese government, which has initiated constructive engagement with Burma, has indicated an interest in the project (subject to the rule that regional initiatives in South-East Asia through the US$30 billion Miyazawa fund are dependent on the use of Japanese technology and technical consultancies). The Japanese state-backed EPDC (Electric Power Development Corporation) has already initiated preliminary studies on the Salween along with Burmese army and Thai surveyors, such as MDX Power Plc (a company already involved in feasibility work for the Kok river with Italian Thai and the Japanese Marubeni Corporation), while the MDX subsidiary GMS (Greater Mekong Sub-Region Power Co. Ltd) is engaged in dam construction planning with the Myanmar Economic Corporation. China has also looked south for investment opportunities, and the Hat Gyi dam on the Salween river was agreed between Burma, China and Thailand in 2006, with construction to begin in November 2007. It is expected to be ready to sell power to Thailand by 2012 (Karen and Karen 2007).

The most promising site near Ta Hsang (Tasang) is close to the Ping and Kok rivers in Thailand. A facilitator for this deal, the developing-country company Thai Sawat, has been granted timber and road construction concessions by the Burmese government in the area and now seeks to negotiate a deal for logging the areas to be flooded. If the water levels of this project are to be sufficient for effective diversion to Thailand, the dam would have to be very high with a large reservoir (estimated to cover 640 square kilometres, but this will depend on whether water transfer is included), which will inevitably have a major impact on agriculture, fisheries and the uncultivated environment, as well as necessitating the construction of waterways and extensive electric power transmission grids. Mediators for MDX, GMS and Southeast Asia Technology Plc have also sought to secure Shan compliance with the survey and feasibility work, although it is suspected that the project will be used to cut off Shan insurgents from access to the border (one of the convenient side effects of the Yedana gas pipeline for the Mon). Based on evidence of previous human rights violations against the Shan and other indigenous peoples, the involvement of the Burmese military means that it is likely that the energy and water projects will entail forced labour and portering, forced relocations – an estimated 300,000 people have already experienced this – torture, (sexual) assaults and extra-judicial killings.

Rapid economic development within the borderland zones has also resulted in exploitation of human resources. There are nearly two million legal and illegal migrant workers from Burma, Cambodia and Laos, employed in a variety of low-paying jobs throughout Thailand. Burmese migrants make up the vast majority of the migrant workforce in Thailand and have a large presence in the northern border provinces. Over the last four decades, millions of Burmese men and women have been fleeing into neighbouring countries to escape a repressive political regime and increasingly difficult socio-economic conditions. Developing-country firms that outsource production are able to intensively exploit these desperate and highly vulnerable people while neglecting labour standards and human rights or keeping them to a bare minimum. At the same time, migrant workers' status as 'immigrant' or 'alien' means that they are at great risk of physical abuse, as well as labour standards and human rights violations.

The busiest entry port for Burmese migrants is the border town of Mae Sot in Tak province, which lies opposite the town of Myawaddy in Karen State. The constant flow of migrants into Thailand's northern border provinces is aided by the relative ease of entry into the country. The fact that one-day passes can be obtained at official checkpoints goes to show how the exploitation of human resources is facilitated by the state. Many migrants use these 'passes' as informal work permits into the country. As Dennis Arnold highlights, the causes of migration are a combination of push and pull factors which, in the case of Burmese migrants, the former involving the need to escape political persecution, displacement and relocation and a dire economic situation, the latter including easy access into Thailand and Thailand's economic advantages and a more favourable social and political climate (Arnold 2004: 3). Unskilled daily workers in Burma, for instance, earn about US$0.48–0.58 per day, while workers in Mae Sot can earn between US$1.50 and $2.00 per day. These wage differentials can thus be seen as a major economic incentive not only from the vantage point of firms but from the vantage point of migrant workers in search of higher-paying jobs (Pangsapa and Smith 2008a).

The growing population of Mae Sot also places considerable demands on the local ecosystem. The rapid growth in the number of factories (21 per cent per annum in the 1990s), which often specialize in labour-intensive outsourced work in garments, plastics and electronics, also generated increased pollution and traffic problems, generating a protest again migrant labour by Thai local residents in 2001. Mae Sot has also had a history of zinc mining since the 1970s, and in 1998 it was discovered by a team led by Robert Simmons (International Water Management Institute) that cadmium pollution from the mine run-off had contaminated local food supplies, particularly the rice fields. Subsequently it was discovered that cadmium exposure was fourteen to thirty times the level recommended as safe by FAO/WHO, that levels in the Mae Tao Creek were seventy times EU standards, and that 65 per cent of rice samples were contaminated. Local medical facilities were also recording urinary cadmium levels, noting weakening of the bones and kidney failure (Itai-itai disease, a form of osteoporosis). As a result, rice for food consumption is now provided by the Thai authorities.

In the context of human, energy and resource flows across borders, there are three main reasons why labour, human rights and environmental issues should be seen as interconnected in South-East Asia:

1 In the networks of the global supply chain, capital investment decisions and outsource contracts are influenced by the availability of cheap labour and ample natural resources combined with the compliance of the local political system (compliance that can lead to corruption and human rights violations). 'Just-in-time' regional factories often have a detrimental effect on local ecosystems through resource extraction, (unregulated) pollution impacts, and disruption of local employment markets serving more sustainable forms of production. In Burma, opposition to these processes has resulted in political and military persecution, adding another push factor for survival migration while at the same time making available a substantial low-wage workforce on the Thai–Burmese border.

2 Within the culture of corporate responsibility, codes of conduct are most often focused on labour standards and environmental sustainability (while human rights are often more important in conflict zones). Living up to the codes of conduct makes corporations more responsive to the pressures of campaigns by Western NGOs on labour and environmental issues. At the WEF in Davos in 2004, only one CEO had been willing to openly question whether companies had social and environmental responsibilities – Peter Brabeck of Nestlé – indicating that corporate decision-making is susceptible to pressure and argument.

3 Resistance networks are emerging that link unions to environmental movements (sometimes as part of broader platforms for social

and political change, such as the Assembly of the Poor in Thailand). Moreover, localized and regional campaigns are developing strategies in coordination with transnational NGOs to initiate consumer boycotts and raise awareness of how corporations are neglecting their responsibilities. For example, challenging the information provided for transnational brand-based corporations by subcontract companies would create more pressure for compliance with the codes of conduct.

Since global networks of corporations operate to produce social and environmental injustice, then critical responses to corporate decision-making would be more effective by developing counteracting networks that benefit from 'movement fusion: the coming together of two movements in a way that expands the base of support for both' (Cole and Foster 2001: 164). The most likely context for achieving fusion and fostering global networks for promoting social and environmental justice is the emerging discourses of corporate responsibility and citizenship – that is through self-regulation rather than through the state. This is especially relevant in South-East Asia since developing countries in the region operate in a global economy while not experiencing the same history of national regulation of capital, labour and the environment characteristic of the twentieth century.

The results of this case study may seem counter-intuitive at first sight (activists tend to see outsourcing as the major problem). In some ways, this is informed by an ethnocentric response, i.e. that representatives of workforces, social justice movements and environmental campaigners are fixated on the relocation of labour from North America and Europe to cheaper markets overseas (commonly described as the 'race to the bottom'). Interestingly, this has created significant opportunities for change – the separation of ownership between transnational brand-name corporations and outsourced manufacturing companies (some of which are local while others are nationally or regionally based) creates mechanisms for intervention by unions, environmental movements, human rights organizations and other NGOs. When considering the effects of the Nam Theun 2 and the Huey Ho dam projects in Laos, a nation characterized by poor governance structures, the controlling role of transnational corporations (as integral to development consortiums) tends to present obstacles to achieving real change or even adequate compensation for affected groups (the relevant constituencies).

Rethinking environmental borders and citizenship

The chapter is a comparative one but it also shows the different ways in which social and environmental injustices are connected, and, in the case of environmental, labour and human rights NGOs, present obstacles to campaign groups achieving their objectives. The case studies are compared to other trans-boundary pollution and resource extraction problems (such as acidification, illegal dumping and deforestation) to highlight how obstacles to effective strategies can be overcome. We have considered the effects of different kinds of borders – porous borders (Thailand), locked borders (Gibraltar/Spain) and borders where responsibility is contested (USA/Canada). The environmental issues are diverse, ranging from water and air pollution to resource depletion, and the challenges posed for environmental movements and NGOs are complicated. Moreover, while the recent literature on citizenship focuses on transnational connections and problematizes the relationship between citizenship and the nation-state, these case studies highlight the continuing relevance of national citizenship for particular environmental issues. The table below provides a general picture of trans-border issues as illustrated by the three cases.

When considering the three cases (as summarized above), in spite of the different types of borders, their locations, the many obstacles and political tensions involved, there are underlying commonalities across all the cases in terms of the issues involved. First, the complex and serious nature of environmental problems affecting peoples and communities on either side of the border. Second, the difficulties in devising solutions to address them. Here we see the emergence of strong activist organizations which are forging broader alliances and networking with a whole host of constituents, attempting to develop trans-boundary cooperation and dialogue on the part of states, NGOs and citizens, and calling for responsibility and accountability on the part of corporations.

Hence we need a conceptual shift to view the concerns of others across borders, in other parts of the world or in future generations, and acknowledge stakeholding in the here and now as having a right to participate but also obligations and duties towards the interests of others and to avoid harm. Nowhere is this more evident than in the global waste trade. This brings us back to the argument we made at the beginning of the chapter – if we began to see peoples in other countries as citizens in a common global community then that would radically alter the basis of how we see our entitlements and obligations. Such an approach or outlook would be a good starting point for trans-border solutions because it allows us to underline our commonalities while also recognizing the differences and the many complexities involved in the issues raised. This means that the role of territorial borders should be geared towards developing effective strategies directed towards a common goal, preventing further

Environmental borderlands

TABLE 6.1 Trans-border issues – different kinds of borders

Border type	Stable	Locked	Porous
Borders	USA/Canada in the Great Lakes Region Contested environmental discourses	Spain/Gibraltar (UK territory) History of blockade but now normalization of relations under way	Thailand/South-East Asia mainland Facilitation of cross-border flows of people and resources (sometimes illegally)
Issues	Shared levels of responsibility in Canada; in USA complex and serious nature of problems (water and air pollution, invasive species, toxic waste hot spots)	Serious nature of environmental problems; a trans-boundary crisis; linking environment and social justice	Export of environmental degradation in SEA. Environmental degradation and exploitation of people on the border areas complicated by concessions by governments of neighbouring countries to exploit their natural resources
Obstacles and challenges	Uncoordinated on the part of country governments; uneven development on the part of responsible citizens, i.e. Canadian residents are often more engaged in acts of environmental responsibility; NGOs playing crucial role in the absence of citizen participation	History of political deadlock; interferes with environmental responsibility (blame game), compounded by long-term animosity between UK and Spain. Responsibility by government officials on both sides remains a problem in the context of strained international relations. Existing but dated industrial developments in Spain; Gibraltar dependent on finance and tourism with a high growth rate; British	Country governments and TNCs as primary actors in the context of poor governance structures. Powerful and influential TN firms able to secure support of IFIs (e.g. ADB and WB). Ease of border access; construction projects displacing families. Thai dependency on energy for foreign revenue. Competition between TN firms and domestic industrialists; knowledge gap (local versus expert)

		military/ naval presence (unclear national boundaries at sea)	Communities engage in reactive campaigns rather than involved (treated as constituencies at best and not as shareholders)
Activism/ activist organizations	Formation of citizen action groups on both sides with intent to form broader alliances but problems of managing the differences between social and environmental justice	Strong activist support base including committed and knowledgeable advisers; cross-border linkages formed between environmentalists and recently labour unions	Environmental movements and human rights groups; strong activist networks and protest campaigns; active NGOs, intensive lobbying efforts. Livelihood campaigns also a key part of local activism (informed by Buddhist values)
Responsibility/ solutions	Strong NGO activism; more trans-boundary cooperation for states and citizen organizations; more accountable and transparent governance process; responsibility must be extended to all affected constituencies	Transnational and regional solutions. Empowering campaigns like Bucket Brigade; cooperation and dialogue; cross-border action; all constituents concerned about general health and well-being	Labour standards, human rights and environmental issues are ultimately interconnected. Factories impact local ecosystems; corporate responsibility pressure to address both labour and environment; activist networks and advocacy groups developing strategies with transnational NGOs to raise awareness and pressurize corporations into compliance

environmental degradation and promoting sustainability. As Jared Diamond explains,

> We need a healthy environment because we need clean water, clean air, wood, and food from the ocean, plus soil and sunlight to grow crops. We need functioning natural ecosystems, with their native species of earthworms, bees, plants, and microbes, to generate and aerate our soils, pollinate our crops, decompose our wastes, and produce our oxygen. We need to prevent toxic substances from accumulating in our water and air and soil. We need to prevent weeds, germs, and other pest species from becoming established in places where they aren't native and where they cause economic damage. (Diamond 2003: 44).

A healthy, sustainable environment is undoubtedly something we all want and something we should all strive for *together* – for ourselves and for future generations. The environment transcends all boundaries, and in our globalized world, where everything is interconnected, our perspective in this regard needs to be radically altered. 'So this blue planet is our only home,' His Holiness the Dalai Lama reminded us during a lecture he delivered to a crowd of 30,000 at the University at Buffalo in September 2006; 'if something goes wrong at the present generation, then the future generations really face a lot of problems, and those problems will be beyond human control; so that's very serious. Ecology should be part of our daily life.' We just want to add that the ecology of distant peoples should be a key part of our consideration as we make our environmental decisions. They hold a stake in our lives just as we hold a stake in theirs.

7 | Insiders and outsiders in environmental mobilizations in South-East Asia

This chapter has a more concrete focus in a particular context. Building on the borderlands case study in the previous chapter, we consider the emergence of environmental campaigns in Thailand and neighbouring countries, focusing on the different kinds of campaign movements, the resources at their disposal, their varied and distinctive social composition and their opportunities for political effectiveness in an emerging system of democratic governance. To do justice to the environmental politics of Thailand and neighbouring countries would require at least an entire book, so here we focus on aspects of civic engagement that can aid our understanding of environment and citizenship. Thailand is a divided country in a number of ways, between urban and rural, between organized workers and unorganized workers, the educated elite and the uneducated poor, between Thai-Chinese and Thais, nouveau-riche business and old-money cliques, bureaucratic officialdom and popular opinion, Thai citizens and stateless migrants from Burma and Laos, Buddhists and non-Buddhists, Thailand as a modernizing country and its less developed neighbours, foreign-educated and Thai-educated (predominantly focusing on linguistic skill), men and women, royalty/nobility and subjects, 'farang' and Thai, or business class and working class.

By mapping these antagonisms in Thai society, we hope to demonstrate how agonistic politics acts as a frame for understanding the complex political situation within which civil organizations engage in political participation. In the last two decades, however, all of these previously fixed boundaries have been subject to transgression and challenges, raising deep questions about cultural identity and the traditional ordering of Thai politics and culture. This is a society experiencing significant transformation, where all that once appeared solid appears now to have melted into air. It is often said that repression, retrenchment and clampdowns are the symbolic manifestations of an old way of thinking and acting, as a result of cultural change desperately coping with new ways of thinking and acting, and the same could be said about Thailand today. We hope that the peaceful coup of 2006 is an illustration of this kind of conjuncture leading to a new phase of permanent democracy, a reordering of the relationship between the public and private spheres, but this process may take a decade and require a generational shift in the

Seven

political class as well as the emergence of new mechanisms for ensuring accountability. What has been startling about politics in Thailand has been the capacity of civil organizations to make a difference, or at least highlight injustices, despite instability in the polity, the threat of military takeover and the problems of establishing a legitimate rule of law. As Chai-Anan Samudavanija has identified in defending the continuing relevance of the state for its capacity to deploy legal powers:

> Asia has seen the rise of Asian civil society, which actually should be termed 'societies' rather than a universal, aggregate 'society,' in the form of oppositional social movements with diverse values. As transnational operations replace the state in controlling and directing economic activities at all levels, elites – political, military and technocratic – lose their most fundamental power over the private sector, namely their regulative authority. Thus the process of globalization is inseparable from good governance: both exert pressure on the state. (By contrast, democratization involves the expansion of political participation, which involves *all* sectors of society.) (Samudavanija 2002: 191–2)

While Chai-Anan Samudavanija considers multinational corporations as 'above' the state, however, and highlights illegal migrants and small-scale traders as 'under' the state, we argue that a key aspect of citizenship is missing from this picture – the emergence of citizen movements alongside the state and sometimes in partnership with local authorities, the government and intergovernmental bodies, as well as corporations and transnational activist networks. He also highlights a fundamental antagonism in Thailand, the bifurcation between the corporate sector concentrated in the major urban areas (particularly in and around Bangkok) and the agricultural sector, which remains village based and has until recently seen few benefits from economic development. For these reasons, we have selected Thailand as a focus because it provides a microcosm for many of the issues arising from environmental mobilization in rapidly developing societies.

Many of the environmental movements in Thailand have been defensive reactions against the effects of development, whether dam construction and power plants to provide the energy supply for the Thai modernization project or the increased reach of transnational agribusiness and biotechnology companies into the rural areas. Chai-Anan Samudavanija also highlights the speedy imposition of legislation on business competition and more transparent accountancy mechanisms compared to the slow and obstacle-ridden path for laws protecting communities and concerned with promoting responsible environmental management. While this sort of inconsistency is common in rapidly developing societies, civil organizations in Thailand have been remarkably effective in keeping up the pressure for legislative measures that seek to counterbalance corporate power. Also, just as different kinds of corporations (local, national, intra-regional and transnational) are now penetrating all levels of Thai society, social movements and NGOs are also moving from more localized and national concerns to thinking in terms of issue-based activism across the region, and forms of coordination with movements and NGOs in Western societies that cannot be described as directed from the West.

One of the reasons for this is the preoccupation of the elite with maintaining a distinctively Thai form of politics and notion of development that take environmental responsibility seriously (such as that expressed in the idea of a sufficiency economy), reinforced by the predominant Theravada Buddhist religious belief system which emphasizes well-being over materialist growth. Jim Taylor (1997) argues that the Buddhist concept of *Kamma*, intentional action with many consequences in the context of Theravada Buddhism, is a key part of understanding environmental issues in Thailand. Everyday understanding of *Kamma* often focuses on the negative consequences of actions, although in Buddhist teachings it often emphasizes learning from mistakes within the context of action, speech and thought. Buddhism also stresses the interdependency of society and nature, the importance of a range of virtues (such as restraint, generosity and kindness), and the need to develop a respectful approach to nature in communal life.

For Swearer et al., whose work focuses on the relationship between Buddhism and environmental problems, the problems created by the asymmetries between globalizers and globalized demand not simply a quantitative answer but a qualitative one based on asking how it is possible to live a good life. In addition, the Buddhist belief system emphasizes the virtues of simplicity, compassion, loving kindness, empathy and an awareness of the suffering of all living things, as well as the land. In the context of South-East Asia, notwithstanding the increase in materialism, Theravada Buddhism remains a key part of everyday discourse, in particular the importance of refraining from doing evil and seeking to do good. Underpinning these virtues and maxims is a belief in the need to maintain a cooperative relationship between society and nature, in which human beings are displaced from the top of the ethical hierarchy (Swearer et al. 2004: 1–2). In many ways this is analogous to some conceptions of ecological citizenship (for example: Smith 1998a: 96–100). For David Engel, in his study of 'injury narratives' in northern

Thailand, Buddhist values led to distinctive ways of settling disputes and remedying harms where locally sanctioned remediation processes existed without rights. The emphasis on duty and obligation applied to the victim as well as the injurer, and where compensation was judged to be appropriate it could sometimes be notional or less than the value of the harm inflicted. Victims would often accept such settlements as just because balance had been restored, in part through their acts of forgiveness and selflessness. As Engel concludes, however, one key problem that exists is the undermining of customary justice without an effective replacement in the Thai legal system (Engel 2007).

In order to address the needs of rural communities, environmental problems arising from development in the provinces and to ensure that the benefits of economic growth were more fairly distributed, rural monks have become involved in community-based projects. These 'development monks' sought to preserve Thai culture by linking Buddhist values to development projects, but also sought to provide a space to defend cultural identity and community rights. Anan Ganjanapan highlights how some ceremonies involving donations also have a redistributive function within communities (Ganjanapan 2000: 6–7).

On the importance of hegemony: rethinking civil society and the state

Academic thought has traditionally overemphasized the power of the state, which is not surprising given the importance of the nation-state from the mid-nineteenth century through to the dominance of the Keynesian welfare state in Western societies in the mid- to late twentieth century. Before and after this period, the state was considered to be an adjunct or partner of civil society, although the precise relationship has often depended on the issues involved. For example, in understanding military actions and geopolitically oriented policy, the state is still regarded as the prime mover. Similarly, in border disputes and questions of security, national sovereignty (with all its attendant notions of responsibility within the terms of territorial sovereignty) is the main focus of discussion. As we have demonstrated in the previous chapter, the linkage between sovereignty and responsibility is a major factor in addressing trans-boundary environmental concerns. In Smith's (2000b) account of pluralist, neoliberal and neo-Marxist state theories, the account of the state in three major traditions of Western thinking is reassessed. Sometimes civil society includes the economy and sometimes it does not. Sometimes the state is an organizing force and sometimes it is the epiphenomenon of other social relations. Sometimes the state is an instrument of specific interests and sometimes it is an arena for bargaining and negotiation. Key to the arguments developed here is that theorization of the state has often depended on thinking about the state as the horizon of what has often been described as civil society or the private sphere. According to Smith:

> While there are clear differences between the state theories in question, both in the way they define the state and in the way they situate the state in the context of wider social relations ... their conceptualizations of the state are closely related to the ways in which they attempt to theorize the social order. For Dahl, the polyarchic potential of political institutions is closely connected to the civic orientations and conceptions of citizenship prevalent in the social system in question, as well as the opportunities for mass participation and organized public participation. ... For Hayek, the state serves as a horizon of catallactic possibilities: the state form is responsible for the degree to which the intersubjective capabilities of human beings can flourish. ... Finally, for Jessop, the state is both the terrain of contestation and a site of strategic interventions, institutionally formed through the simultaneous interplay of structures and strategies. As the nation-state is redefined as part of the networks of governance through which social life is organized, these state theories offer fertile ideas and conceptual tools for rethinking our conceptions of the state and its relationship to other social spheres. (ibid.: 241–2)

We want to pose the view that when we consider the state, then we are addressing what we referred to earlier as the sociality of politics (i.e. the state is always conceived in terms of how we define civil society; ibid.), just as when we consider civil society or civic engagement we are addressing 'the political' within 'the social' (Mouffe 1992). As we saw in Chapter 2, the idea of civil society emerged in liberal accounts of citizenship representing one side of the coin of the institutional separation of the state from other social relations. This notion of the state tends to emphasize its mediating role through institutional ensembles such as 'rule of law', political parties' regulatory practices and the branches of governance. The shift of focus from government to governance in academic research also prompts us to consider the flows and relations that exist between institutions formally designated as public and private. One of the key features of the debate on ecological citizenship (see Chapters 1–3) has been the problematization of the distinction between public and private spheres, whether this is in terms of the role of civic engagement and the development of participatory democracy, Mouffe's distinction between politics and the political (Mouffe 1992, 2005), the feminist critique of androcentric notions of politics and the growing importance of the feminist ethics of care (MacGregor 2006), or the opening up of a new ethico-political terrain in which entitlements and obligations are seen as existing in a complex relation that binds actors in all parts of a society, as well as globally and in terms of time.

This has important implications when addressing the research literature on social movements, NGOs and the state in Thailand. Bruce Missingham (2003) recognizes the ambiguity of civil society in this context and the importance of spatial metaphors, highlighting Kevin Hewison's description of the space as an 'autonomous sphere of political space in which political forces representing constellations of interests in society have contested state power'. Nevertheless, this still portrays the state as above and beyond civil society, as well as suggesting that the interests of civil organizations are somehow independent of the state. Here, we want to conjecture that these interests are discursively and materially constructed through the relations between public and private institutions and organizations, which as a matter of course are always relations of power. Civic engagement practices, some of which could involve contestation between for-profit and not-for-profit civil organizations (whether the state institutions are the focus of action or not), are also acts of power, even if they merely lead to the empowerment of movements and communities in terms of their resources and forms of organization. In addition, as Missingham (ibid.) highlights in the case of Thailand, NGOs and international organizations seeking to remedy social and environmental injustices can engage in acts of power that disengage (and at worst infantalize) communities, groups and movements in developing societies from direct involvement in politics (see Hirsch 1997).

Environmental activism and the popular-democratic assemblies

The history of Thai environmental movements is often portrayed as riven by division between rural-based livelihood movements and NGO-coordinated campaigns on broader environmental issues (often with an urban or, recently, an industrial focus) in a way that mirrors Western political research of outsider and insider groups. The distinction is a simplified one, as Wyn Grant (2000) states, but it has some utility as a basis for comparison. While it may have been a convenient distinction in the 1970s and early 1980s, developments in this context suggest that a more nuanced framework is needed, especially as the effects of development have spread throughout the country and the region. Peasant-based rural movements have had a long history of activism in Thailand since the establishment of free speech and free association in the political liberalization of the late 1970s. For the most part, the campaigns were non-violent and drew in the emerging NGO community in South-East Asia. In addition, co-activism between farmers and unions dates back to 1974, when 20,000 farmers demonstrated on behalf of textile workers in Bangkok, leading to the formation of the Peasants' Federation of Thailand, campaigning on land rights, excessive rents and indebtedness (Pangsapa and Smith 2008a). Following this and the Kho Cho Ko initiative to relocate poor villages, environmental activist strategy shifted to developing networks linking the material grievances of the affected groups to government programmes, aiding the emergence of the Assembly of the Poor (Missingham 2003; Sivaraksa 2002). Tim Forsyth (2001) suggests that environmental movements in the 1980s were, for the most part, urban elite based but fixated on traditional environmental concerns of environmental protection, especially deforestation.

While this is accurate in terms of Western portrayals of NGO politics in the period, it still neglects the emergence of a variety of campaigns that are sometimes designated as development NGOs or livelihood and land rights movements and, as a result, are not often portrayed as having an environmental orientation. A closer look, however, will reveal that they just see the environment as an inhabited one where people and nature are interdependent and need to live in balance. It should also be noted that similar movements in developed societies, such as the slow food movement (see Andrews 2008), also link livelihood to quality of life and reducing environmental impacts. Nevertheless, peasant-based movements have been widespread, and often the issues they raise have an important environmental dimension. When considering the attention given by the *Bangkok Post* to different environmental campaigns, Forsyth highlights the equivalence of coverage generated by middle-class, working-class and peasant movements, as well as the relatively low middle-class involvement in what he defines as the brown environmental agenda (urban and industrial issues such as the effects of electricity generation plants or toxic waste storage and disposal). One qualification should be added here. Quantitative analysis of reports may produce only a partial picture of actual movements for the newspaper in question. Other press outlets, such as *The Nation*, define newsworthiness in terms of metropolitan issues, and the gatekeepers in the media have a close relationship with the urban elite, shaped by their own social composition and social connections with business, the monarchy and the interfamilial networks of the PLO ('people like ourselves') in Bangkok. In other words, media preoccupations may not be representative of actual environmental action.

Prior to these environmental campaigns, the Enhancement and Conservation of National Environmental Quality Acts (1975, 1978, 1979) had already put in place a basis for environmental protection, with the 1978 Act establishing the National Environmental Board (NEB), an advisory body for the Prime Minister's Office, but which lacked the power to enforce necessary rules on environmental sustainability. The increased focus on environmental issues in the 1980s, concern about deforestation and continuing pressure from ongoing environmental campaigns changed the political agenda. Soil erosion due to rapid deforestation over previous decades was highlighted in the devastating floods of 1988 as a major factor in deaths and damage to property, resulting in the blanket logging ban of 1989 (although as we saw in the previous chapter the logging companies have moved into neighbouring countries). The fact that the previous legislation had clearly failed led to its repeal, the passage of the National Environmental Quality Act (1992) and the creation of an environment department (the Office of Environmental Policy and Planning, OEPP), incorporating some NEB tasks within the reorganized Ministry of Science, Technology and Environment (MOSTE). Project approval required the completion of an Environmental Impact Assessment (EIA). Initially all projects are screened by MOSTE and the NEB to consider if an EIA is necessary, and once the EIA is completed, it requires approval by the licensing authority, the Environmental Impact Evaluation Department of the OEPP, an Expert Review Committee (sometimes including NGO and academic members), and in some cases, when state enterprises and government agencies are involved, the NEB and the cabinet. The 1997 constitution also added the right of access to public information (with Section 59 concerned specifically with environmental quality and public health). As in many consolidated ministerial departments, environmental protection did not always sit easily with the imperatives of scientific and technological development (such as biotechnology and the promotion of GMO flora). In 2002, the Thaksin administration created a separate Ministry of Natural Resources and the Environment to consolidate and coordinate environmental policy departments and agencies, with the OEPP becoming the Office of Natural Resources and Environmental Policy and Planning (ONEP). The new ministry also contains dedicated departments for environmental quality promotion, pollution control and for a variety of ecological resources. As Tim Forsyth has stated, however, competing environmental discourses in the Thai government, and the disjuncture between the technocratic bureaucracy and the political appointments that have pursued pro-business interests in the context of Thai 'money politics', have presented a series of obstacles to progress on coordination and on developing mechanisms for public participation (Forsyth 2002b).

NGOs engaged in advocacy work, project development and activism in Thailand, such as the long-established Thailand Rural Reconstruction Movement (formed in 1967 under royal patronage), Wildlife Fund Thailand and initially Greenpeace Southeast Asia (bearing in mind that linking social and environmental justice has since become a priority), have been primarily concerned with the effects of economic development on rural livelihoods and the step-by-step encroachment of environmental resources that have hitherto been treated with respect by the communities sustained by them. The attitude of local Thais to forests in many areas of the north is to view them as sacred places. In line with Buddhist beliefs, those that draw on the forests and land are inhabited by spirits or guardians, requiring the performance of rituals to request permission before they engage in foraging, collecting wood, tree-felling or constructing buildings –the forest and land have spiritual value. This encourages respect for the environment but also helps to create a sense of responsibility to ensure that the same resources will be available in the future. Bruce Missingham portrays the alternative development movement as an important precursor of the Assembly of the Poor, suggesting that:

> Out of the theory and practice of alternative development during the 1980s a focus on promoting villagers' organizations (*ongkon chao-ban*) emerged as a central strategy of NGO development work that has had growing political implications and a critical role in the development of villagers' movements of the 1990s ... They see their main role as supporting villagers' own local organizations by providing advice, information, and resources. (Missingham 2003: 31)

Furthermore, Missingham highlights the emphasis placed on linking the solution of environmental problems to action on economic and political issues by members of the Project for Ecological Recovery (PER). In this context there is a long history of linking campaigns for social and environmental justice, although it should be added that rural grievances constituted the majority of the campaigns' concerns and occupational health was marginal in the movement. In addition, he highlights the crucial role played by NGOs as mediators between grassroots activism and more generalized political structures, academics in universities and research institutes, and the mass media. By far the most important relationship here is that between local needs and national policy, especially in the light of the actions by state officials and the military in the Kho Cho Ko programme to resettle village communities in areas severely affected

Insiders and outsiders

217

by deforestation. Some relocations took the form of forced displacement with the military engaged in actions that ensured that the villages could not be easily re-established, producing large-scale protests in Bangkok. The Assembly of the Poor also set up a more or less permanent 'village of the poor' as a space for political demonstration outside Government House in Bangkok. Between April 2002 and April 2003 Thai photographer Manit Sriwanichpoom took pictures of mass protest rallies that were held every Tuesday outside the gates of Government House. The demonstrators included the young and the elderly, men and women who travelled long distances with their children and grandchildren from rural provinces to demand compensation for farmlands they lost from flooding as a result of dam construction projects, forced displacement or encroachment of residential land signed over to Buddhist monasteries. Their inventive demonstration tactics included lying flat out in rows on the pavement to imitate corpses, raising detailed placards explaining their situation, placing life-size papier mâché figures of monitor lizards symbolizing human vileness in the creation of hydroelectric power plant and irrigation projects that destroy the land and marine environment, releasing real monitor lizards in front of the Government House gates, parading mock coffins around the House, and displaying photos of ailing local residents who were affected by ash and dust from the rock explosions caused by the construction of hydroelectric power plants.

The proposed Nam Choan dam on the Khwae Yai river (within the Thung Yai Naresuan Wildlife Sanctuary in Kanchanburi province) generated widely endorsed protests that brought together urban and rural campaigners in 1982/83 and more so in 1986/87 until the project was cancelled in 1988. As a result, communities affected by hydroelectric projects initiated similar protests over dams in Kaeng Krung, Kaeng Sua Ten and Pak Mun (although the urban support here was considerably less given the absence of deforestation as a key issue). Water is often seen as a rural issue linked to livelihood and irrigation rather than as an environmental issue; also, hydroelectric power (HEP) projects are often viewed by urban-based environmental groups as cleaner and therefore preferable to coal-, oil- and gas-generated power, which have severe air pollution consequences for proximate communities. In addition, urban environmental campaigns are often staffed by people possessing social capital and in some cases with links to political parties and policy communities partially embedded within the state. The linking of livelihood campaigns to more influential groups in terms of environmental policy-making at the national level is, however, an ongoing process that can be fostered even if the results fall short of the demands of the movements concerned. As a result, the Assembly of the Poor ensured that 'more NGOs became involved in resource issues and became advocates for rural people in environmental disputes ... and encouraged them to join in broader networks for their campaigns' (ibid.: 32).

Similarly, local social movements became active against the Rasi Salai dam (initially a 'rubber weir' to avoid EIA but ending up as a concrete dam), the Khong-Chi-Mun (KCM) irrigation project in north-east Thailand promoted by Chavalit in his Green Isaan (Isaan Kiew) plan and Thaksin's Water Grid Project in 2003. EGAT's successful linking of the Pak Mun dam to the KCM project also aided its approval. This US$5 billion mega-project is for a water grid planned to provide 11 million rai (approximately 4.4 million acres) of fully irrigated land to promote rice production and 25 million rai (approximately 10 million acres) of partially irrigated land for other crops alongside a nationwide tap water system. The primary aim was poverty alleviation, as with previous initiatives in the north-east. Questions were raised throughout 2004/05 as to the feasibility of the project (especially given increased salinity in the dry season) and about the need to use water from international waters as well as from Laos. Initially, it was delayed by divisions within TRT on which faction of the party would be responsible (the ministers of agriculture and the environment were competing for the leadership role) and the projects were shelved as a result of the 2006 coup. As Molle and Floche (2007) have argued, the proposals overemphasized the capacity of the state to deliver poverty alleviation and may be more to do with maintaining political support than practicality. Environmental responsibility in these contexts has to lead to much closer attention to the concrete conditions of the ecosystems and, likewise, future research needs to take local situations more into account.

Conflicts over forest, land and water resources, as in the development of hydroelectric dams on Thai rivers, led to ongoing protests, especially in times of drought such as 1993, while the 1989 logging ban supported by conservationist environmental discourses (as part of a strategy for reforestation) ignored considerable encroachment by established interests that are linked to the main political parties, but still severely restricted the ability of rural communities to use forest resources. Where the ban was enforced it had a disproportionate effect on the rural poor and the hill tribes in the border regions. Deane Curtin (1999) has highlighted similar examples in South Asia where wildlife conservation measures often deprive local communities of customary rights to livelihood.

According to Pinkaew Laungaramsri (2002), movements against the Nam Songkram dam developed a broad base of support by mobilizing cultural identity. She highlights the sentimental form of identification, *Watthanatham Pladaek*, or the culture of fermented fish, *pladaek*, which highlights how culture is understood as a practice of doing rather than an ossified set of beliefs, and stresses the vital role of river resources in daily life in Isaan culture (although the urban classes call fermented fish *plalah* instead of *pladaek*, which is used primarily by provincial peoples or rural farmers, referred to as *chao baan, chao na*). In the protests covered by Manit Sriwanichpoon, Assembly of the Poor members repeatedly stressed the importance of fermented fish culture as part of their livelihood and would hold up jars of the strong-smelling fish (comparable to fermented cheese) as they marched in front of Government House against the decision that would allow the Pak Mun dam sluice gates to be open for only four months a year. One woman farmer held up a placard that was a symbolic expression of their plight. The placard read 'Don't Destroy Fermented Fish Culture' and displayed a picture of 'a natural rock pool that reemerged from under the dam lake after the sluice gates were open, allowing villagers to go fishing there as they used to' (Sriwanichpoom 2003: 142). Villagers also acted out plays in front of Government House in an attempt to give those in power 'some understanding of their traditional fishing life' (ibid.: 143).

Also in the north-east, there have been repeated reports of pollution in the Nam Phong river from the Phoenix pulp and paper plant. Ironically the plant was set up to provide ecologically sound paper supplies for the American market, initially using kenaf and later eucalyptus and bamboo. To ensure adequate supplies, forest areas were cleared, displacing a considerable local population. Despite the zero-discharge rule of the Thai government, there have been reports that chlorinated as well as other inorganic by-products have been discharged into the river system, and when the waste water was used in irrigation projects this led to soil acidification in the surrounding fields. The company settled compensation claims from local farmers in 1995/96 and local fishermen in 1997/98. This is a classic case of good intentions all round (including Thai policy-makers promoting development in the north-east) having a range of different ecological effects on local ecosystems, communities and the river system. The supply of bamboo pulp to the Fox Paper company and Lyons Falls was discontinued owing to the activities of the NGO ReThink Paper but also as a result of increased market prices. The Phoenix paper company has since been subject to a takeover, has reviewed its practices and is seeking ISO 14001 certification.

Moving on from predominantly provincial issues, there had also been successful protests against mining concessions granted to TEMCO (Thailand Exploration and Mining Company), a company controlled by Union Carbide, in 1974/75 (Hirsch and Lohmann 1989). In addition, a partially completed tantalum processing plant was burned down by protesters in 1986 to protect tourism in Phuket. The deaths of fourteen workers in 1994 due to Lumphun industrial pollution was also significant in highlighting occupational safety and environmental impacts, although the scientific causal attribution of these cases has been contested. By far the most attention has been devoted to the Mae Moh lignite mine and EGAT-run power plant (near Lampang in the northern provinces and operating since 1992), which have had a dual effect. The open-cast mine producing 40,000 tons a day already covers 135 square kilometres, while the ADB-funded power plant began to have a significant effect on local health within a very short period, with dizziness, nausea and respiratory problems caused by sulphur dioxide emissions (some estimates have suggested that 42,000 people have suffered breathing difficulties). NGOs have also reported that sulphur emissions have damaged local crops (for which compensation was agreed in 2004). The long-term effects of this giant power plant through fly ash containing mercury, arsenic, lead and chromium, and the effects of mine dust on local ecosystems and water supplies, have yet to be fully established. To date, NGOs claim that over three hundred local villagers have died as a result of pollution, which appears to worsen in some atmospheric conditions. As with the Phoenix case, EGAT has attempted to introduce retrofit measures to reduce sulphur emissions (the lignite used has a high sulphur density). A separate development has been the formation of activist networks such as the Occupational Patients Rights Network of Mae Moh (geared to promoting compensation cases) and People Against Coal, which links campaigns against existing and planned coal-fired power stations throughout the country. Together with Greenpeace Southeast Asia and Mekong Watch, these NGOs have also initiated a campaign to prevent ADB funding for projects that have delivered adverse social and environmental effects.

It should also be added that industrial environmental issues are much more difficult to resolve. Tim Forsyth (2001) suggests that industrial pollution campaigns have not had the success seen on other environmental issues, and effectiveness depends as much on scientific expertise as it does on activism. There are good reasons for this difficulty: the government pressing for increased power generation as part of modernization and export-led economic growth, the vested interests of the industrial sector finding expression through politicians or directly lobbying ministerial departments, the concentration of industry in particular economic

Box 7.1 Community campaigns against toxic cocktails

In October 2005, a joint Greenpeace Southeast Asia (GPSEA), Campaign for Alternative Industry Network (CAIN) and Global Community Monitor (GCM) report, *Thailand's Air: Toxic Cocktail – Exposing Unsustainable Industries and the Case of Community Right-to-know*, was launched to demonstrate the extent of pollution released by the facilities in the Map Ta Phut 176,000-acre industrial zone (Rayong province, on the eastern coast of Thailand). Using Bucket Brigade techniques, the report claimed that the local communities experience airborne toxic chemicals between 60 and 3,000 times higher than EPA standards. This technique, highlighted in Chapter 6, focuses on community-based environmental monitoring involving 'simplified "grab sampling" that simulates the lung's breathing in of foul chemical odours and allows for detailed testing of their chemical makeup ... [enabling] communities to turn their everyday observations into hard evidence that cannot be dismissed by corporate public relations agents or misinformed bureaucrats' (GCM 2005: 9). This also allowed communities to develop 'do-it-ourselves pollutant inventories' and test for the mix of chemicals from samples collected over eight months in 2004. The key findings are summarized below:

Benzene (a known human cancer-causing agent) detected in four of the five samples exceeded the US EPA Annual Ambient Air Screening Level by as much as sixty times.

Vinyl chloride (a known human cancer-causing agent) detected in two samples exceeded the EPA Annual Ambient Air Screening Level by as much as eighty-six times.

1, 2-Dichloroethane (EDC) (a known probable human cancer-causing agent) detected in two samples exceeded the EPA Annual Ambient Air Screening Level by as much as 3,380 times.

Chloroform (a known probable human cancer-causing agent) detected in a sample was in excess of the EPA Annual Ambient Air Screening Level by 119 times.

zones, and the underlying problems of movements seeking to make a difference in a political system that has a long history of graft and corruption. We should also bear in mind that large-scale protests may be an indicator of weakness rather than strength, for all the possibilities have been exhausted. The Map Ta Phut industrial estate already has forty-five

A total of twenty different toxic chemicals was identified in the five air samples. At least six and up to twelve VOCs (Volatile Organic Chemicals) and sulphur compounds were detected in each sample, and at least two of the toxic chemicals were in excess of one or more health protective standards or screening levels, giving proof of the toxic cocktail inhaled in Map Ta Phut.*

* '1 Benzene's health effects are irritation of eyes, skin, nose, respiratory system, dizziness, headache, nausea, staggered gait, anorexia, lassitude (weakness exhaustion), dermatitis, bone marrow depression, and potential occupational carcinogen. The target organs are eyes, skin, respiratory system, blood, central nervous system, and bone marrow. Cancer site: bone marrow (Leukemia). 2 Vinyl Chloride's health effects are weakness, exhaustion, abdominal pain, gastrointestinal bleeding, enlarged liver, pallor or cyanosis of extremities, liquid: frostbite; [potential occupational carcinogen]. Its target organs are liver, central nervous system, blood, respiratory system, and lymphatic system. Cancer site: liver. 3 1, 2-Dichloroethane causes eye problems, headache, feelings of drunkenness, fatigue, central nervous system depression, convulsions, pulmonary oedema (excessive fluid in the lungs), unconsciousness and death from respiratory and cardiac failure, skin irritation. Long-term exposures may cause damage to the liver, kidneys, lungs and adrenal glands. Target organs are eyes, skin, kidneys, liver, central nervous system, and cardiovascular system. Cancer site: [in animals: fore-stomach, mammary gland and circulatory system cancer]. 4 Chloroform may be released to the air as a result of its formation in the chlorination of drinking water, wastewater and swimming pools. Other sources include pulp and paper mills, hazardous waste sites, and sanitary landfills. The major effect from acute (short-term) inhalation exposure to chloroform is central nervous system depression. Chronic (long-term) exposure to chloroform by inhalation in humans has resulted in effects on the liver, including hepatitis and jaundice, and central nervous system effects, such as depression and irritability. Chloroform has been shown to be carcinogenic in animals after oral exposure, resulting in an increase in kidney and liver tumours. EPA has classified chloroform as a Group B2, probable human carcinogen' (GCM 2005: 11–15).

petrochemical facilities, twelve fertilizer factories, eight coal-fired power plants and two oil refineries in the mix of companies based there, so, with such a startling environmental problem located in one place, perhaps we should not be too surprised that in September 2007 the Thai energy ministry approved eleven new petrochemical facilities, even though one coal-fired power station plan has recently been withdrawn (considered later in the chapter).

During the more formal democratization of Thailand after 1992, environmental movements allied with rural farmers and unions and NGOs (including aid agencies and human rights organizations) demonstrated their political credibility. In a series of campaigns they succeeded in embarrassing successive governments on issues of forest degradation and the effects of dam and reservoir construction (including the decimation of fishery stocks in some river systems), as well as highlighting the inadequacy of access to health and educational resources for the rural poor. While they were not always successful in securing their immediate demands (such as keeping the sluice gates of dams open to enable fish migration for spawning), the high visibility of mass protests such as those at Government House in Bangkok ensured that their interests had to be taken seriously in future.

The traditional approach of environmental management has been oriented towards state control of resources, although many communities living in designated conservation areas have often discovered that environmental policy has ignored or had adverse effects on their needs. The environmental movements based in urban centres such as Bangkok have tended to be more concerned with environmental issues such as traffic management and air pollution, while rural movements have been focused on defending and maintaining local production, land rights and access to resources such as timber and fisheries (with communities viewing national parks as a form of encroachment on their way of life). Sometimes the two meet at a crossroads, as in Charles Greenberg's analysis of an eclectic environmental movement in the Greater Bangkok Metropolitan Region, where the environment was no longer just an urban issue but intrinsically a regional one (Greenberg 1997: 178). In demonstrating the diversity of such an environmental movement, Greenberg cites the 1991 case of a massive public park scheme unveiled by former PM Anand Panyarachun, which resulted in mass protests and rallies on the part of local residents, who called upon NGOs and local academics for support. Along with over ten thousand activists, the residents fought 'successfully to retain their land and halt further park planning' (ibid.: 177). This highlights how movement diversity can enable flexibility and coalition-building that could potentially broaden the base of urban movements in Bangkok, but can create obstacles for the generation of coherent platforms.

Sophon Suphaphong, along with other leading political and business figures, sponsored the Thailand Environment Institute (TEI) (established in 1993), a think tank devoted to linking grassroots activism to scientific and policy work in order to provide environmental training and awareness. It also has close connections within the urban elite, including the president of TEI, Phaichitr Uathavikul, former minister of MOTSE. More recently, the TEI has become an important advocate of public–private partnerships and the participatory approach to environmental responsibility, while at the same time focusing on poverty alleviation. An interesting feature of TEI work is the linkage with transnational initiatives on political participation and stakeholding. Like the Thailand Development Institute, the TEI has a technocratic orientation that ensures that many of their policy proposals are geared towards general rules for environmental management and information systems rather than working with individual groups and localized information.

As top-down environmental legislation and standard-setting have met with poor implementation within the context of Thai 'money politics', these think tanks have shifted their focus to corporate responsibility and polluter-pays schemes (although in many cases the state has stepped in, as with the rice provision for villagers in Tak province). As demonstrated in Chapter 5, corporate responsibility also has its problems, and since 2000 there has been a shift towards stakeholder involvement as a means of drawing in citizens to participate in environmental policy.

We should also bear in mind that many NGOs playing a stakeholding role are unrepresentative of the groups they seek to protect. Many NGOs were founded outside Thailand, such as WWF and Greenpeace. While they often provide movements with valuable social capital, their social composition and the backgrounds of key workers and volunteers are often quite different from those of the communities with which they engage and which they seek to represent. Nevertheless, they often provide an important link between grassroots movements, political authorities and corporations, as well as providing skills that local movements lack, such as report-writing, lobbying and coordination (Pfirrman and Kron 1992; Hirsch 1998). In terms of issue focus, environmental NGOs have also found that campaign allies are likely to be preoccupied with community and livelihood issues. For NGOs heavily influenced by Western environmental issues there is also the problem of discursive dissonance between their stated objectives of environmental protection (sometimes regarding the environment as a pristine space that should not be interfered with rather than an evolving ecosystem inhabited by existing stakeholders) and the concerns of local communities, peasant farmers and local NGOs run by local leaders and, in some cases, by monks. In turn, local campaigners concerned with social justice issues have at times viewed environmental NGOs as having views that are too distanced from conditions on the ground.

High-society (hi-so) initiatives and NGO environmental activism

Given that this book highlights corporate responsibility and the role of social entrepreneurs from the 'for-profit' private sector, we want to highlight examples that develop this theme. As a rapidly developing society, Thailand was until recently marked by a considerable division between an urban and cosmopolitan elite and a mass of peasants in the countryside with relatively low levels of education, a division that became more stark following the economic growth in the cities during the 1970s through to the 1990s. This became more entrenched through the practice of vote-buying by political parties, which ensured that the demands for change for the majority of the population in the provinces were rarely addressed. Hence, it is not surprising that some of the early environmental campaigners were social entrepreneurs from some of the wealthiest families. Khunying Chodchoy Sophonpanich's (daughter of the founder of Bangkok Bank) campaign emerged when Bangkok was classed as one of the five dirtiest cities in the world. The Ta Viset ('Magic Eyes') anti-litter campaign initially campaigned for children to police their parents' and community's behaviour, then later diversified into recycling projects.

The Magic Eye campaigns established links between children, school-teachers, families and communities to promote awareness of the need for recycling when there were few opportunities and no statutory require-ment – Magic Eye's glass-bottle campaigns aimed to reduce landfill by 8 per cent. The campaign was formally instituted as an NGO, the Thai Environmental and Community Development Association (TECDA), in 1986. TECDA has a capacity-building focus, initially working in Bang-kok and later in the province's schools, but now only becomes directly involved when new schools join. The campaigns have also diversified into environmental education, such as the Prem Tinsulanonda Centre's 'Magic Eyes' barge programme, which creates outdoor opportunities for children to study wildlife and the ecosystem of the Chao Phraya river. The campaign now works on environmental awareness of water pollu-tion and deforestation as well as project consultancy, such as advising on integrated waste management systems in Phuket. The success of the programme in promoting personal and community responsibility has, in part, been the result of the campaign tapping into Thai culture – in particular the shame of losing face (*seayah naah*), citizens being embar-rassed if they were seen dropping litter, thus linking values to action

Figure 7.1 The people are watching: Filipino unionists, nurses and environmental campaigners draw on the rhetoric of popular environmental surveillance in South-East Asia to press home their demands for accountability © Greenpeace/Gigie Cruz-Sy

through citizens coming to understand underlying reasons but also being able to ensure compliance through moral coercion.

Magic Eyes is also remarkable in using personal connections within the Thai elite to bring together corporate support and media companies with political authorities and NGOs; 126 organizations were involved in planning the Love the Chao Phraya campaign, of which the barge project is a part. In addition, once the street litter scheme was beginning to be successful they turned their attention to the sorting of household and business waste, which was rapidly filling Bangkok's remaining landfill sites. They consulted widely with stakeholders and sought to include a group previously viewed by the police as thieves and vagrants – the 'Saleng' (second-hand dealers in recycled materials and junk businesses). Coordination between this informal work sector and environmental NGOs has led to an improvement in their status; the occupation carries certain risks, however, such as cuts and infections, respiratory illnesses and the possibility of involvement in traffic accidents (all of which can lead to time off work without welfare support). Phornthep Phornprapha (former president of Siam Motors) founded the Think Earth project in 1991 in order the promote environmental awareness among the young, but also to develop environmental knowledge alongside other sciences and Thai cultural values. In the case of this NGO, citizen participation is developed through activities such as tree-planting and coastal conservation projects.

Earlier we considered the Thailand Environment Institute (TEI). Key member Sophon Suphaphong had a long record of promoting the idea of the self-sufficient economy and resigned from his position as president of Bangchak Petroleum PLC when the company moved towards inviting foreign investment. He has also appealed for the corporate sector to take social and environmental responsibility more seriously: 'The world's markets just won't buy products that are cheap and good quality if they are manufactured by countries that exploit child labor; that are dictatorial; and that destroy the environment. Eventually, business people will have no choice but to take part in the process of resolving our social problems' (Tansubhapol 1996). A key feature of his managerial style was to encourage company staff to be involved in projects involving health, nutrition and protecting street children. As part of eradicating corruption in a sector previously owned by the defence ministry, in 1990 he created distribution franchise systems that included community ownership and which provided marketing, technical and financial support and a safety net if some of the franchises ran into difficulty. In addition, Bangchak allowed drivers to lease company trucks and roadside food and convenience retailing (Lemon Tree and Lemon Farm cooperatives and Lemon Green minimarts) to promote individual and community self-reliance. This diversification strategy, part of a wider trend towards the development of micro-enterprises in rural areas, with over six hundred affiliated outlets created in the 1990s (managed by a combination of community organizations, cooperatives, women's associations and peasant farmer groups – roughly one million households), also enabled Bangchak to ride out the Asian crisis of 1997 as it was returning to profitability. At the same time it continued to encourage social and environmental entrepreneurs. Also, a similar number of outlets were established in a conventional way, although they were not able to generate the same levels of consumer loyalty. These micro-enterprises also provided contexts for raising environmental awareness, political meetings, workshops on Buddhist teachings and Thai culture and health promotion through organic and macrobiotic foods. This range of activities also created the basis for the Environment and Development Network (TADNET), linking over two hundred organizations for the purpose of sharing knowledge between scientific researchers, activists, corporate executives and politicians.

What was unusual about this company was that it was a state enterprise rather than being in the private sector. In the privatization programme initiated as part of the conditions for securing a loan from the IMF following the Asian crisis, the Leekpai government proposed the sale of 32 per cent of its stock. Sophon resigned as president of the company in protest against the 'farangization' (increased non-Thai ownership) of the company and joined a wider campaign organized by the Bangchek Lovers Club (BLC) against the sale of state assets to non-Thai investors. Subsequent attempts to raise Thai investment by the BLC were followed by a proposal to break up the company because the refineries were no longer profitable owing to higher oil prices and the energy sector moving to gas-generated power. It was proposed that the community-based subsidiaries and marketing arm of Bangchek become a separate company under the name Bai Chak. The Thaksin government approved the restructuring of the company (which is now 20 per cent owned by the state) into Bangchak petrochemicals and Bangchak Green Net, although, since the 2006 coup, these arrangements have been subject to investigation by the Assets Scrutiny Commission. While the restructuring creates a sound basis for the development of community and environmental responsibility, in line with the idea of the sufficiency economy, the continuation of the refinery plant has become a matter of national pride. Other companies have also followed in these footsteps, such as DTAC and UCOM, to promote the Sam Nuk Rak Ban Kerd ('to know you love your home town') project founded by Boonchai Bencharongkul in 1998. This fosters community development, forest protection, local agricultural produce (through the Rak Ban Kerd convenience shops) and education. It should be added that community-oriented diversification not only provides evidence of corporate responsibility but also reduces costs for the parent companies, since locally sourced products are cheaper and they no longer have to pay franchise and branding fees to transnational companies.

In conclusion, while some movements are based on community-led initiatives in the rural provinces (including those participating in broader alliances, such as the Assembly of the Poor), they are also rooted in the PLO ('people like ourselves'), based on the familial networks of the establishment and located primarily in Bangkok. As Philip Hirsch has identified, environmental politics has often been articulated by the progressive and internationally educated middle classes, the main media outlets (such as the Nation Multimedia Group and the *Bangkok Post*), the universities (Chulalongkorn, Mahidol and Thammasat) and overlapping activist networks that are concerned with cultural as much as environmental change. The resources that can be mobilized by these different campaigns are also distinctive. Rural campaigns tend to be based on ethnic identity and emerge as a direct result of immediate environmental issues such as the relocation of communities caused by energy generation and irrigation schemes, as well as generating linkages between movements concerned with rural poverty, labour standards, human rights and environmental sustainability. Urban-based campaigns are more likely to deploy the media-savvy strategies of contemporary Western social movements, drawing on their own or associates' skills as artists, graphic designers, marketing executives, journalists, documentary film-makers, performance artists and photographers, as well as on the academic research community located primarily in the cities. As a result, urban movements have been able to mount high-profile media campaigns with a transnational impact, such as the anti-golf movement and protests against the problems generated by ecotourism. Rural-based campaigns are therefore often more localized, but are also concerned with labour and land-use issues (offering opportunities for co-activism or 'movement fusion'), as well as making connections between social and environmental injustice. Rural movements often lack access to more sophisticated forms of political campaigning, but have nevertheless developed innovative forms of protest and have achieved their objectives through transnational activist networks.

Participatory environmental research

Participatory research has been used by activist-researchers to identify environmental impacts more accurately, contributing to both movement formation and consolidation. Research by NGOs, research institutes and government departments tends to focus on specialized problems, whereas participatory research often produces more integrated or holistic knowledge on local conditions, linking water, land and forests and capturing the community wisdom. The main focus has been how to maintain or develop sustainable livelihoods. Anan Ganjanapan highlights two community-oriented traditions in environmental activism (in addition to the role of development monks considered at the start of the chapter). The first is the community culture approach developed by local projected-oriented NGOs, which placed a special emphasis on wisdom. This approach focuses on consciousness-raising as well as indigenous knowledge of the local environment and its uses (Anan highlights agroforestry and folk medicine such as herbal remedies). One of the key mechanisms for achieving this is participatory research, where as part of the development project or environmental monitoring programme, communities rediscover and/or reaffirm their cultural identity. It is also suggested that the communities are empowered by the process, generating evidence that is much more comprehensive and detailed than that produced by outsiders, and research outputs that help similar projects elsewhere as well. For Anan, the second approach builds on the first but places an additional emphasis on culture as dynamic and in process: 'it modifies the concept of local or folk wisdom to cover not only a value and a belief system but also a mode of thinking and system of rationality concerned with two fundamental rights: communal or collective rights of common property; and customary rights in communal organizations and social management of social resources' (Ganjanapan 2000: 13).

The results in this case go beyond protecting traditions and encourage civic engagement with NGOs, scientific researchers and political authorities. This is not often an easy process because national legal systems emphasize individual private property ownership and technocratic environmental policy-makers often portray open-access commons as a problem for resource management (ibid.: 7–18). In addition, the Thai national government has been reluctant to accept that communities have group rights for the reasons identified in Chapter 2, in particular when dealing with ethnic minority communities in the border regions. Similarly, Thai state authorities are sometimes reluctant to recognize the value of indigenous knowledge when dealing with local people. Santita Ganjanapan (1997) highlights the fact that the classificatory practices of scientists often do not map on to those of indigenous knowledges – what different actors mean by environmental degradation can vary enormously, and this often leads to very different kinds of environmental management solutions being proposed (see Tables 7.1. and 7.2 below). As she explains,

> ... villagers are still able to retain the sense of communality by asserting the rights of human guardians of resources. Only those who protect and look after their resources have rights to benefit from them. Therefore, outsiders who do not take care of resources have no rights to use and must be excluded. (ibid.: 263)

She emphasizes that local peoples should therefore be given the opportunity to work in collaboration with the state and should be granted the right to manage their own resources. Likewise, Bruce Missingham indicates that on environmental issues the Assembly of the Poor 'is principally concerned with defending people's livelihoods and community rights to manage and control local resources such as land and forests' (Missingham 2003: 55).

In another case study, Nitasmai Tantemsapya explores the sustainable agriculture movement to consider how indigenous resource uses are sometimes at odds with state resource management. She highlights the key role of local NGOs in promoting sustainable agriculture in Thailand but points out that while a diverse set of social actors have become interested in sustainable agriculture as an environmental alternative, 'the extent to which it could serve as an alternative on a wide scale has yet to be tested' and that it is 'likely to sit uneasily with the dominant trends of ever greater marker orientation, diversion of labor from agricultural to industrial and service sector occupations, vertically integrated production through agribusiness and new developments' (Tantemsapya 1997: 284–5).

Along the same lines, Philip Hirsch investigates community forestry as a social movement from the perspective of marginal groups and points out that because community forestry is a contested issue between local people and state authorities, it needs to be approached in 'a more inclusive way' (Hirsch 1998: 16). For Hirsch,

> the community in community forest is simultaneously a level at which forestry is locally managed (local rather than central); a unit within which forest is managed but one that is always going to be contested and whose territorial and social boundaries cannot be assumed; and a *discourse* counter to state management that is at once reactive ... and forward looking. (ibid.)

Malee Lang (2003) investigated a grassroots movement against the Pak Mun dam in Thailand and discovered how local fishers, by relying on traditional knowledge and experience, were able to produce their own research, which they used as a means of negotiation with the state and as a challenge to the experts' knowledge:

> A small group of fishers ... began to collect fish samples both by themselves and by buying big quantities of fish from other fishers. They took photographs and tried to identify the fish species by consulting available scientific literature about fish taxonomy in the Mekong basin ... The research also affirmed that fisheries in the Moon River depend on the replenishment of natural stock from the Mekong, and that fish migrate between the Mekong and the Moon ... the Tai Ban Research group ... consists of 195 local researchers representing each of the 65 affected villages along the Moon River ... The researchers in each village had the task of collecting fish samples in their villages and recording the data including fish name, size, the place where the fish was caught, and fish prey ... A monthly meeting was held to discuss the research progress and problems and to jointly identify details about fish characteristics, behaviour, habitat and lifecycle ... These research findings are truly impressive ... The depth of the local fishers' ecological knowledge presented in the

counter-research is striking. To mention just the Tai Ban fish study, 156 fish species returned to the Moon when the dam was open. Of these, 25 species were endemic to the Moon, and 123 were migratory fish from the Mekong, of which 97 species remained in the Moon as they could not migrate back in time before the water dropped. The studies documented two biological patterns: the feeding and spawning behaviour. There were 54 species feeding at the rapids, 33 in the whirlpools near the rapids, 69 in the pools below the rapids, 17 at the submerged reefs and shoals, and 35 in the tributaries of the Moon. Many of them could extend their habitat and feeding grounds to more than one type of habitat. There were 33 species spawning at the rapids, 25 species in the deep pool below the rapids, 40 species in the long stretch between two rapids, 22 species in the pool adjacent to the rapids, 24 species in caves in the shoals, 9 species in the submerged reefs, 15 species in the tributaries and 56 species in the riverbank's seasonally flooded forests. Some species have more than two types of spawning habitat. There were 18 endemic species relying solely on the rapids type of habitat. (ibid.: 2–3)

The sheer wealth of detail expressed through this form of indigenous knowledge will rarely be captured by external scientific experts in their assessment of a particular river system. This small-scale exercise merely demonstrates the return of marine biodiversity following the opening of the sluice gates of the Pak Mun dam (described above as the 'Moon River') and provides tangible justification for the maintenance of a more active flow of water through the river course and the facilitation of spawning by migrating fish species, much of which has previously been lost as a

TABLE 7.1 Indigenous land classification of Thawangpha

Terrains	Soil textures and colours	Land uses
teud (lowland)	*din dam, din dak, din hae, din khi pong, din ruan, din pon hin*	paddy
term or *merng* (gentle slopes)	*din daeng, din sai* and *din pon hin*	paddy and upland crops
jing (steep slopes)	no available data	forest
tad (cliff)	no available data	forest
san (mountain tops or ridges)	no available data	upland crops, forest

TABLE 7.2 Scientific land classification of Thawangpha village[1]

Terrains	Soil series	Nomenclature	Paddy suitability	Land suitability for upland crops
floodplains	alluvial soils	not available	PI, PIIs	UIVd
semi-recent terraces	Hang Dong	TypicTropaqualfs	PI	UIIId
old terraces	Mae Rim	Oxic Paleustults; loamy-skeletal, mixed	PVt	UVIs
mountains	slope complex	not available	PVt	UVIIe

Source: Ganjanapan (1997: 252)

Note: 1 Codes used are as follows:

1. Soil Suitability Grouping for Paddy Rice (P): PI = soils very well suited for paddy land, having no significant limitations for rice production. There is sufficient water available from rainfall and/or irrigation for at least one high-yielding crop of rice in most years; PIIs = soils moderately suited for paddy land, having moderate limitations that restrict their use of rice production and/or require special management. In this case, s = soil limitations in the root zone, such as shallowness, unfavourable texture, stoniness or low fertility that is difficult to correct; PVt = soils generally not suited for paddy land, having very severe limitations that preclude their use for rice production with ordinary methods. In this case, t = unfavorable topography. They are soils of which relative position or relief (macro or micro) limits use for crops and paddy in particular.

2. Land Capability Classification for Upland Crops (U): UIVd = soils poorly suited for upland crops, having severe limitations that restrict the choice of crops and/or require very careful management. In this case, d = impeded drainage. These are soils of which use for upland crops is limited by excess water fur to high water table, slow permeability or slow surface drainage or a combination of all three limitations; UIIId = soils moderately suited for upland crops, having moderate limitations that reduce the choice of crops and/or require special management. "d" has the same meaning as in UIVd; UVIs = soils having severe limitations which make them generally unsuited for cultivation and limit their use to pasture, woodland, wildlife food and cover and water supply. "s" = soil limitations in the root zone similar to PIIs; UVIIe = soils and land types having limitations that preclude their use for commercial plant production and restrict their use to recreation, wildlife food and cover and water supply. "e" = erosion. These are soils with an erosion hazard or past erosion damage (Ganjanapan 1997: 252–3).

result of the construction of the dam, affecting livelihoods and forcing population displacement among peoples that had relied on this food source for generations.

In another example, local community members, along with Greenpeace activists in Thailand, have been demonstrating against the state-funded coal-fired power plant of Mae Moh in the northern province of Lampang. This energy plant is considered to be one of the worst of its kind in Asia, having inflicted serious damage upon both the health of local residents and the environment since 1978. Because the livelihoods of local communities are at stake, we need a sober analysis of *whose* livelihoods are affected. The issues involved here are fisheries and the local ecology upon which local communities are dependent. Examples like this prompt us also to acknowledge rural–urban interdependence. The urban population relies on food supplies from the local agricultural sector, i.e. environmental damage to rural communities should be a concern for everyone.

After Thaksin and the generals: the new political context in Thailand

Until recently, Thai politics was characterized by more effective dialogue and communication between NGOs, local authorities, policy-makers and local stakeholders, including academic institutions, trade unions and labour advocacy groups, and industry representatives. Suddenly, the political situation in Thailand underwent a profound transformation. Thaksin Shinawatra's political party, Thai Rak Thai (Thais love Thais, TRT) built support among the rural poor in the north of Thailand, constructing a new electoral alliance that led to the first TRT government in 2001. Despite the government's pro-business leanings and traditional vote-buying, this was not only the first political party to appeal to the livelihood and social justice concerns of the rural poor, it was also the first government to try to deliver on electoral promises to the rural poor. The reaction by the urban middle class in Bangkok was initially shock and then horror. By comparison with previous administrations, Thai Rak Thai's record on pro-poor policies is impressive – subsidized and affordable healthcare policies for the first time, initiatives to promote local crafts, income-contingent student loan programmes and financial assistance to lift farmers out of debt. The results (agricultural incomes increasing by 40 per cent and a reduction in the number of Thais in poverty by more than half from 13 million in 2000) help to explain Thaksin's populist power base. Of course, not all policies were pro-poor or respected the environment, but the sheer weight of support in the subsequent elections in 2005 (plus the absorption of minority parties) produced not only the unique re-election of a Thai prime minister but a landslide electoral victory for the first time. As a result, the popular press dubbed Thaksin the Berlusconi of Asia. Accusations of financial corruption concerning the sale of the Shinawatra family company's shares in the Shin Corporation (a telecommunications firm built up by Thaksin but controlled by family members since he became prime minister) generated a political crisis. The shares were sold to a Singaporean investment fund managed by Ho Ching, the wife of the Singapore prime minister, Lee Hsien Loong, as part of a tax-free liability buy-out. This has been seen by many elitist nationalist Thais as an act of betrayal. The transaction, three days after the implementation of the Telecommunication Act permitting such sales by individuals without tax liability, generated $1.88 billion for the Shinawatra family. The urban elite response was sustained protests spurred on by the media firebrand Sondhi Limthongkul, portraying Thaksin as either the reincarnation of Hitler or a Chinese demon, while at the same time appealing to the revered King of Thailand, Bhumibol Adulyadej (King Rama IX), to intervene to resolve the political crisis. Underlying the rhetoric used in the protests was an urban elitist fear of the influence of the poor and to some extent latent xenophobia – anti-Singaporean feeling, anti-Chinese racism and urban distrust of the Thai Rak Thai party's perceived capacity to 'buy the votes' of peasant farmers.

Environmental campaigns disappeared as the protests organized by the People's Alliance for Democracy (PAD) brought together students, urban unionists, professional workers (including civil servants) and the supporters of the opposition parties (the Democratic Party, the Thai Nation Party and the Mahachon Party). Accusations of corruption and misrepresentation were filed by all sides. Even the normally apolitical monks have taken sides with the Dharma Army, joining the anti-Thaksin protests, while others helped to look after the crowds at pro-Thaksin rallies, which on one occasion mustered twice as many people as the PAD. In the end, the election was annulled and then the military acted on 19 September 2006 on the grounds of instability to suspend democratic rule. Interestingly, only the opposition's claim that TRT party members have bankrolled the smaller opposition parties that had not joined the election boycott was regarded as legitimate, leading to the dissolution of TRT and the suspension from politics of 111 of its leading members. Much of the rhetoric of the protest movement focused on the manipulation of uneducated and simplistic peasants as well as the lack of sophistication of TRT officials. The only other large party, the Democrats, are seen as the party of the 'blue blood' establishment that has always neglected the interests of the poor. Deep social cleavages remain, and the reconfiguration of the political party system continues as the military government moves towards scheduled elections in December 2007.

Following the coup, civil organizations have had much less freedom to organize. Even after January 2007, martial law was still in place in thirty-five of the seventy-six Thai provinces, particularly in the north and the border regions. Thai labour unions, however, have maintained a visible presence following large-scale job lay-offs and factory closures as a result of the effects of the coup on the domestic economy. In May 2007, 10,000 labour union members marched on May Day in Bangkok in protest against the military, and as the garment workers experienced increased lay-offs in the summer, the protests took a new turn when women union protesters from the Inter Moda plant threw their knickers into the compound of Government House and ten women staged a naked protest at the gates against the absence of severance pay. Localized environmental movements have subsequently taken heart from the easing of military rule in the central regions.

The planned development of a IRPC Plc coal-fired electrical plant in Rayong led to a protest of between 1,000 and 10,000 villagers and small business owners on 3 September 2007. The presence of the small business sector in this cross-class environmental activism also endowed the movement with financial resources that many environmental protests in the past have lacked – enough to cover the costs of organizing a 15,000-signature petition, transportation, coordination, vehicles for blockade purposes, and staffing for a long-term campaign. The campaign has also opted for focused demonstrations at ministry buildings in Bangkok to generate media coverage about their concerns, which relate to both human health and environmental impacts. On their part the company was willing to discuss mitigation and consider EIA with the protest movement, but not the termination of the project itself. Within the terms of the Thai Government's power auction, however, the bid was subsequently withdrawn. Similar movements are emerging to protest against the EGAT power plant in Bang Kaew and the joint venture between the Thai company Loxley and Babcock and Brown (an Australian investment company) in Mae Klong (Samut Songkhram province).

This builds on earlier successful protests against the air pollution of coal-fired power stations in Prachuab Khirikhan (190 miles south of Bangkok) in 2002, which linked environmental NGOs and village groups. As identified above, however, other smaller-scale but pollution-heavy development projects have been approved under the military regime. It appears that protest movements have been more successful in discouraging transnational corporations than government institutions and are more likely to have an impact on international lending institutions such as the ADB. What happens if democracy is restored is a different matter, however.

The new constitution proposed by appointed prime minister Surayud Chulanont and the military government in Thailand offers an interesting mix of obstacles and opportunities for democratic participation. The reintroduction of appointed senators in half the upper chamber places limits on popular sovereignty while the introduction of multi-party constituencies inhibits the possibility of single-party government. Combined with this, the dissolution of TRT, a five-year ban on political activities for 111 of its leading members on the part of the Electoral Commission and the subsequent reconfiguration of political parties is likely to lead to multi-party coalition government following new elections. The dissolved TRT has also fragmented into the People Power Party and a range of smaller former TRT factions attempting to galvanize a third-party force in the political centre ground. Many of these factions have only limited regional support, and their policy platforms are unlikely to provide a basis for securing broad-based rural support in the way achieved by TRT.

The rapid development of Thailand has changed the political landscape for environmental movements (now broadly defined to include livelihood projects and land rights campaigns). The location of the Mae Moh plant in the rural north has generated opportunities for linking environmental issues often regarded as urban to movements such as People Against Coal which network NGOs such as the Forum for the Global South could capitalize on. In addition, the military government's concern with a sufficiency economy has allowed some insider groups such as the Thailand Environment Institute to press for the new constitution to contain articles on citizens' right to access information, environmental safety for communities and participation in decisions that affect them. They also pressed for an environmental court to solidify the law in this area. These hopes were only partially realized in the final version of the constitution submitted for the 2007 referendum (Sections 55 and 56, 65 and 66, and 84 respectively). While citizen and community involvement are specified, the term 'participation' is largely restricted to political institutions and economic development plans (although consultation with private bodies is specified under human rights). EIA has been retained along with the requirement of public hearings for projects causing serious environmental impacts. How environmental movements and NGOs respond to these challenges and how case law evolves in legal disputes remains to be seen.

8 | The new vocabulary of ecological citizenship

Introduction

This final chapter reconsiders the meaning of environmental and ecological citizenship in the light of previous explorations of responsibility. These explorations have raised issues of justice, responsibility and/or civic engagement, and now is the right time to reconsider entitlements and obligations, rights and duties and the relationship between norms and values in concrete practical situations. Rather than doing this in the abstract we want to highlight some additional areas of concern and use them to flag up issues that are likely to become increasingly important, such as local environmental action, the appropriate use of research methods, and the importance of environmental ethics in informing but not dominating environmental action and policy. Inevitably much of this book has been devoted to institutional developments, the effects of campaigns, the resources they mobilize and the role of political discourses. So it seems opportune now to rethink the conceptual landscape of these new discourses and provide guidelines for new research in the field, not only to fill the many gaps but also to consider how environmental movements and NGOs can become more internally democratic and inclusive, drawing in new constituencies, and thus become more accountable and broaden their resource base. After all, that is exactly what they repeatedly expect from governments and private corporations, so why should this not apply to them? The increased concern with environmental and ecological citizenship means that the analytic focus has now shifted to finding ways in which citizens understand why certain actions are virtuous, right or good, so that the desired changes in behaviour become more stable; that they stick! Only by developing an ethical sense, a better understanding of why certain outcomes are desirable, when rights should be applied to all and which virtues should be cultivated in particular situations, can they help create a firm commitment to new obligations in a lasting way.

Cleaner, safer but not always greener – does it have to be this way?

In the 1990s, the key buzzwords among NGOs, environmental movements and academics were *environmental justice*, or, rather, highlighting environmental injustices. The Environmental Justice (EJ) movement in the USA advocates not only policy prescriptions but also a vocabulary for political action that only makes sense if participants are directly involved in the decisions that affect their constituencies. The movement's evolution from one of protest to policy informing civic engagement highlights something of which we should take note – by using the American discourse of civil rights they managed to articulate their standpoint and develop a degree of legitimacy that is often very hard to achieve for oppositional movements. Within the environmental movements, there are already significant attempts to bridge the gap between backyard or grassroots local environmental justice campaigns and the policy communities concerned with sustainability (by which we mean co-activism rather than merely rainbow coalition building) to good effect on specific campaigns on 'just transportation' (Bullard and Johnson 1997; Conservation Law Foundation 1998), urban and city sustainability strategies (Bullard et al. 2000; Evans et al. 2005) and precautionary principles in cleaning production processes (Rachel's Environment and Health News 1998). To illustrate, not only does the inner urban population experience a disproportionate impact from pollution such as toxic waste, but spending on transport is often higher in the suburbs than in minority and low-income neighbourhoods.

The EJ movement initially grew out of the concern with the storage and disposal of hazardous waste in neighbourhoods with low socio-economic status (overlaid by ethnic identity) and low levels of civic engagement, compounding social and environmental injustice. As a grassroots or 'bottom-up' movement, however, its trajectory has differed from that of other advocacy campaigns concerned with sustainable development in state and international policy formation, simply because it has moved into civic engagement, and its constituencies have increasingly become stakeholders. As a result, they have become empowered. In 'broad-focus civic environmentalism' issues such as civic disengagement, segregation, urban disinvestment, unemployment, environmental degradation are intimately linked. Julian Agyemen describes the movement as having 'many streams contributing to the river' of EJ bringing together local communities, farm-workers' unions, anti-toxins movements, traditional environmentalists, Native American struggles for self-determination, black civil rights movement, eco-feminist groups, academic researchers and so on (interview with Mark Smith, 2004). What is common to all these constituencies is that they feel that their interests are harmed and that their voices are not being or have not been heard, though the precise form of harm and exclusion can vary enormously. The goals of justice expressed by union campaigns and community activism are no longer seen as incompatible with those of environmentalists. Active citizenship focuses on our obligations to foster the social, environmental and economic health of communities, and while recognizing that procedural processes (such as deliberative democracy, consensus conferencing and so on) are important at the same time to acknowledge that they should not be separated from substantive goals and outcomes. As the EJ movement shifted its focus to institutional lobbying and private–public partnership, it has become a participative mechanism in environmental governance.

The same problems have been identified in many developing societies such as China, Thailand and the Philippines, as indicated in previous chapters. All these examples indicate that rather than fixating on the environmental issues arising from protecting pristine wilderness, which Joan Martinez-Alier (2002) even goes so far as to call the 'cult of the wilderness' in much of environmental thought, we need to devise a practically grounded environmental ethics suited to diverse contexts. There are relatively few such wilderness areas left, and many environmental contexts subject to protection are not pristine but are managed and highly adapted to human intervention. Joan Martinez-Alier's *Environmentalism of the Poor* (ibid.) raises similar questions about linking environmental and social justice in South Africa. In this context, the traditional concerns with conservation were poorly equipped for thinking through the problems of a society where a majority had been excluded from many of the economic benefits of apartheid society (see Figure 2.1). The heavy focus on overpopulation as the key environmental problem in the region also took little account of how large parts of the population were artificially concentrated within designated areas, leading to concentrated resource use and land erosion problems. Thus traditional conservationism gave way to strategies for using resources in a way that sought to conserve the habitat and species while offering incentives for the local community through, for example, ecotourism. This highlights the importance of doing research in the context of application and developing innovative and inclusive solutions that promote environmental objectives while generating reasons for local people to invest in these projects.

After all, as Westergaard and Resler (1976) stated, *power is visible in its consequences.* So, if a socially and politically marginalized community experiences most of the environmental 'bads' and few environmental 'goods', then even if it is hard to provide causal attribution, we can still say that power has been exercised in a tragic way (i.e. through the remorseless working of things). Today an environmental stench permeating the experience of the poor is as rank as the sweatshops of the Industrial

Revolution. Where there are people forcibly displaced or losing their livelihoods, living downstream of a dam or mine, living downwind of sulphur or benzene emissions, having homes in close proximity to polluting factories, working for punishing hours with no concern for health and safety, then it is very likely that social and environmental injustice will be found cheek by jowl. This is not consigned to history but with us now, even if hidden by distance. Drawing from just some of the examples discussed in previous chapters we want to highlight these issues for all future researchers. Just ask the Burmese factory workers of Mae Sot, rural migrants in the Pearl River delta industrial zone in China or the South Indian leather workers toiling up to their waists in chemicals (banned in developed countries) and leather slurry, providing the sanitized and cheap products that Westerners buy in every supermarket and fashion outlet. When we try on a new pair of shoes, we should consider in whose ecological footprints we are walking.

In Chapter 2, we highlighted the Dudley Street Neighbourhood Initiative (DSNI) as the first community not-for-profit private organization in the USA to be granted eminent domain authority over abandoned land in its territorial area. Residents angry at urban decline (crime, arson, disinvestment, the impact of redlining and property speculation) were increasingly frustrated with the inability of political leaders to find solutions. In partnership with Community Development Corporations, this initiative brought together neighbourhood organizations, companies, private charities, religious groups, banks and state officials to implement plans that drew on residents' wishes, pushing through not just the usual mix of green spaces, play areas, urban gardens and vegetable plots, to repeat from earlier, not just affordable housing, but energy-efficient affordable housing for those least able to afford high energy bills – a 'just sustainability' (Agyeman 2005; Agyeman et al. 2003, Agyeman and Evans 2006: 191–2). So, in this example, the members of the group were transformed from a constituency into a 'stakeholding constituency', prompting local companies to acknowledge obligations to the welfare of the local community and other local constituencies, developing a long-lasting partnership for mutual benefit (i.e. co-activism or movement fusion that works). In this example of 'broad focus civic environmentalism', environmental injustice is not a result of a lack of access (a narrow-focus approach concentrating on rights) but a result of the inability of communities to be responsible for and develop active strategies that promote economic vitality, ecological integrity, civic democracy and social well-being, so constituting 'just sustainability', a practical solution that simultaneously addresses social justice as well as environmental justice. This movement is thus not just concerned about dumping or the development of LULUs ('locally unwanted land uses', such as waste transfer facilities) in these neighbourhoods, it is also concerned about creating access to environmental quality – increasing access to goods such as the countryside and urban green spaces. Environmental debate is articulated with existing political discourses, so attention is needed to find the most appropriate means of communication. While in the UK town planning and conservationist discourses dominate, in the USA it is the civil rights discourse against racism while in South-East Asia it is expressed through the Buddhist understanding of suffering and balance. Each context is already occupied by discourses that regulate the production of meaning, and we need to recognize the crucial role they play in environmental communication and mobilization.

The UK: responsibility in context

According to the Environment Agency in the UK, social deprivation measures usually coincide with poor air quality, flood hazards and emissions. In the UK, areas where the most deprived 10 per cent live also have five times as many Integrated Pollution Control (IPC) sites and seven times as many emission sources, exacerbated by the presence of more offensive and harzardous pollutants. Where these factors combine, such as in 'pollution-poverty hot spots' in London, Manchester, Sheffield, Nottingham and Liverpool, then these impacts are much more serious (Environment Agency 2003). In terms of experiencing environmental 'bads', the causes are usually deep seated as a result of communities historically forming (or at least moving in when property prices and rents are relatively low) around specific industries and transport routes. On the other side of the environmental equation, in terms of the ability to secure environmental 'goods' (including access to green spaces), the most deprived and socially excluded citizens are less likely to have the resources to enjoy green spaces or live on affordable transport routes in order to access them. In a similar way, areas with high traffic, the main contributor to poor air quality and resulting poor health consequences, also have the lowest car ownership. While social class has historically been seen as a more significant indicator of environmental quality, the shifting demographic profile combined with employment and housing opportunities for migrants in the last twenty years highlights a link between ethnic inequalities and environmental inequalities (Walker and Bickerstaff 2001; Social Exclusion Unit 2000). The excluded, whether in terms of class or ethnic identity, are more often the victims of pollution rather than the cause.

Local strategic partnerships and community planning have had some positive impacts, but the primary concern has often been public safety. Stoneham Park near Brighton was reclaimed by Hove City Council, Hove YMCA and the Poets Corner resident society from being a space dominated by drug and alcohol abuse, youth gangs and vandalism. In order to encourage local families and vulnerable citizens to use the space (especially encouraging the presence of adults in the evenings through 'Park Safe'), the preference for art projects (to cover graffiti), play areas for children, community festivals, a community café staffed by volunteers, grassy rather than woodland areas and pruned undergrowth in order to ensure higher visibility makes this a highly managed solution in an area where many local residents in multi-person-occupation housing lacked their own gardens. Urban green spaces like these are usually heavily managed, primarily to encourage local families and vulnerable citizens to use them, especially where residents in multi-person-occupation housing lack gardens. In addition, unmanaged woodlands in urban spaces are regarded as unsafe, as 'muggers' paradises', as media reports describe them.

As a result, the community initiatives that improve shared environmental spaces are more often focused on safer and cleaner rather than greener environments. In addition, as a result of the housing market, the improvements in the end lead to rising property prices and so displace the most deprived to areas where the improvements have not yet taken root. The environment was clearly transformed for the better in the Stoneham Park case, contributing to neighbourhood renewal, but not in a way that generates wilder woodlands expansion and closer consorting with nature or addresses all of the marginalized. These kinds of initiatives improve the shared spaces but also seem to be more concerned with changing the social balance of the area, especially through housing market renewal and gentrification. INclude, in Liverpool 8 (a postal district in the UK), with the support of Liverpool City Council, combines urban safety, crime reduction, street cleaning and grounds maintenance (through urban environmental rangers) with the aim of creating 50:50 social and owner-occupied housing (from its previous balance of 80:20).

There is an older story that many current environmentalists do not often acknowledge. The story of environmental awareness predates the 1960s but was wrapped up in campaigns for social justice and the improvement of urban habitats. If we look back at the social entrepreneurs of the late nineteenth and early twentieth centuries, such as the garden city movement, there was a conscious attempt to integrate the positive elements of urban environments and those of the countryside to create a model of harmony between interests and a flexible framework for creating environments suited for purpose, a healthier and happier community. By way of parallel, initiatives like Welwyn Garden City and, in a more limited way, the leafy suburbs of Hampstead Heath were future-thinking attempts to address the effects of industrial restructuring (at that time deteriorating slum conditions in the inner cities and public health scandals, notably infant mortality peaks, provided the impetus). The attempts to create wooded areas in urban spaces or easy access to other environmental amenities were a key part of the message. Bottom-up movements combined with the impassioned motives of ecologists and town planners helped to temper the early reactions against working-class enjoyment of the benefits of the rural environment by romantic conservative environmentalists such as John Ruskin.

Although the picture is uneven and patchy, we can conclude that the environmental movements of the last forty years have had a considerable impact on human practices, and many things that have been advocated along the way have found their way into mainstream political consciousness (although some were initially regarded as impracticable or politically impossible). Today, the reconstruction of urban spaces that has resulted from deindustrialization, neoliberal policies and economic globalization of the economy presents similar problems: brownfield sites have lain unreclaimed with a preference for the gradual encroachment of green spaces on the edges of the cities, the acceleration of suburban housing expansion whittling away at woodland areas and even impinging on the remaining areas of ancient woodland. Woodland expansion in the UK, in recent decades, has in large part been driven by the expansion of conifer plantations, an investment that matures more quickly than deciduous woodlands.

This has more pertinence since the European Landscape Convention, which entered into force following its tenth ratification in March 2004, with the UK becoming a signatory in February 2005. Within the terms of the Convention, landscape is defined as 'an area, as perceived by people, whose character is the result of the action and interaction of natural and/or human factors' (Council of Europe 2000). The landscape and biodiversity minister, Jim Knight, stated that the UK was 'already fulfilling the requirements of the Convention, which is the first to deal solely with landscape – and importantly, that covers the whole landscape: rural, urban, and peri-urban; both everyday and extraordinary' (DEFRA 2006). A proposal to ratify still requires agreement from the European Policy Committee prior to implementation, however, and we await a Regulatory Impact Assessment to aid these deliberations. When ratified, the terms of reference of the Convention are heuristic for the new woodlands initiative, although the terminology is top-down – in terms of landscape policy, decisions depend on 'competent public authorities taking specific measures aimed at the protection, management and planning of landscapes'. In terms of quality objectives, the Convention states that these bodies are best suited to express the 'aspirations of the public'. It also has a primarily static approach, however; under landscape protection, it seeks to 'conserve and maintain', focusing on heritage value; and under landscape management, it focuses on 'regular upkeep of a landscape, so as to guide and harmonize changes which are brought about by social, economic and environmental processes'. More promisingly, under landscape planning, it seeks to foster 'strong forward-looking action to enhance, restore or create landscapes'. When considering awareness of the issues, it also lags behind, suggesting that the role of signatory members is to raise awareness in civil society, private organizations and public authorities. Recognizing social entrepreneurialism in this field, this poses the question of whether the signatory bodies have more to learn than to teach or impart. A more inclusive approach that recognizes the benefits of civil society organizations as primary agents of change as well as reservoirs of local, regional and trans-frontier knowledge and interests would be welcomed.

There is also a danger that the identification and assessment of landscapes by national, regional and local authorities (or combinations of these) will lead to landscape designation that fails to take account of how ecological systems operate and situations where the boundaries between administrative authority interfere with the conservation and maintenance of these landscapes. For example, many citizens who value the Ashdown Forest in East Sussex live in West Sussex, Surrey and Kent. In addition, citizens in neighbouring counties may value this woodland and heath area for very different reasons: rambling, wood collection, foraging for mushrooms, ornithological interests, pony-trekking, orienteering, to mention a few (in the past the forest even served as a venue for naturist walks). Each constituency has its own distinctive and specialized knowledge of this specific landscape. The same applies to the relevant constituencies in the Lake District, the Peak District, the New Forest or urban woodlands such as Oxleas Wood in south-east London. The constituencies that should be welcomed as stakeholders in this process are geographically dispersed and united by common passions rather than having residence in a specific territory. Moreover, the property values in many of these areas are often prohibitive for socially excluded groups, so the consultation process would focus overwhelmingly on the local

Eight

246

population and established NGOs rather than the diverse groups using these areas for various recreational purposes. The effective consultation of users demands a more innovative approach. If this Convention is to have real impact in terms of the expansion of urban and rural woodlands, then a more bottom-up perspective would alert policy-makers to the need for local and regional authorities, as well as representatives of proximate interests, to acknowledge many fellow stakeholders, or merely to operate as deliberative facilitators rather than the hubs of policy-making.

In the UK, the Woodlands Trust has initiated an ambitious project to restore woodlands from a land area of 12 per cent to something closer to the EU average of around 40 per cent. In the Lake District, there are opportunities for expanding woodland areas as a result of rural de-population and the vacant hill farms, which may mitigate soil erosion and, combined with the decline in sheep farming (which inhibits the growth of saplings), create opportunities for fen woodland, with oak planting on the valley sides and yew and holly on the screes and crags. These woodlands would create niches for the expansion of biodiversity to include wild deer, cattle and boar, although this would contradict the expectations of tourists in search of open views and a panorama characterized by dry-stone walls. This involves a different strategy from the expansion of conifer plantations (as in Grizedale, Eskdale and Thirl-mere). It would also take considerable time for woods in the wetlands to extend on to the valley flats, and at least a century for a high forest of birch, juniper, hazel and oak to take root. The western Lake District, less frequently visited by day-trippers to Windermere and Ambleside, has already shown some signs of woodland regeneration in the Furness Fells, and there are opportunities to expand on what is left of ancient woodland, a key niche for diverse ferns, lichens and Atlantic mosses alongside plants, flowers and small mammals. Allowing unruly nature to take its course will also mean that introduced species (such as larch, spruce and rhododendron) will compete when ecological opportunities arise. The expansion of woodlands in these places does not have to impact severely on human livelihoods and could enhance tourism in National Parks, creating new employment for local people in woodcrafts and possibly biomass harvests for local power production. As a result, woodlands expansion would demand different approaches in urban, suburban, peri-urban and rural contexts. Some isolated woodlands (that is, isolated by human-made obstacles) are valuable biodiversity niches, while at the same time they are vulnerable to exposure to new forms of competition from other species of tree or flower. The presence of inva-sive species in the gardens of urban and suburban areas also presents additional complications. Some green spaces are ecological oases for species that are either unusual or endangered, such as black-necked grebes or red squirrels. Using urban woodlands to establish connections between oases could allow for the spread of marginalized indigenous species of tree as well as mammals and butterflies, but could also leave them susceptible to intense competition. Each oasis therefore has to be subject to careful investigation on a case-by-case basis. Other species, such as foxes, have adapted so well to urban spaces that they can present a threat to wild species in more specialized habitats. Woodlands expansion should therefore include a precautionary approach towards specific habitats, and decisions on woodlands expansion need to draw in all relevant constituencies.

We also need to adopt a transnational approach to the expansion of woodlands as part of a global trading system. Deforestation in India, South-East Asia and China, as these developing societies industrialize, adds to the increased demand for resources from already industrialized societies. One recent unintended consequence of international trade is that Chinese trading vessels bringing imports to the UK are returning with over a third of the waste paper and plastics collected by local authorities, supermarkets and businesses (200,000 tonnes of plastic and 500,000 tonnes of paper in 2004), without regard for the health implications of sorting and sifting the potentially contaminated materials by low-cost labour. A further unintended consequence of this is the shrinking recycling sector in the UK. Similar quirks are likely to arise in the timber trade, i.e. woodlands expansion may be driven by market forces towards more extensive use of conifer plantations to match market demands. Perhaps one solution is to develop guidelines for appropriate mixes of woodlands in different contexts. Another issue is whether after twenty to thirty years we pat ourselves on the back and then realize that woodlands expansion in Western societies has diverted resources that could be better deployed to avoid the loss of biodiversity and the indigenous knowledge of the varied ecologies of specific habitats in developing societies following the growing of cash crops for external markets. The expansion of woodlands in the UK and elsewhere in Europe within a global context should be a variable-sum rather than a zero-sum or even negative-sum game in terms of biodiversity – where the UK becomes a major exporter of timber to newly developed societies where conservation measures have failed.

All these concerns are brought together in one of the most significant new debates in recent years, the debate on the precise meaning of citizenship and what it means as a 'politics of obligation'. Much of the twentieth century was taken up with the specification of entitlements and rights while the other side – obligations, duties and responsibility – was neglected. The debate on the environment and citizenship forces us to rethink the relationship between entitlements and obligations and question the assumption that other members of the biotic community can be protected only if they have rights. As the debate has unfolded, two currents have emerged: one that tries to maintain a distinction between morality and politics, conceptual clarification being the prime objective, and another that treats the questions in a more strategic way (Norton 2003). The latter argues that the lived experience of environmental politics demands that we see ethics and citizenly relations as intertwined. Both the changes in tactics and the more fragmented and fluid political structures (both internally but also in partnerships with business and governments) point to three new features of environmental politics. First, a clearer focus on the informal, unorthodox mechanisms of participation as well as the formal mechanisms. Second, an awareness of the need to address human duties, responsibilities and obligations as well as rights and entitlements. Third, a sensitivity to the importance of everyday meanings in shaping the agenda on the environment and in helping people see the reasons for ecologically beneficial activities. In the next section, we turn to how environmental ethics can help us address these concerns.

Values and the environment

Environmental philosophy has often been concerned with the preservation of natural things by allowing natural habitats to evolve in their own way – that is, by preventing human intervention. For conservationists, human intervention and management are seen as necessary to ensure biodiversity. Arguments for conservation can be made on materialistic grounds or in terms of aesthetic values. Similarly, some preservationist arguments are based on the attribution of rights to natural things; others ground their claims in human obligations to, for example, animals, butterflies and trees. We should be careful, first, to distinguish those issues that affect everyone from those that affect specific groups, such as landowners or indigenous tribes; and second, to distinguish those that affect present generations only from those that also affect future generations. Some reasons for developing conservation and preservation strategies include the following.

- The loss of potential resources through species extinction, including as yet undiscovered medical treatments based on the chemical components of particular plants and insects.

- The decline of biodiversity involves a loss of potential benefits (i.e. a cost) which exceeds the immediate or short-term benefits. For example, converting tropical forest to agricultural land yields benefits for just two to five years' use before soil exhaustion sets in, after which erosion and other processes ensure that recovery is slow and partial.

- The argument that forests should be preserved for the benefit of future generations, whether this refers to future generations of the indigenous peoples who live there, future generations of hardwood users in the West, or future generations more generally, is not often made explicit (Humphreys 1999). We should also be careful to remember that we are focusing on future generations in the medium term (for, given the right conditions, in the distant future, forests can regenerate).

The importance of maintaining biodiversity highlights a theme developed within many environmentalist texts and philosophical works – that nature is an interdependent 'web' or 'system' that human beings have disrupted. Such accounts argue that all natural things have an 'intrinsic value'. This is conveyed either through an identification of the way in which trees are also living things *or* in terms of the part they play within the ecosystem in which they exist. For instance, it is one thing to argue that we should set aside a portion of wilderness because it serves the human function of recreational pleasure (an instrumental view of nature) and another to suggest that human activities should never violate the sanctity of ecosystems (that ecosystems have an intrinsic value in some way independent of human needs and interests). Just as there are a variety of ways in which the environment can be valued for human needs, however, there are different ways in which the 'intrinsic value' of natural things can be understood (see Box 8.1).

All convey a sense of unease at the disruption and violation of a 'natural order'. With respect to intrinsic value 3, there is the logical question of whether it is possible to think about intrinsic value independently of human valuation. Whereas deep ecology claims that natural things possess rights, Aldo Leopold (1949) was concerned with human motives in the treatment of the environment, with a strong focus on human obligations. For Leopold, values are seen as a product of human practices and the meanings we attach to them in everyday life. He endorses the meaning of intrinsic value 1 and recognizes the complex properties of natural things (intrinsic value 2). This account of the natural world, however, is one which recognizes that the source of valuation is a human one, so there is little sign of an endorsement of intrinsic value 3. Deep ecologists like Arne Naess, however, stake a claim for intrinsic value

> **Box 8.1 Understanding the intrinsic value of natural things**
>
> John O'Neill identifies three common uses of the idea of intrinsic value in the environmental research literature (although they can be combined in various ways in many writings).
>
> - Intrinsic value 1 – that a natural thing is an end in itself, not a means to an end. This is the most frequently cited meaning of intrinsic value as a direct opposite to instrumental valuation.
> - Intrinsic value 2 – refers to the inherent properties of a thing that exists by virtue of the very structure and properties of a rock, a mountain, a stream, water and so on – just as we often value people because of their properties. This recognizes the intrinsic complexities and distinctive qualities of ecosystems.
> - Intrinsic value 3 – when intrinsic value is taken as a synonym for 'objective value', i.e. a natural object has value that is independent of the ways in which human beings value it. As O'Neill argues, much depends on what we mean by independent, but such an awareness draws our attention to the process of valuation. It also offers some ecological activists a basis for countering the claim that the value of a natural thing can be ascertained through a price.
>
> *Sources*: O'Neill (1993); Smith (1998a)

in the strong sense (that is, in all three versions simultaneously). So, while Leopoldians emphasize obligations, deep ecologists focus more on the rights of natural things to flourish in conditions of diversity. This 'rights-based approach' is based on what Devall and Sessions describe as two 'ultimate norms': biocentric equality and self-realization. While the idea of biocentric equality undermines the sense of human superiority and uniqueness associated with many approaches to the environment, this is combined with an appeal to redefine the human self, i.e. this account has a double-barrelled impact: 1) natural things are entitled to greater respect; 2) people will also benefit. Although there is a strong endorsement of intrinsic value, Devall and Sessions still fall back on the idea that the activity of valuation remains a human one and, as such, cannot be as objective as has sometimes been claimed.

Nevertheless, this concern with the rights of natural things has generated some interesting interventions. Christopher D. Stone considers the implications of integrating the rights of natural things into the legal process and addresses how these rights would be protected. He sees this as a long-term objective and explores the ways in which obligations could be established in the meantime. Stone considers a legal case which considered whether (and how) the interests of trees could be legally represented when a private company wished to engage in a development project in a National Park in the early 1970s. The case went as far as the US Supreme Court, and although it was finally judged by the majority of justices that trees could not be seen as legal entities, a minority report supported Stone's case for legal guardianship on behalf of the trees concerned. Stone argues that if we look at the history of the expanding moral community we can see many precedents for extending rights to natural things. The lesson from history is that legal rights have been denied in the past on fairly arbitrary grounds. For instance, slavery was sustained and women were excluded from voting or other elements of citizenship without recourse to anything other than 'this is the way things are'. As Stone points out, the 'rights of rightless things' are always unthinkable before they are thought through (Stone 1972, 1987).

The processes through which we value things and produce meaning are also important. In order to make sense of writers as different as Pinchot and Leopold, we have to be clear about the criteria through which they make judgements about environmental practice. In Western societies, three ways of making judgements have emerged in environmental discussion. These three kinds of judgement have generated three disciplines or fields of philosophical knowledge: science, ethics and aesthetics. In each area, there is a concern to find a demarcation criterion that can serve as a solid reference point for identifying what is valuable (and perhaps also what is taken seriously) and what is not. (For a comparison with the way ethical judgements creep into scientific ones, see Smith 1998b: 284–6.) This criterion, it has been argued, would be universal in scope – that is, it must apply in every situation, and it must be detached from all personal or subjective interests. In discussions about scientific knowledge this involves establishing the demarcation criteria between 'truth' and 'falsehood'; in ethics, the 'good' from the 'bad'; and in aesthetics, the 'beautiful' from the 'ugly'. Here we are concerned primarily with ethics, but it is useful to spot when the other kinds of criteria are at work at the same time. While Leopold draws upon aesthetics, the conservationist advocate of scientific management Gifford Pinchot relies on scientific truth to define the collective good of present and future generations. We should also bear in mind that the demarcation criteria that are plausible and sensible only in historically and socially specific cultures can masquerade as universal ones (although it must be added that if we believe them to be real, and act as if they are, then they are real enough in their consequences).

In the philosophical writings of Holmes Rolston III (1988), we can see how it is possible to shift the focus of the debate from rights to human obligations, a position that is much closer to Leopold. Rolston's account of values highlights how the distinction between anthropocentric and ecocentric is often inappropriately seen as clear cut – i.e. the clarity of the distinction is based on an oversimplification. Instrumental and intrinsic value can be defined in different ways, and if the value of a natural thing is purely in terms of the ends that are served, much depends on the objectives of the society in question and the values upon which outcomes are based. J. Baird Callicott, the promoter of Leopold's land ethic, suggests: 'We are animals ourselves, large omnivorous primates, very precocious to be sure, but just big monkeys nevertheless. We are therefore part of nature not set apart from it. Chicago is no less a phenomenon of nature than is the Great Barrier Reef' (Callicott 1992: 17). Nevertheless, he retains an element of human uniqueness, for he also argues that we need to take account of one distinctive human quality – we are 'conscious beings' who can value (we can make a judgement as to what is valuable or not), which means that a distinction between humans and nature is feasible. Callicott sees values as human generated rather than necessarily human centred (as anthropogenic rather than necessarily anthropocentric). As a result, *intrinsic value* is a product of human encounters with the natural, grounded in human feelings and tethered to the long history of human experience. This is still a form of non-instrumental valuation, for the value of the environment is an end in itself, not a means to an end, and indeed brings aspects of nature into the field of moral vision. The most obvious criticism is that this approach does not provide a basis for sifting and sorting the various obligations and duties that we have for different kinds of things from higher-order animals to insects or from woodlands to mountain ranges. It's difficult to treat the intrinsic value of all 'natural things' as if they are the same. For Rolston, however, Callicott's approach is problematic, for it considers intrinsic value as merely a metaphor, i.e. the projected subjective values do not themselves reside in nature (for Rolston, in Callicott's account, value is mislocated or misplaced). Rolston claims his own approach is simpler for it merely seeks to discover intrinsic value that is already present in nature (values that existed before human beings even came on to the scene); *rejecting anthropogenic intrinsic value by calling for autonomous intrinsic value*. Rolston also worries about the

253

implications of dropping the dualism of the natural and social, claiming that Callicott merely ends up naturalizing all culture. If you follow this through to its logical conclusion, it even makes human destruction of woodlands and forests natural.

Bryan Norton (2003) takes us in a different direction by suggesting that trying to find intrinsic value in nature is ultimately a task that is doomed to failure; nor should we believe that the only credible response to the exploitation of nature is to assert its independent value. He also challenges Callicott's attempt to ground values in a Cartesian notion of self or knowing/judging subject. For Norton, the search for intrinsic value is a bit of a distraction from the more important task of developing a new ecological worldview that goes beyond the idea of a conscious subject in opposition to an external reality (incidentally, he argues that advocates of anthropocentrism and ecocentrism are both guilty of this error). Environmentalists, he argues, are preoccupied with the claim that their values and goals are objective because they want people to believe their claims as true (a common feature in all 'worthy projects' for change). In response, he develops a new vocabulary and style of thinking that reject foundations, recognizing anthropocentricity as an inevitable part of constructing 'nature', but asserting non-instrumental values. In summary, Norton highlights two kinds of intrinsic value (IV) approach in environmental ethics (the first bearing some resemblance to the definition of intrinsic values considered earlier):

1 *autonomous IV* – strong or heroic conception of intrinsic value; natural objects or things have value entirely independently of the conscious human mind (seeking to avoid accusations of cultural relativism), whereby philosophers in the tower agree on the principles that can be passed down to activists in the streets;
2 *attributed IV* – a less heroic conception where valuation is a conscious act and whereby *value is only inherent* in nature but also remains independent of the goals or ends of human valuers, an attribution of value that is culturally specific and projected in a culture-laden context.

Norton's answer is that we need to go beyond objective and subjective accounts of value in order to escape this debate. He is not trying to show that IV does not exist, he hopes it does, but is more concerned to ask whether appeals to IV are going to be effective and persuasive on policy issues such as reforestation and biodiversity when some predictions point to the extinction of a quarter of species in the next two decades. Just as Leopold recognized that his conception of the biotic community was too intangible for policy-makers and turned to future generations as a justification, so Norton argues that environmentalists need to be more strategic rather than imagining that an intellectual case for a unified morality for environmentalists is going to emerge. To achieve this we need to take the specifics of each ecological location more seriously.

On the importance of ethnographic research on social and environmental justice

The research techniques associated with ethnography (direct observation, participant observation, in-depth interviews and participatory research) and also environmental journalism, sometimes in conjunction with quantitative methods, provide a more adequate account ('witness-cum-recording of human events' – Willis and Trondman 2002) of particular events and relationships in ways that aid the development of ecological citizenship. It is also crucial to add that, like many areas of environmental research, ethnography is keen to address how quantitative data sources are constructed – i.e. they should not always be regarded as unquestionable resources but as topics for research, as the result of authoritative decisions taken by actors in research institutes and government departments. Ethnographic research is used to access data on the lives of groups that are difficult to study by any other means, particularly social groups that are marginalized and suspicious of the intentions of researchers, a key issue in developing-society environmental movements when dealing with the victims of environmental degradation (such as indigenous peoples in Asia and Latin America, communities without a history or experience of civic engagement, or workers and their families living in close proximity to polluting industries and waste facilities).

During our field research, we have encountered very different responses by grassroots environmental activists towards their experiences of encounters with academic researchers. Some have been heavily indebted to the expertise and practical help that scientific advice has provided, but others, after bearing their souls and providing valuable evidence on their campaigning experiences and the issues involved, have concluded they were misrepresented and used when they have seen the final outputs, particularly when the researchers have been more concerned to fit the evidence within Western-centred academic debates. If we can speak the language of responsibility, researchers who act as a voice for such movements have an obligation to establish stronger connections between the lived experiences of these movements and communities and their research outputs. Nor should researchers and NGO activists use research associates and consultants in arbitrary ways in order to achieve their

The new vocabulary of ecological citizenship

research goals. In all cases, we would argue that researchers' obligations should be as stringent and respectful as they would expect from transnational corporations following their codes of conduct (if necessary, they should rethink their obligations as having the status of duties).

Within the ethnographic tradition, there are two approaches that we feel can act as a partial remedy for addressing issues of justice on the ground. First, mundane phenomenology, which stresses that the first-order constructs of the people studied should be represented by the second-order constructs of the researcher and that the end result should be intelligible to them (the postulate of adequacy). Second, critical ethnography, which makes a crucial link between the work of researchers and the empowerment of the people studied. Michael Burawoy argues that ethnographic researchers should document diverse forms of resistance or struggles that are taking place in order to highlight the common problems and issues while also acknowledging the normativity of ethnographic research practice (Smith and Pangsapa 2007). By studying the effects of environmental problems on the everyday lives of indigenous peoples, urban pollution victims or migrant communities, it is possible to build up a holistic account that tries to link all parts of a particular situation. Baszanger and Dodier recently developed a new way of considering how ethnographers try to do this by distinguishing between:

1 *Integrative ethnography*: following the anthropological tradition, this constructs units of collective belonging for individuals.
2 *Narrative ethnography*: by contrast, this offers readers a first-person narrative of events for each different field.
3 *Combinative ethnography*: by working simultaneously in different fields, this brings together a casebook that can be used to identify the different forms of action in which people may engage, along with the possible combinations between them (Baszanger and Dodier 2004: 10).

Integrative ethnography often takes place in cultural and social anthropology as well as sociological ethnographic studies of subcultures, where the research gradually builds up an account based on reflections during the process of research while attempting to empathize and stand in the shoes of the participants. Some describe the acquisition of this total picture as an 'internal revolution' (Lévi-Strauss 1963), if you like a eureka moment in which all the fragments of long and painstaking research come together, while others see it as more gradual or even mechanical, like putting together a jigsaw without a picture to work from, and with some parts being clear at an early stage. Narrative ethnography takes place in many areas of ethnographic work that view the relationship between researcher and participants as a dialogue, sometimes to the extent that much of the research output focuses on these encounters rather than acting as an account of a particular context. This approach places a special emphasis on the writing process, with the researcher acting as a visible narrator in the text, and the research process is conveyed in the sense of a journey towards understanding or as a history of unfolding events. The following excerpt is a good example of how environmental journalism as a form of narrative ethnography can press all the right buttons:

> I had already spent nearly a week in Mae Hong Son during the hot summer month of June 1995. I was investigating a tip that hardwood logs were illegally imported into the province from just across the border in Burma. Not only was the trade contributing to deforestation in Burma but the smuggling traffic was also reportedly interfering with the flow of refugees fleeing the war-torn country. It was a sensitive subject in the province; but after talking with various Burmese and Thai sources in town, I had managed to confirm the existence of the illicit logging trade, and I had also been told where the timber was allegedly crossing the border. I'd even discovered the name of the local logging kingpin. Then I'd spent several days wandering around Thai government offices ... where I badgered local officials until they grudgingly made some of their files and records available. According to the documents, there were not supposed to be imports of timber in this area ... nor were there supposed to be any active sawmills. I had even met with the governor of the province, who had assured me that no legal border trade took place in the area. Now I had to prove that the logs were indeed being smuggled. Pictures of timber coming across the border and run through a Thai sawmill would give me a major scoop ... I could hear the sawmill, but couldn't see it ... After crossing a patchwork of rice fields ... I came to a small stream ... The mill was close now ... but I still couldn't see it. A dead tree with long-hanging branches seemed to offer a good vantage point, so I began to climb. About fifteen feet off the ground, I was able to spy over the surrounding bushes into the mill yard, where several trucks and a pile of timber were heaped against the mill itself ... So I started taking pictures, one arm wrapped around the trunk for support. SNAP! I was suddenly in midair plummeting. I landed in a heap on the ground with a solid thump ... (Fahn 2003: 109–11)

Fahn's perilous work in the north of Thailand sustained by the virtue of courage provides a vivid and intricate picture of how human rights violations, social injustices and environmental degradation are closely connected. In his narrative ethnographic account of the Assembly of the Poor, Bruce Missingham highlights the following experiences when observing the formation of the 'village of the poor':

> When I first arrived at the protest two days after it commenced, people were still pouring into the site, lugging tattered bags of clothes, old sacks full of rice and food, and the odd cooking pot and charcoal stove. Metal barricades and protest banners mark the entrances to the rally from Phitsanulok Road. Riot police standing guard nearby paid no notice as I walked past them with the flow of people and in through the barricades. Just inside stood a makeshift medical tent under a blue tarpaulin, staffed by white-uniformed nurses from a nearby hospital and already receiving patients. Rows of portable awning-style tents and make-shift shelters stretched away along both sides of the street, backing onto the mosquito-infested canal on one side, and the black, grey walls of the Civil Service Commission building on the other ... Under the tents villagers had piled their provisions together and sat or sprawled on old tattered reed mats. Banners and display boards hung everywhere, making a backdrop of protest rhetoric, mostly in Thai, some in English. I continued along the pathway through the middle of the ramshackle encampment. From loudspeakers somewhere a stream of announcements blared out over the site, drowning out traffic noise from Phitsanulok Road. I came upon a stage that had been erected among the jumble of tents, protesters, and provisions. A large elaborately painted backdrop rose behind the stage, featuring a giant fist rising beside the words: 'The Assembly of the Poor demands what was promised'. Under these words, the painting depicted a sea of angry faces staring out, and interspersed among them, placards naming the main grievances of the Assembly: Dams, Forest and Land, State Projects, Slums, Alternative Agriculture ... I continued on past the stage, moving with the constant circulation of people throughout the rally site. Many of the protesters had set up small stalls selling fruit, vegetables, boodles, *som tum* (papaya salad), and chicken and fish grilled over earthenware charcoal stoves. Mostly these stalls consisted only of a reed mat on which produce was laid out for sale. The air was heavy with the smell of roasting chicken and fish, and the sour, acrid odor of fermented fish (Lao: *pladaek*). (Missingham 2003: 121–2)

Finally, combinative ethnography is portrayed by Baszangar and Dodier as the navigation through fragmentary resources and is common in (symbolic) interactionist accounts. Particular cases, forms of action or types of activity are seen as illustrations of more general patterns and relationships. The context of the events observed is considered neither as a 'whole' to be discovered (integrative ethnography) nor as a grounding point for an individual history (narrative ethnography), but as a disparate collection of resources between which individuals have to navigate. Unlike in the cultural approach, we do not presume here that the resources mobilized by people in their behaviour can be linked up to a coherent whole. Unlike in narrative ethnography, we leave behind the first-person account, the aim being to generalize from the study (Baszangar and Dodier 2004: 18).

In his discussion of the extended case method, Burawoy (Burawoy et al. 1991) argues that the significance of a case study lies in its ability to tell us about the world in which it is embedded. This approach provides us with a more in-depth context within which to look at social change and allows us to consider how social research can improve people's lives. This approach was developed to deal with marginalized groups, and the same applies to all peoples in the world who suffer from environmental degradation, such as the men, women and children in Guiyu, China, who spend their lives retrieving precious metals from discarded hard drives, and others who simply want to work with nature in the way that their parents and many previous generations were able to, and many more who want a better quality of life but don't want to see the environment of their childhood disappear.

Future research should not only focus on wage issues and labour violations but should also include investigations of the working environment inside and outside the workplace – local communities and neighbourhoods where workers live and the environmental impacts caused by the factories where they are employed. Documentation of occupational health hazards such as dust, noise pollution, weakened eyesight, hearing loss and other common ailments suffered by industrial workers is just as important as the many pollutants factories discharge from their operations into external communities. Key questions include the following: Does the factory treat its waste? Where does the waste go? What kinds of emissions are being released? It is important for researchers to identify these factors as well, and to hold companies accountable for labour and environmental violations. The consequences of urban industrial manufacturing on workers' health and their quality of life are very much interconnected – harmful work environments along with low wages and long hours affect every aspect of a worker's life and well-being, and companies need to realize that labour issues cannot be divorced from environmental issues. In developing societies, we should remember that most family members (often from a young age) are engaged in employment as well as experiencing the broader environmental effects of production. Labour standards have to be more than just wages and conditions. Labour issues are also environmental issues, and both are human rights issues, which is why there is an urgency to make sure that companies make these connections as well. What we need henceforth is a genuinely trans-disciplinary approach, and one that also links activists to scholarly research.

The environment is central to all aspects of human life, which means that we need to avoid the choice of addressing environmental issues or alleviating poverty because the solution to environmental issues requires that social injustices are addressed as well. Environmental issues always had and will continue to have a social justice dimension, and since environmental impacts are driven by development, issues concerning labour and social welfare they cannot be easily or sensibly separated. People, their families and their communities are entitled to clean air and water and they too have to participate to reduce their environmental impacts. The time has come and the time is now for environmental activists to engage in practical workable solutions to address an urgent and immediate problem that ultimately affects everyone, producers and consumers. There is only one standpoint that binds activists and their 'enemies', and that is recognizing the links between environmental and social justice. All actors have an obligation to act responsibly because everyone should have rights to safe and clean work conditions and everyone should have access to clean air, water and green spaces. If companies are responsible then they should be minimally obliged to address these issues.

We have developed a colour-coded classification of the kinds of partnerships and networks that are being and can be established between transnational private organizations (Figure 8.1). Drawing on the useful distinction made by Hawken et al. (1999) between pro-marketers, socialists and labour unions, environmentalists and synthesists who adopt a path of integration, reform, respect and reliance, we mapped out the networks across different sectors which highlight the diversity of contemporary transnational activist networks (Pangsapa and Smith 2008a).

Companies must be obliged to enforce environmental regulations – treating effluent discharge from their factories or curbing emission and other pollutants that are released into the air, into waterways and into the ground where workers and their families live. They must also recognize their obligations to ensure that their suppliers provide cleaner and safer working environments for their workers, and suppliers must be at least obliged to abide by labour standards and environmental regulations (unless the codes of conduct are more demanding) since they are just as responsible for sticking to these standards and codes of conduct as

Hawken et al. (1999: 311–12) make a useful distinction between:

Blues – pro-marketers

Reds – socialists and labour unions

Greens – environmentalists

Whites – synthesists 'adopting a path of integration, reform, respect and reliance' who do not agree with or completely oppose the blues, reds and greens

Drawing on this idea, the networks across different sectors can be characterized as turquoise (green-blue networks), purple (blue-red networks) and browns (red-green networks), as well as others.

Greens – deep ecology, bioregionalism, Earth First, Greenpeace

Reds – socialists and labour unions varying from dark to light red (social democratic and reformist movements)

Saffrons – Human rights, anti-(child)slavery/trafficking, pro-citizenship movements, self-determination movements

Browns –oppositional alliances (whistle-blowing, exposing, coordinated pressure) and co-activism (movement fusion)

Turquoises – ecological modernization and Green consumerism, Global Compact on Sustainable Development, Sierra Club/Friends of the Earth/Future Forum (incorporation of eco-establishment), Green conservatism

Purples – companies engaged in fair trade and at least respecting labour standards (better factories), Global Compact on Labour

Magnolias – labour, human rights and environmental movements together

Limes – companies acting with human rights groups (primarily in conflict zones), businesses respecting human rights concerns

Dark blues – corporations opposing corporate responsibility, environmental scepticism

Blues – corporations endorsing corporate responsibility but only to avoid adverse publicity, signatories of global compacts that have weak codes of conduct or ones that are inadequately implemented, monitored and enforced – shareholders' dividends and profit are the bottom line unless responsibility provides increased profitability and/or increased market share (constituencies excluded from stakeholding)

Light blues/aquatics – responsible corporations who initiate stakeholding initiatives, bringing a wider range of constituencies and promoting corporate citizenship, rigorous and implemented/monitored/enforced codes of conduct

Figure 8.1 Colour-coded partnerships and networks between transnational private organizations

are their clients, and states must be obligated to strictly enforce and implement standards and regulations. In other words, the politics of obligation must be observed at every level in the global supply chain.

Throughout this book we have focused heavily on responsibility, obligations and duties, but this does not mean that rights and entitlements should be marginalized. What matters is how they work together in concrete strategic situations. Given the changing political and institutional patterns that have followed from economic globalization, we are coming to realize that the less formal motivations that govern actions have increased in importance (especially when considering the acts of citizens, movements, NGOs and corporations). If we fall back into the oppositional rhetoric and treat corporations as 'enemies' then we risk the politics of empty gestures. The illustrations used throughout this text point to how both public and private institutions can make a difference. This does not mean that the actors involved can always be regarded as 'friends' or even fellow travellers, and the many environmental impacts we have described should highlight how for-profit and possibly quite a few not-for-profit civil organizations are still adversaries as we search for better solutions. By adversaries, we mean organizations that have interests that should be respected but which can be redirected, pushed and prodded in new directions to mitigate their effects, or even to find new ways of developing sustainable approaches. There is also the ethico-political question of how to find bridges between personal life and the bigger issues that affect us in communities, countries, regions and globally. We have explicitly indicated that no one moral compass is available; there is no single right course of action, good outcome or virtuous activity. Much depends on the environmental issue with which we are concerned and its cultural context. What is right simply because it applies to all equally in one context is unlikely to apply elsewhere. What is a good outcome for the members of a particular collectivity, acknowledging that this means assessing the costs and benefits to them, is unlikely to be relevant to another group of people.

The virtue ethics approach similarly has some weaknesses because in different cultural locations some virtues are privileged over others. Nevertheless, if we start from the assumption of virtue pluralism and draw upon specific virtues that offer guidance for living in balance with the environment according to their relevance then we stand a chance of getting things right and achieving the good. In addition, the focus on virtues and the grounding of environmental action in the concrete strategic context of each ecological problem mean that the ethical virtues have a much better chance of producing positive outcomes. Moreover, virtues can be combined in many ways, as in Gandhi's development of temperance, simplicity, prudence, contemplation and courage. It is often said that virtues are ways of cultivating the personalities of citizens through their engagements with other citizens and in acting within the public sphere. The interesting outcome of this approach to ecological citizenship is that each environmental issue may demand a different (combination of) virtue(s), which opens the way for multicultural and even multi-faith approaches to environmental actions. It must be clear by now, however, that ecological citizenship is above all a politics of obligation that links the personal and the private to the public, which focuses on the ties that bind and bond between different actors, links the informal and sometimes barely expressed entitlements and obligations to the more formally specified rights and duties, and is as demanding of citizens as it is of civil organizations, governments and intergovernmental bodies. We argue here that this does not harbour an incipient eco-authoritarianism (a limit on freedom or liberty) but that it provides a pathway for finding solutions that work and address the combined injustices that affect us. Being aware of these injustices is not, of course, enough, for they act as the motivation of civic engagement and the promotion of environmental responsibility. In the worst cases, these injustices involve a combination of human rights and labour standards violations alongside environmental degradation, all operating side by side. As a result, then, there is an obligation on all researchers to seek ways of informing environmental debate that bring these concerns together and are at the same time respectful of the first-order constructs of everyday experiences of the people who are studied. It is often said that knowledge is power, but this only ever really becomes true if that knowledge draws on these experiences, represents them in good faith, and provides outcomes that are intelligible to the people who serve as the focus of inquiry. If we can come back to the opening questions, then it is not so much that the environment matters, but why, how, where and when it matters. If we start and end on these questions then we can act.

Bibliography

Addo, M. (1999) *Human Rights Standards and the Responsibility of Transnational Corporations*, New York: Springer.

Adler, J. (1995) *Environmentalism at the Crossroads: Green Activism in America*, Washington, DC, Capital Research Center.

Agyeman, J. (2000) 'Environmental justice: from the margins to the mainstream', *Tomorrow Series*, London: Town and Country Planning Association.

— (2002) 'Constructing environmental (in)justice: transatlantic tales', *Environmental Politics*, 11(3): 31–5.

— (2005) *Sustainable Communities and the Challenge of Environmental Justice*, New York: New York University Press.

Agyeman, J. and B. Evans (2003) 'Towards just sustainability in urban communities: building equity rights with sustainable solutions', *Annals of the American Academy of Political and Social Science*, 590: 35–53.

— (2004) 'Just sustainability: the emerging discourse of environmental justice in Britain', *Geographical Journal* 170(2): 155–64.

— (2006) 'Justice, governance and sustainability: perspectives on Environmental Citizenship from North America and Europe', in A. Dobson and D. Bell (eds), *Environmental Citizenship*, Cambridge, MA: MIT Press.

Agyeman, J., R. D. Bullard and B. Evans (2003) *Just Sustain-abilities: Development in an Unequal World*, London: Earthscan.

AMRC (Asia Monitor Resource Centre) (2003) 'A decade of denial, 10th anniversary of Kader fire and proceedings of the 2003 ANROAV annual meeting', 25–27 July, Bangkok, Thailand, Hong Kong: Asia Monitor Resource Centre, Kowloon, <www.anroav.org/pdf/>, accessed 15 August 2007.

Anable, J. (2005) 'Complacent car addicts or aspiring environmentalists? Identifying travel behaviour segments using attitude theory', *Transport Policy*, 12: 65–78.

Anable, J., A. Kirkbride, L. Sloman, C. Newson, S. Cairns and P. Goodwin (2005) 'Soft measures – soft option or smart choice?', Bristol: UWE, January.

Anderson, M. S. and D. Liefferink (eds) (1997) *European Environmental Policy: The Pioneers*, Manchester: Manchester University Press.

Andrews, G. (2008) *Slow Food Movement*, London: Pluto Press.

Annan, K. (1999) Address to the World Economic Forum in Davos, <www.un.org/News/Press/docs/1999/19990201.sgsm6881.html>, accessed 26 March 2008.

Arnold, D. (2004) 'Work, rights, and discrimination against Burmese workers in Thailand', Southeast Asia Research Centre, Working Paper Series no. 71, Hong Kong: City University.

Baird Callicott, J. (1992) 'La Nature est morte, vive la nature', Hastings Centre report, 22(5): 16–23.

Baker, S. (1997) 'The evolution of European Union environmental policy: from growth to sustainable development?', in S. Baker, M. Kousis, D. Richardson and S. Young (eds), *The Politics of Sustainable Development: Theory, Policy and Practice within the European Union*, London: Routledge.

— (2001) 'Environmental governance in the EU', in G. Thompson (ed.), *Governing the European Economy*, London: Sage.

Baker, S., M. Kousis, D. Richardson and S. Young (eds) (1997) *The Politics of Sustainable Development: Theory, Policy and Practice within the European Union*, London: Routledge.

Bales, K. (2004) *Disposable People: New Slavery in the Global Economy*, Berkeley: University of California Press.

Ball, R. and N. Piper (2006) 'Trading labour-trading rights: the regional dynamics of rights recognition for migrant workers in the Asia-Pacific', in K. Hewison and K. Young (eds), *Transnational Migration and Work in Asia*, London: RoutledgeCurzon.

Barr, S. (2003) 'Strategies for sustainability: citizens and responsible environmental behaviour', *Area*, 35(3): 227–40.

— (2006) 'Environmental action in the home: investigating the "value–action" gap', *Geography*, 91(1): 43–54.

Barry, B. (1978) 'Justice between generations', in P. Hacker and J. Raz (eds), *Law, Morality and Society*, Oxford: Clarendon Press.

Barry, J. (1999) *Rethinking Green Theory*, London: Sage.

Bartelmus, P. (1994) *Environment, Growth, and Development: The Concepts and Strategies of Sustainability*, London: Routledge.

Baszanger, I. and N. Dodier (2004) 'Ethnography: relating the part to the whole', in D. Silverman (ed.), *Qualitative Research: Theory, Method and Practice*, 2nd edn, London: Sage.

Beck, U. (1992) *Risk Society: Towards a New Modernity*, London: Sage.

— (1995) *Ecological Politics in an Age of Risk*, Cambridge: Polity Press.

— (2000) *What is Globalisation?*, Cambridge: Polity Press.

Been, V. (1994a) 'Unpopular neighbours: are dumps and landfills sited equitably?', *Resources*, 115, Spring.

— (1994b) 'Locally undesirable land uses in minority neighbourhoods: disproportionate siting and market dynamics?', *Yale Law Journal*, 103(6): 1383–422.

Bell, D. (2003) 'Environmental citizenship and the political', Paper presented to the ESRC Seminar Series on Citizenship and the Environment, 27 October, Durham.

— (2005) 'Liberal environmental citizenship', *Environmental Politics*, 14(2): 179–94.

Bello, W. and S. Rosenfeld (1990) *Dragons in Distress: Asia's Miracle Economies in Crisis*, San Francisco, CA: Institute for Food and Development Policy.

Bemidji Statement on Seventh Generation Guardianship, Guardians of the Future, <www.guardiansofthe future.org/bemidji>, accessed 10 December 2007.

Benach, J., Y. Yasui, J. M. Martinez, C. Barrell, M. I. Pasarin and A. Daponte (2004) 'The geography of the highest mortality areas in Spain: a striking cluster in the southwestern region of the country', *Occupational and Environmental Medicine*, 61: 280–81.

Blowers, A. (1997) 'Environmental policy: ecological modernization or risk society?', *Urban Studies*, 34(5–6): 864–71.

— (1999) 'Radioactive waste: an inescapable legacy', in M. J. Smith (ed.), *Thinking through the Environment*, London: Routledge.

Blunden, J. (1999) 'Fresh water: a natural resource issue for the twenty-first century?', in M. J. Smith (ed.), *Thinking through the Environment*, London: Routledge.

Boehmer-Christiansen, S. and J. Skea (1991) 'Acid politics: environmental and energy policies in Britain and Germany', London: Belhaven.

Bromley, S. and M. J. Smith (2004) 'Transforming international order?', in W. Brown, S. Bromley and S. Athreye (eds), *Ordering the International: History, Change and Transformation*, Milton Keynes: Open University.

Bryson, V. (1999) *Feminist Debates: Issues of Theory and Political Practice*, Basingstoke: Macmillan.

Bullard, R. D. (1990) *Dumping in Dixie: Race, Class and Environmental Quality*, Boulder, CO: Westview Press.

Bullard, R. D. and S. Johnson (1997) *Just Transportation*, Gabriola Island, BC: Island Press.

Bullard, R. D., G. Johnson and A. Torres (2000) *Sprawl City: Race, Politics and Planning in Atlanta*, Washington, DC: Island Press.

Burawoy, M., A. Burton, A. Ferguson, K. J. Fox, J. Gamson, N. Gartrell, L. Hurst, C. Kurzman, L. Salzinger, J. Schiffman and S. Ui (1991), *Ethnography Unbound: Power and Resistance in the Modern Metropolis*, Berkeley: University of California Press.

Burningham, K. and M. O'Brien (1994) 'Global environmental values and local contexts of action', *Sociology*, 28: 913–32.

Burningham, K. and D. Thrush (2001) *Rainforests are a Long Way from Here: The Environmental Concerns of Disadvantaged Groups*, York: York Publishing Services Ltd.

Cahoone, L. (2004) 'Hunting: personal predation in civilised society', Paper presented to the Eighth Annual Meeting of the International Association of Philosophers, October.

Cairns, S., L. Sloman, C. Newson, J. Anable, A. Kirkbride and P. Goodwin (2004) 'Smarter choices. 1: Changing the way we travel', 'Sustainable Travel' section of <www.dft.gov.uk>, London: Department for Transport.

Callicott, J. B. (1992) 'La nature est morte, vive la nature!', *Hastings Center Report*, 2(5) (September–October), 16–23.

Caney, S. (2001) 'International distributive justice', *Political Studies* 49(5): 974–7.

Castells, M. (2000) *The Rise of the Network Society*, 2nd edn, Oxford: Blackwell.

CEM (Campaign for Ethical Marketing) (2005) <www.babymilkaction. org/pdfs/cemdec05.pdf>, accessed 25 March 2008.

Chesterton, G. K. (1908) American Chesterton Society, <www. chesterton.org>, accessed 1 July 2007.

Chin, C. B. N. (1998) *In Service and Servitude*, Columbia, NY: Columbia University Press.

Christian, J. J. (1983) 'Love Canal's unhealthy voles', *Natural History*, 8: 8–16.

Christoff, P. (1996) 'Ecological citizens and ecologically guided democracy', in B. Doherty and M. de Geus (eds), *Democracy and Green Political Thought: Sustainability, Rights and Citizenship*, London: Routledge.

Clark, A. (2001) *Diplomacy of Conscience: Amnesty International and Changing Human Rights Norms*, Princeton, NJ: Princeton University Press.

Clarke, N. (2002) 'The demon seed: bioinvasion as the unsettling of environmental cosmopolitanism', *Theory Culture & Society*, 19(1–2): 101–26.

Cole, L. W. and S. R. Foster (2001) *From the Ground Up: Environmental Racism and the Rise of the Environmental Justice Movement*, New York: New York University Press.

Commission on Racial Justice of the United Church of Christ (1987) *Toxic Waste and Race in the United States*, in D. E. Newton (1996), *Environmental Justice: A Reference Handbook*, Santa Barbara, CA: ABC-CLIO Inc., pp. 20–21.

Committee for Asian Women (1998) *Dolls and Dust*, Kowloon, Hong Kong.

Connolly, J. (2006) 'The virtues of environmental citizenship', in A. Dobson and D. Bell (eds), *Environmental Citizenship*, Cambridge, MA: MIT Press.

Conservation Law Foundation (1998) *City Routes, City Right: Building Livable Neighborhoods and Environmental Justice by Fixing Transportation*, Boston, MA: Conservation Law Foundation.

Cooper, T. and S. Evans (2000) 'Products to services', Report for Friends of the Earth, Centre for Sustainable Consumption, London: Sheffield Hallam University.

Cotgrove, S. and S. Duff (1981) 'Environmentalism, values and social change', *British Journal of Sociology*, XXXII(1): 92–110.

Crossley, N. (2002) *Making Sense of Social Movements*, Milton Keynes: Open University Press.

Couldry, N. (2006) 'Culture and citizenship: the missing link?', *European Journal of Cultural Studies*, 9(3): 321–39.

Council of Europe (2000) *European Landscape Convention*, European Landscape Convention, <www.coe.int/t/e/cultural_co-operation/environment/landscape/presentation/9_text/02_convention_en.asp#P29_977>, accessed 8 January 2007.

Curtin, D. (1999) *Chinnagounder's Challenge: The Question of Ecological Citizenship*, Bloomington: Indiana University Press.

Dahrendorf, R. (1959) *Class and Class Conflict in Industrial Society*, London: Routledge.

Dales, J. H. (1968) *Pollution, Property and Prices: An Essay in Policy-Making and Economics*, Toronto: University of Toronto Press.

Damon, W. (2004) *The Moral Advantage: How to Succeed in Business by Doing the Right Thing*, San Francisco, CA: Berrett-Koehler Publishers.

Dawson, G. (2001) 'Governing the European macroeconomy', in G. Thompson (ed.), *Governing the European Economy*, London: Sage/Open University.

DEFRA (2006) 'UK signs European

Landscape Convention', Department for Environment, Food and Rural Affairs, <www.defra.gov.uk/news/2006/060224a.htm>, accessed 8 February 2007.

Deleuze, G. and F. Guattari (1987) 'A thousand plateaus: capitalism and Schizo 22', *Environments*, 33(3).

— (1994) *What is Philosophy?*, New York: Columbia University Press.

Devall, B. and G. Sessions (1985) *Deep Ecology*, Utah: Peregrine Smith Books.

Diamond, J. (2003) 'The last Americans: environmental collapse and the end of civilization', *Harper's*, June.

Dobson, A. (2003a) *Citizenship and the Environment*, Oxford: Oxford University Press.

— (2003b) 'Social justice and environmental sustainability: ne'er the twain shall meet?', in J. Agyeman, R. D. Bullard and B. Evans, *Just Sustainabilities: Development in an Unequal World*, London: Earthscan.

— (2003/04) 'Educating environmental citizens', *Society Matters*, 6, Autumn/Winter, Milton Keynes: Open University, <www.open.ac.uk/socialsciences/about-the-faculty/society-matters/society-matters.php>.

Dobson, A. and D. Bell (eds) (2006) *Environmental Citizenship*, Cambridge, MA: MIT Press.

Doppelt, B. (2003) *Leading Change toward Sustainability: A Change-Management Guide for Business, Government and Civil Society*, Sheffield: Greenleaf Publishing.

Douglas, M. (1996) *Purity and Danger: An Analysis of Pollution and Taboo*, London: Routledge.

Dryzek, J. S. (1997) *Politics of the Earth: Environmental Discourses*, Oxford: Oxford University Press.

Eckerberg, K. and W. Lafferty (1998) 'Comparative perspectives on evaluation and explanation', in W. M. Lafferty and K. Eckerberg (eds), *From the Earth Summit to Local Agenda 21: Working towards Sustainable Development*, London: Earthscan.

Edelstein, M. (1989) 'Psychosocial impacts on trial: the case of hazardous waste disposal', in D. L. Peck (ed.), *Psychosocial Effects of Hazardous Toxic Waste Disposal on Communities*, Springfield, IL: Charles C. Thomas Publishers.

Engel, D. M. (2007) 'Globalization and the decline of legal consciousness: torts, ghosts, and karma in Thailand', *Thailand Law Journal*, (10)1.

Environment Agency (2003) *Environmental Quality and Social Deprivation*, Technical Report to R&D Project 12615.

Esping-Anderson, G. and M. Regini (eds) (2000) *Why Deregulate Labour Markets?*, Oxford: Oxford University Press.

ETF (Ecumenical Task Force of the Niagara Frontier Love Canal Collection) (1998) 'Annual report: 1985–1986 – Ecumenical Task Force of the Niagara Frontier', University Archives, University Libraries, Buffalo, NY: State University, pp. 3–8.

European Parliament (2006) 'Parliament adopts REACH – new EU chemicals legislation and new chemicals agency', European Parliament-Environment, 13 December, <www.europarl.europa.eu/news/expert/infopress_page/064-1496-345-12-50-911-20061213IPR01493-11-12-

2006-2006-true/default_en.htm>, accessed 1 September 2007.

Evangelista, O. L. (1998) 'Biography of Sophon Suphapong', Ramon Magsaysay Award Foundation, <www.rmaf.org.ph/Awardees/ Biography/BiographySuphapong Sop.htm>.

Evans, B., M. Joas, S. Sundback and K. Theobald (2005) *Governing Sustainable Cities*, London: Earthscan.

Fahn, J. D. (2003) *A Land on Fire: The Environmental Consequences of the Southeast Asian Boom*, Boulder, CO: Westview Press.

Fishman, C. (2006) *The Wal-Mart Effect: How the World's Most Powerful Company Really Works – and How It's Transforming the American Economy*, New York: Penguin.

Fletcher, T. H. (2003) *From Love Canal to Environmental Justice: The Politics of Hazardous Waste on the Canada–US Border*, Peterborough, Ont.: Broadview Press.

Foek, A. (1997) *Sweatshop Barbie: Dynamics Factory in Thailand*, January/February, <www.hartford-hwp.com/archives/54/086.html>, accessed 8 August 2007.

Forsyth, T. (2001) 'Environmental social movements in Thailand: how important is class?', *Asian Journal of Social Sciences*, 29(1): 35–51.

— (2002a) 'Environmental social movements in Thailand: a critical assessment', *Asian Review*, 15: 106–27.

— (2002b) 'What happened on *The Beach*? Social movements and governance of tourism in Thailand', *International Journal of Sustainable Development*, 5(3): 326–37.

— (2004) 'Social movements and environmental democratization in Thailand', in S. Jasanoff and M. Long (eds), *Earthy Politics: Local and Global in Environmental Governance*, Cambridge, MA: MIT Press.

— (2007a) 'Are environmental social movements socially exclusive? An historical study from Thailand', *World Development* (forthcoming).

— (2007b) 'Sustainable livelihood approaches and soil erosion risks: who is to judge?', *International Journal of Social Economics*, 34(1/2): 88–102.

Forsyth, T. and C. Johnson (2002) 'In the eyes of the state: negotiating a "rights-based approach" to forest conservation in Thailand', *World Development*, 30(9): 1591–605.

Foucault, M. (1980) *Power/Knowledge: Selected Interviews and Other Writings 1972–1977*, Brighton: Harvester Press.

— (1982) 'The subject and power', in H. L. Dreyfus and P. Rabinow (eds), *Michel Foucault: Beyond Structuralism and Hermeneutics*, Brighton: Harvester Press.

Fraser, N. and L. Gordon (1994) 'Civil citizenship against social citizenship? On the idea of contract versus charity', in B. van Steenbergen (ed.), *The Condition of Citizenship*, London: Sage.

Freeden, M. (1996) *Ideology and Political Theory*, Oxford: Oxford University Press.

Fuji Xerox (2004a) 'Fuji Xerox environmental activities', <www.fujixerox.co.jp/eng/ecology/index.html>, accessed 18 August 2007.

— (2004b) 'Fuji Xerox formulates environmental, health and safety requirements for paper procurement: toward universal procurement standards in accord with Europe and the United States', 30 November, <www.fujixerox.co.jp/eng/headline/2004/1207_paper_procurement.html>.

— (2006) 'Interview with the engineer vol. 3, Repelle System – recycling system for a recycling-oriented society', 23 February, <www.fujixerox.co.jp/eng/company/technical/interview/recycle/index.html>, accessed 31 August 2007.

Ganjanapan, A. (2000) *Local Control of Land and Forest: Cultural Dimensions of Resource Management in Northern Thailand*, Regional Centre for Social Science and Sustainable Development, Chiang Mai: Chiang Mai University.

Ganjanapan, S. (1997) 'Indigenous and scientific concepts of forest and land classification in northern Thailand', in P. Hirsch (ed.), *Seeing Forests for Trees: Environment and Environmentalism in Thailand*, Chiang Mai: Silkworm Books.

GCM (Global Community Monitor) (2005) 'Thailand's air: poison cocktail – exposing unsustainable industries and the case for community right to know and prevention', Campaign for Alternative Industry Network, Greenpeace Southeast Asia, Global Community Monitor, October, <www.bucketbrigade.net/downloads/thailand_toxic_cocktail.pdf>, accessed 25 March 2008.

GECP (2000) *Risky Choices, Soft Disasters: Environmental Decision Making under Uncertainty*, Global Environmental Change Programme of the Economic and Social Research Council, Brighton, April, also at <www.gecko.ac.uk>.

Gibbons, M., C. Limoges, H. Nowotny, S. Schwartzman, P. Scott and M. Trow (1994) *The New Production of Knowledge: The Dynamics of Science and Research in Contemporary Societies*, London: Sage.

Gibbs, L. M. (2006) '25 years of an inspirational journey: from Love Canal to the nation', Bioneers Conference plenary presentation, Marin Center, San Rafael, CA, 20 October.

Giddens, A. (1990) *The Consequences of Modernity*, Cambridge: Polity Press.

Gleckman, H. and R. Krut (1998) *A Missed Opportunity for Sustainable Global Industrial Development*, Stylus Publishing.

Goodpaster, K. (1983) 'On being morally considerable', in D. Scherer and T. Attig (eds), *Ethics and the Environment*, Englewood Cliffs, NJ: Prentice Hall.

Grahl, J. (2001) '"Social Europe" and the governance of labour relations', in G. Thompson (ed.), *Governing the European Economy*, London: Sage/Open University.

Grant, W. (2000) *Pressure Groups and British Politics*, London: Palgrave-Macmillan.

Greenberg, C. (1997) 'The varied responses to an environmental crisis in the Extended Bangkok Metropolitan Region', in P. Hirsch (ed.), *Seeing Forests for Trees: Environment and Environmentalism in Thailand*, Chiang Mai: Silkworm Books.

Greenpeace (2007) 'Waste survey exposes extent of plastic pollution in Manila Bay,' <www.greenpeace.org/seasia/en/press/releases/waste-survey-exposes-extent-of#>, accessed 15 August 2007.

Greiner, T., M. Rossi, B. Thorpe and

B. Kerr (2006) *Healthy Business Strategies for Transforming the Toxic Chemical Economy*, A Clean Production Action Report, Montreal.

Guttal, S. (2000) 'Public consultation and participation in the Nam Theun 2 hydroelectric project in the Lao PDR', International Rivers Network, <www.irn.org/programs/mekong/shalmaliwcd0904.pdf>, accessed 21 August 2007.

Guttal, S. and B. Shoemaker (2004) 'Manipulating consent: the World Bank and public consultation in the Nam Theun 2 hydroelectric project', *Watershed*, 10(1).

Hajer, M. A (1995) *The Politics of Environmental Discourse: Ecological Modernisation and the Policy Porcess*, Oxford: Clarendon Press.

— (1996) 'Ecological modernization as cultural politics', in S. Lash, B. Szerszynski and B. Wynne (eds), *Risk Environment and Modernity: Towards a New Ecology*, London: Sage.

Hall, P. (1986) *Governing the Economy: The Politics of State Intervention in Britain and France*, Cambridge: Polity.

Haugestad, A. (2003) 'The Dugnad: sustainable development and sustainable consumption in Norway', Paper presented at the 6th Nordic Conference on Environmental Social Sciences, <www.home.online.no/~akhauges/docs/Ppr6.doc>, accessed 8 October 2006.

Havel, V. (2007) 'Our moral footprint', *New York Times*, 27 September.

Hawken, P., A. Lovens and L. H. Lovens (1999) *Natural Capitalism: Creating the Next Industrial Revolution*, London: Earthscan.

Hay, B. L., R. N. Stavins and R. H. K.

Vietor (eds) (2005) *Environmental Protection and the Social Responsibility of Firms: Perspectives from Law, Economics, and Business*, Washington, DC: Resources for the Future Press.

Hayek, F. A. (1960) *The Constitution of Liberty*, London: Routledge.

Heffernan, R. (2001) 'Building the European Union', in S. J. Bromley (ed.), *Governing the European Union*, London: Sage/Open University.

Held, D. (2002) 'Globalization, corporate practice and cosmopolitan social standards', *Contemporary Political Theory*, 1(1): 59–78.

Heller, A. (1987) *Beyond Justice*, Oxford: Blackwell.

Hill, A. B. (1965) 'The environment and disease: association or causation?', *Proceedings of the Royal Society of Medicine*, 58: 295–300.

Hirsch, P. (1997) *Seeing Forests for Trees: Environment and Environmentalism in Thailand*, Chiang Mai: Silkworm Books.

— (1998) 'Community forestry revisited: messages from the periphery', in M. Victor, C. Lang and J. Bornemeier (eds), *Community Forestry at a Crossroads: Reflections and Future Directions in the Development of Community Forestry*, Bangkok: RECOFTC.

Hirsch, P. and L. Lohmann (1989) 'The contemporary politics of environment in Thailand', *Asian Survey*, 29(4): 439–51.

Hirschmann, N. J. (1996) 'Rethinking obligation for feminism', in N. J. Hirschmann and C. Stegano (eds), *Revisioning the Political: Feminist Reconstructions of Traditional Concepts in Western Political Theory*, Boulder, CO: Westview Press, pp. 157–80.

Huber, J. (1982) *Die Verlorene Unschuld der Okologie* (The Lost Innocence of Ecology), Frankfurt am Main: Fischer Verlag.

Humphreys, D. (1999) 'Forest policy: justice within and between generations', in M. J. Smith (ed.), *Thinking through the Environment*, London: Routledge.

Humphreys, D. R. (2007) *Logjam: Deforestation and the Crisis of Global Governance*, London: Earthscan.

Ignatieff, M. (1995) 'The myth of citizenship', in R. Beiner (ed.), *Theorizing Citizenship*, Albany: State University of New York Press.

Imhof, A. and S. Lawrence (2005) 'An analysis of Nam Theun 2 compliance with World Commission on Dams strategic priorities', Joint paper for International Rivers Network/Environmental Defense, <www.irn.org/programs/mekong/pdf/namtheun/NT2WCDExec-Summary2005.pdf>, accessed 30 August 2007.

— (2006) 'Letter to World Bank and Asian Development Bank', Joint response of the International Rivers Network and Environmental Defense, 7 February.

Irwin, A. (1995) *Citizen Science: A Study of People, Expertise and Sustainable Development*, London: Routledge.

Isin, E. F. (2000) *Democracy, Citizenship and the Global City*, London: Routledge.

— (2002) *Being Political: Genealogies of Citizenship*, Minneapolis: University of Minnesota Press.

— (forthcoming) 'Citizenship in flux: sites, scales, and acts'.

Isin, E. F. and G. M. Nielsen (eds) (2008) 'Introduction: Acts of Citizenship', in E. F. Isin and G. M. Nielsen (eds), *Acts of Citizenship*, London: Zed Books.

Isin, E. F. and B. S. Turner (eds) (2002) *Handbook of Citizenship Studies*, London: Sage.

Jacob, M. and T. Hellstrom (eds) (2000) *The Future of Knowledge Production in the Academy*, Buckingham: Society for Research into Higher Education/Open University Press.

James, W. (1890) *The Principles of Psychology*, vol. II, New York: Holt.

Janicke, M. (1985) *Preventive Environmental Policy as Ecological Modernisation and Structural Policy*, Berlin: Wissenschaftszentrum.

Jenkins, R., R. Pearson and G. Seyfang (2002) *Corporate Responsibility and Labour Rights: Codes of Conduct in the Global Economy*, London: Earthscan.

Jose, A. V. (ed.) (2002) *Organized Labour in the 21st Century*, International Institute for Labour Studies, Geneva: International Labour Organization.

Kaplan, A. (1964) *The Conduct of Inquiry*, New York: Chandler Publishing.

Karen, K. and S. Karen (2007) 'EGAT resumes Hat Gyi Dam studies', *Mizzima News*, 19 July, <www.mizzima.com/MizzimaNews/News/2007/July/44-July-2007.html>, accessed 10 September 2007.

Kavka, G. and V. Warren (1983) 'Political representation for future generations', in R. Elliot and A. Gare (eds), *Environmental Philosophy*, Milton Keynes: Open University Press.

Keck, M. E. and K. Sikkink (1998) *Activists beyond Borders: Advocacy Networks in International Politics*,

Ithaca, NY: Cornell University Press.

Kell, G. (2003) 'Guide to the Global Compact: a practical understanding of the vision and Nine Principles', United Nations, <www.uneptie.org/outreach/compact/docs/gcguide.pdf>, accessed 8 February 2007.

King, Y. (1989) 'The ecology of feminism and the feminism of ecology', in J. Plant (ed.), *Healing the Wounds: The Promise of Ecofeminism*, Philadelphia, PA: New Society.

Kirk, G. and M. Okazawa-Rey (2006) *Women's Lives: Multicultural Perspectives*, 4th edn, New York: McGraw-Hill.

Knorr-Cetina, K. (1981) *The Manufacture of Knowledge*, Oxford: Pergamon.

Koo, H. (2001) *Korean Workers: The Culture and Politics of Class Formation*, Ithaca, NY: Cornell University Press.

Korten, D. C. (1995) *When Corporations Rule the World*, West Hartford, CT: Kumarian Press.

Kousis, M. (1997) 'Grassroots environmental movements in rural Greece: effectiveness, success and the quest for sustainable development', in S. Baker, M. Kousis, D. Richardson and S. Young (eds), *The Politics of Sustainable Development: Theory, Policy and Practice within the European Union*, London: Routledge.

Krasner, S. D. (1983) *International Regimes*, Ithaca, NY: Cornell University Press.

Kruger to Canyons Biosphere (2007) 'Bridge construction impedes Peace Park progress', <www.kruger2canyons.com/2006/04/bridge-construction-impedes-

peace-park.htm>, accessed 9 June 2007.

Kuhn, T. (1970) *The Structure of Scientific Revolutions*, 2nd edn, Chicago, IL: University of Chicago Press.

Kymlicka, W. (1995) *Multicultural Citizenship*, Oxford: Oxford University Press.

Kymlicka, W. and W. Norman (eds) (2000) *Citizenship in Diverse Societies*, Oxford: Oxford University Press.

Lafferty, W. M. and K. Eckerberg (eds) (1998) *From the Earth Summit to Local Agenda 21: Working towards Sustainable Development*, London: Earthscan.

Lakatos, I. (1970) 'Falsification and the methodology of scientific research programmes', in I. Lakatos and A. Musgrave (eds), *Criticism and the Growth of Knowledge*, Cambridge: Cambridge University Press.

Lang, M. T. (2003) 'Tai Ban research: local knowledge as negotiation in the policy process', *Thailand Human Rights Journal*, 1: 227–36.

Latour, B. and S. Woolgar (1978) *Laboratory Life*, Princeton, NJ: University of Princeton Press.

Laungaramsri, P. (2002) 'Competing discourses and practices of "Civil Society": a reflection on the environmental movement in Thailand and some implications for the Mekong Region', Presented at the Mekong Dialogue Workshop International transfer of river basin development experience: Australia and the Mekong Region, 2 September, Regional Centre for Sustainable Development and Social Science, Faculty of Social Sciences, Chiang Mai: Chiang Mai University.

Bibliography

Ledgerwood, G. and A. Broadhurst (1999) *Environment, Ethics and the Corporation*, Basingstoke: Macmillan.

Lee, C. K. (2006) *Working in China: Ethnographies of Labor and Workplace Transformation (Asia's Transformations)*, London: Routledge.

— (2007) *Against the Law: Labor Protests in China's Rustbelt and Sunbelt*, Berkeley: University of California Press.

Leipziger, D. (2003) *The Corporate Responsibility Code Book*, Sheffield: Greenleaf Publishing.

Leipziger, D. and E. Kaufman (2003) 'SA 8000: human rights in the workplace', in R. Sullivan, *Business and Human Rights: Dilemmas and Solutions I*, Sheffield: Greenleaf Publishing.

Leopold, A. (1949) *A Sand County Almanac – and Sketches Here and There*, Oxford: Oxford University Press.

Lévi-Strauss, C. (1963) *Structural Anthropology*, New York: Basic Books.

Lichtenberg, J. (1981) 'National boundaries and moral boundaries: a cosmopolitan view', in P. Brown and H. Shue (eds), *Boundaries: National Autonomy and Its Limits*, New Jersey: Rowman and Littlefield.

Liefferink, D. and M. K. Anderson (1998) 'Greening the EU: national positions in the run-up to the Amsterdam Treaty', *Environmental Politics*, 7(3): 66–93.

Linklater, A. (1998) *The Transformation of Political Community: Ethical Foundations of the Post-Westphalian Era*, Cambridge: Polity Press.

Lisansky, J. (2005) 'Fostering change for Brazil's indigenous people: the role of the pilot programme,' in A. Hall (ed.), *Global Impact Local Action: New Environmental Policy in Latin America*, London: Institute for the Study of the Americas.

Litvin, D. (2003) *Empires of Profit: Commerce, Conquest and Corporate Responsibility*, New York: Texere.

Lord, C. (2001) 'Democracy and democratization in the European Union', in S. Bromley (ed.), *Governing the European Union*, London: Sage/Open University.

Lovelock, J. E. (2000) *Gaia: A New Look at Life on Earth*, Oxford: Oxford University Press.

Lowe, P. and S. Ward (eds) (1998) *British Environmental Policy and Europe: Politics and Policy in Transition*, London: Routledge.

MacGregor, S. (2006) *Beyond Mothering Earth: Ecological Citizenship and the Politics of Care*, Vancouver: University of British Columbia Press.

McIntosh, M., S. Waddock and G. Kell (eds) (2004) *Learning to Talk: Corporate Citizenship and the Development of the UN Global Compact*, Sheffield: Greenleaf Publishing.

Malinas, G. (1980) 'On justifying and excusing coercion', in D. Mannison, M. McRobbie and R. Routley (eds), *Environmental Philosophy*, Canberra: ANU Publication.

Maneepong, C. (2006) 'Regional policy thinking and industrial development in Thai border towns', *Labour and Management in Development Journal*, 6(4), Asia Pacific Press, Australian National University.

Mannison, D., M. McRobbie and R. Routley (eds), *Environmental*

Philosophy, Canberra: ANU Publications.

Markham, A. (1994) *A Brief History of Pollution*, London: Earthscan.

Marshall, T. H. (1950) *Citizenship and Social Class, and Other Essays*, Cambridge: Cambridge University Press.

Martell, L. (1994) *Ecology and Society*, Cambridge: Polity Press.

Martinez-Alier, J. (2002) *The Environmentalism of the Poor: A Study of Ecological Conflicts and Valuation*, Cheltenham: Edward Elgar.

Meadows, D. H., D. L. Meadows, J. Randers and W. Behrens (1972) *The Limits to Growth: A Report for the Club of Rome's Project on the Predicament of Mankind*, London: Pan.

Meens, R. (1995) 'Pollution in the early middle ages', *Early Medieval Europe*, 4(1): 3–19.

Melucci, A. (1989) *Nomads of the Present: Social Movements and Individual Needs in Contemporary Society*, London: Radius.

Mewes, H. (1998) 'A brief history of the German Green Party', in M. Mayer and J. Ely (eds), *The German Greens: Paradox between Movement and Party*, Philadelphia, PA: Temple University Press.

Mez, L. (1998) 'Who votes green? Sources and trends of green support', in M. Mayer and J. Ely (eds), *The German Greens: Paradox between Movement and Party*, Philadelphia, PA: Temple University Press.

Midgeley, M. (1996) *Utopias, Dolphins and Computers: Problems in Philosophical Plumbing*, London: Routledge.

Mies, M. and V. Shiva (1992) *Ecofeminism*, London: Zed Books.

Mills, T. A. (2007) 'Russia goes for Pole at ice station Putin', *Sunday Times*, 5 August, <www.timesonline.co.uk/tol/news/world/europe/article2199335.ece>, accessed 25 March 2008.

Missingham, B. (2003) 'Forging solidarity and identity in the Assembly of the Poor: from local struggles to a national social movement in Thailand', *Asian Studies Review*, 27(3), September.

Mitchell, L. E. (2004) *Corporate Irresponsibility: America's Newest Export*, New Haven, CT: Yale University Press.

Molle, F. and P. Floche (2007) 'Water, poverty and the governance of megaprojects: the Thai water grid', Mekong Programme on Water Environment and Resilience, <www.mpowernet.org/download_pubdoc.php?doc=3271>, accessed 10 January 2007.

Mouffe, C. (ed.) (1992) *Dimensions of Radical Democracy: Pluralism, Citizenship, Community*, London: Verso.

— (2000) *The Democratic Paradox*, London: Verso.

— (2005) *On the Political*, London: Routledge.

Muir, J. (1901) *Our National Parks*, Boston, MA: Houghton Mifflin.

Mulkay, M. (1991) *Sociology of Science: A Sociological Pilgrimage*, Buckingham: Open University Press.

Mullally, G. (1998) 'Ireland: does the road from Rio lead back to Brussels?', in W. M. Lafferty and K. Eckerberg (eds), *From the Earth Summit to Local Agenda 21: Working towards Sustainable Development*, London: Earthscan.

Naess, A. (1973) 'The shallow and the deep, long-range ecology movement', *Inquiry*, 16: 95–100.

Newton, D. E. (1996) *Environmental Justice: A Reference Handbook*, Santa Barbara, CA: ABC-CLIO Inc.

Nijhuis, M. (2007) 'Dead end: the borderlands', *Audubon*, 109(5): 64–70.

Norton, B. G. (2003) *Searching for Sustainability: Interdisciplinary Essays in the Philosophy of Conservation Biology*, Cambridge: Cambridge University Press.

Novak, M. (2002) 'The moral heart of capitalism', Opening remarks to a panel on corporate responsibility at President Bush's Economic Forum in Waco, Texas, 10 September, *The Insider*, <www.insideronline.org/archives/2002/nov_dec02/moral_heart.pdf>.

Nowotny, H., P. Scott and M. Gibbons (2001) *Re-thinking Science: Knowledge and the Public in an Age of Uncertainty*, Cambridge: Polity Press.

O'Neill, J. (1993) *Ecology, Policy and Politics*, London: Routledge.

O'Riordan, T. (1981) *Environmentalism*, London: Prion Press.

O'Riordan, T. and H. Voisey (eds) (1998) *The Transition to Sustainability: The Politics of Agenda 21 in Europe*, London: Earthscan.

O'Rourke, D. and G. P. Macey (2003) 'Community environmental policing: assessing new strategies of public participation in environmental regulation', *Journal of Policy Analysis and Management*, 22(3): 383–414.

Paine, L. S. (2003) *Value Shift: Why Companies Must Merge Social and Financial Imperatives to Achieve Superior Performance*, New York: McGraw-Hill.

Pangsapa, P. (2007) *Textures of Struggle: The Emergence of Resistance among Garment Workers in Thailand*, Ithaca, NY: ILR Press.

Pangsapa, P. and M. J. Smith (2008a) 'The political economy of Southeast Asian borderlands: migration, environment, and developing-country firms', *Journal of Contemporary Asia*, forthcoming, 38(4).

— (2008b) *Responsible Politics: Bringing Together Labor Standards, Environment, and Human Rights in the Global Corporate Economy*, New York: Palgrave Macmillan.

Peace Parks Foundation (2007a) 'What are peace parks/TFCAs?', <www.peaceparks.org>, accessed 9 June 2007.

— (2007b) 'Great Limpopo overview', <www.peaceparks.org/pdf.php?mid=164&pid=147>, accessed 9 June 2007.

Pearce, F. (2003) 'Rhino rescue plan decimates Asian antelopes', *New Scientist*, 12 February, <www.newscientist.com/channel/life/endangered-species/dn3376>, accessed 30 August 2007.

Pepper, D. (1996) *Modern Environmentalism*, London: Routledge.

Perlez, J. and R. Bonner (2005) 'Below a mountain of wealth, a river of waste', *New York Times*, <www.nytimes.com/2005/12/27/international/asia/27gold.html?ex=1293339600&en=fba5e5cb62 6e7d5c&ei=5088&partner=rssnyt &emc=rss>, accessed 8 November 2007.

Pfirrman, C. and D. Kron (1992) *Environment and NGOs in Thailand*, Thai NGO Support Project and Friedrich Naumann Stiftung, Bangkok.

Phongpaichit, P. and C. Baker (1998) *Thailand's Boom and Bust*, Chiang Mai: Silkworm Books.

— (2004) *Thaksin: The Business of Politics in Thailand*, Chiang Mai: Silkworm Books.

Pinchot, G. (1901) *The Fight for Conservation*, New York: Harcourt Brace.

Porter, G. and J. W. Brown (1991) *Global Environmental Politics*, Boulder, CO: Westview Press.

Prokhovnik, R. (1998) 'Public and private citizenship: from gender invisibility to feminist inclusiveness', *Feminist Review*, 60: 84–104.

Prügl, E. M. (1999) 'What is a worker? Gender, global restructuring, and the ILO Convention on Homework', in M. K. Meyer and E. M. Prügl (eds), *Gender Politics in Global Governance*, Lanham, MD: Rowman & Littlefield.

Pun, N. (2005) *Made in China: Women Factory Workers in a Global Workplace*, Durham, NC: Duke University Press.

Rachel's Environment and Health News (1998) 'The Precautionary Principle', 19 February, <www.rachel.org/bulletin/index.cfm?St=2>, accessed 10 October 2007.

Rawls, J. (1993) *Political Liberalism*, New York: Columbia University Press.

— (1999) *Theory of Justice*, Cambridge, MA: Belknap Press.

Rees, S. and S. W. Wright (2000) *Human Rights, Corporate Responsibility*, Sydney: Pluto Press.

Regan, T. (1984) 'The case for animal rights', in P. Singer (ed.), *Applied Ethics*, Oxford: Oxford University Press.

Regional Institute (2000) 'Equity 9.10 residential segregation', University of New York at Buffalo, <http://regional-institute.buffalo.edu/sotr/Indicator.cfm?Indicator=6c1ff8dd-6da1-4-ce4-aa8c-bfa9f1ab206c>, accessed 9 January 2007.

Reisenberg, P. (1992) *Citizenship in the Western Tradition: Plato to Rousseau*, Chapel Hill: University of North Carolina Press.

Richter, J. (2001) *Holding Corporations Accountable: Corporate Conduct, International Codes, and Citizen Action*, London and Sterling, VA: Zed Books.

Riska, G. (1999) 'NGOs in the GMS: involvement related to poverty alleviation and watershed management', Regional Environmental Technical Assistance 5771, Poverty Reduction & Environmental Management in Remote Greater Mekong Subregion (GMS) Watersheds Project (Phase 1).

Ritzer, G. (2008) *The McDonaldization of Society 5*, Thousand Oaks, CA: Pine Forge Press.

Roche, M. (1992) *Rethinking Citizenship: Welfare, Ideology and Change in Modern Society*, Cambridge: Polity Press.

Rodriguez-Garavito, C. A. (2005) 'Global governance and labor rights: codes of conduct and anti-sweatshop struggles in global apparel factories in Mexico and Guatemala', *Politics & Society*, 33(6): 203–33.

— (2007) 'Sewing resistance: globalization and labor transnationalism in the North American apparel commodity chain (1990–2005)', 102nd Annual American Sociological Association Meeting, New York City, 13 August.

Rolston, H., III (1988) *Environmental Ethics: Duties to and Values in the Natural World*, Philadelphia, PA: Temple University Press.

Rosenthal, S. B. (1999) *Rethinking*

Business Ethics: A Pragmatic Approach, Oxford: Oxford University Press.

Roth, R. and D. Murphy (1998) 'From competing factions to the rise of the realos', in M. Mayer and J. Ely (eds), *The German Greens: Paradox between Movement and Party*, Philadelphia, PA: Temple University Press.

Ryder, G. (2003) 'Behind the ASEAN power grid: analysis of the Asian Development Bank's master plan for regional power', Interconnections and Power Trade in the Greater Mekong Subregion, Energy Probe Research Foundation, Toronto, December.

Sadler, P. (2002) *Building Tomorrow's Company: A Guide to Sustainable Business Success*, London and Milford, CT: Kogan Page Business Books.

SAI (Social Accountability International) (2001) *Setting Standards for a Just World*, New York: SAI.

Samudavanija, C. (2002) *Thailand: State-building, Democracy and Globalization*, Bangkok: Institute of Public Policy Studies.

Saunders, P. (1993) 'Citizenship in a liberal society', in B. Turner (ed.), *Citizenship and Social Theory*, London: Sage.

— (1995) *Capitalism: A Social Audit*, Buckingham: Open University Press.

Schütz, A. (1932 [1967]) *The Phenomenology of the Social World*, Evanston, IL: Northwestern University Press.

— (1953) 'Common-sense and scientific interpretation of human action', *Philosophy and Phenomenological Research*, 14(1): 1–38.

Schwartz, P. and B. Gibb (1999) *When Good Companies Do Bad Things: Responsibility and Risk in an Age of Globalization*, New York: Wiley.

Scott, A. (1990) *Ideology and New Social Movements*, London: Unwin Hyman.

Scott, A., A. Stirling, N. Mabey, F. Berkhout, C. Williams, C. Rose, M. Jacobs, R. Grove-White, I. Scoones, I. and M. Leach (1999) 'Precautionary approach to risk assessment', *Nature*, 402, 25 November.

Scruton, R. (2004) 'First, skin your squirrel ...', *Guardian*, 14 April, <www.guardian.co.uk/g2/story/0,,1191223,00.html>, accessed 21 August 2007.

Seager, J. (1993) *Earth Follies: Feminism, Politics and the Environment*, Washington, DC: Island Press.

Sevenhuijsen, S. (1998) *Citizenship and the Ethics of Care: Feminist Considerations on Justice, Morality and Politics*, London: Routledge.

— (2000) 'Caring in the third way: the relation between obligation, responsibility and care in Third Way discourse', *Critical Social Policy*, 20(1): 5–37.

Shiva, V. (1989) *Staying Alive: Women, Ecology and Development*, London: Zed Books.

— (1992) 'The greening of global reach', *Ecologist*, 22(6): 258–9.

Shoemaker, B. (1999) 'NGOs and natural resource conflict: in whose interests?', *Watershed*, 4(2).

Sivaraksa, S. (2002) 'Assembly of the Poor: Siam's poor take action on their own behalf', Special feature on 'Engaged Buddhism', *Social Policy*, Fall.

Smith, M. J. (1998a) *Ecologism: Towards Ecological Citizenship*, Buckingham: Open University Press.

— (1998b) *Social Science in Question:*

Towards a Postdisciplinary Framework, London: Sage.

— (1999) 'Thinking through ecological citizenship', in M. J. Smith (ed.), *Thinking through the Environment*, London: Routledge.

— (2000a) *Rethinking State Theory*, London: Routledge.

— (2000b) *Culture: Reinventing the Social Sciences*, Buckingham: Open University Press.

— (2001) 'Rethinking normality through postdisciplinary practices: philosophies of pathology', in D. Hook and G. Eagle (eds), *Psychopathology and Social Prejudice*, Cape Town: University of Cape Town Press.

— (2005a) 'Territories of knowledge: the deterritorialization and reterritorialization of the social sciences', *International Studies in Philosophy*, 37(2): 159–80.

— (2005b) 'Obligation and ecological citizenship', *Environments*, 33(4): 9–23.

— (2008) 'Friends, adversaries and enemies: agonistic democracy and ecological citizenship', forthcoming.

Smith, M. J. and P. Pangsapa (2007) 'New controversies in phenomenology: between ethnography and discourse', in W. Outhwaite and S. Turner (eds), *The Sage Handbook of Social Science Methodology*, London: Sage.

— (2008) 'The political economy of borderlands: migration, environment, and the responsible conduct of developing-country firms on the Southeast Asian mainland', *Journal of Contemporary Asia*, forthcoming.

Sneddon, C. (2003) 'Reconfiguring scale and power: the Khong-Chi-Mun project in northeast Thailand', *Environment and Planning A*, 35(12): 2229–50.

Snell, D. (2007) 'Beyond workers' rights: transnational corporations, human rights abuse, and violent conflict in the Global South', in K. Bronfenbrenner (ed.), *Global Unions: Challenging Transnational Capital through Cross-Border Campaigns*, Ithaca, NY: ILR Press.

Social Exclusion Unit (2000) 'National strategy for neighbourhood renewal: minority ethnic issues in social exclusion and neighbourhood renewal', London: HMSO.

Sontag, S. (1989) *AIDS and Its Metaphors*, New York: Farrar, Straus & Giroux.

Soonok, C. (2003) *They are Not Machines: Korean Women Workers and Their Fight for Democratic Trade Unionism in the 1970s*, Burlington, VT: Ashgate.

Sriwanichpoom, M. (2003) *Protest*, Bangkok: Manit Sriwanichpoom.

Stead, J. G. and W. E. Stead (1992) *Management for a Small Planet: Strategic Decision Making and the Environment*, London: Sage.

Steegman, A. T., Jr (2001) 'History of Love Canal and SUNY at Buffalo's response: history, the university role, and health research', *Buffalo Environmental Law Journal*, 8(2): 174–94.

Steiger, U. (ed.) (2004) *Business of Sustainability: Building Industry Cases for Corporate Sustainability*, Basingstoke: Palgrave.

Stein, R. (2004) *New Perspectives on Environmental Justice: Gender, Sexuality, and Activism*, Rutgers, NJ: Rutgers University Press.

Stevenson, N. (ed.) (2001) *Culture and Citizenship*, London: Sage.

Bibliography

— (2003a) 'Cultural citizenship in the "cultural" society: a cosmopolitan approach', *Citizenship Studies*, 7(3): 331–48.

— (2003b) *Cultural Citizenship: Cosmopolitan Questions*, Buckingham: Open University Press.

— (2006) 'Technological citizenship: perspectives in the recent work of Manuel Castells and Paul Virilio', *Sociological Research Online*, 10(3).

Stone, C. D. (1972) 'Should trees have standing?', *Southern California Law Review*, 45(2): 450–501.

— (1987) *Earth and Other Ethics: A Practical Politics of the Environment*, London: Routledge.

Suzuki, N. (1996) 'The truth about The Body Shop', *Compass Online*, <www.tsujiru.net/compass/compass_1996/reg/suzuki_noriko.htm>, accessed 16 August 2007.

Swearer, D. K., S. Premchit and P. Dokbuakaew (2004) *Sacred Mountains of Northern Thailand and Their Legends*, Chiang Mai: Silkworm Books.

Tansubhapol, K. (1996) 'From austerity to prosperity', *Bangkok Post*, August.

Tantemsapya, N. (1997) 'Sustainable agriculture in Thailand', in P. Hirsch (ed.), *Seeing Forests for Trees: Environment and Environmentalism in Thailand*, Chiang Mai: Silkworm Books.

Taylor, A. (1992) *Choosing Our Future*, London: Routledge.

Taylor, J. (1997) 'Thamma-chat: activist monks and competing discourses of nature and nation in northeastern Thailand', in P. Hirsch (ed.), *Seeing Forests for Trees: Environment and Environmentalism in Thailand*, Chiang Mai: Silkworm Books.

Tesner, S. (2000) *UN and Business: A Partnership Recovered*, New York: St Martin's Press.

Tewari, M. and P. Pillai (2005) 'Global standards and the dynamics of environmental compliance in India's leather industry', *Oxford Development Studies*, 33(2): 245–67.

Thai Constitution Drafting Assembly and the Constitution Drafting Committee (2007) *Thai Draft Constitution 2007*, Thai Parliament, <www.parliament.go.th/parcy/sapa_db/sapa25-upload/25-20070517151204_2007.pdf>, accessed 10 March 2007.

Thompson, G. F. (2005) 'Global corporate citizenship: what does it mean?', Paper presented at the Open University, Milton Keynes.

Thongleua, S. and T. Castren (1999) 'Timber trade and wood flow-study Lao PDR', Mekong Info, <www.mekonginfo.org/mrc_en/doclib.nsf/0/E72071FDB8DE1819C725683400358BA7/$FILE/FULLTEXT.html>, accessed 7 April 2005.

Tilly, C. (1994) 'Social movements as historically specific clusters of political performances', *Berkeley Journal of Sociology*, 38: 1–30.

Trask, M. (1992) 'Native Hawaiian historical and cultural perspectives on environmental justice', in G. Kirk and M. Okazawa-Rey (2006), *Women's Lives: Multicultural Perspectives*, 4th edn, New York: McGraw-Hill.

Tulder, R. van and A. van der Zwart (2006) *International Business-Society Management: Linking Corporate Responsibility and Globalization*, London: Routledge.

United Nations (2003) 'The UN & Business: the Global Compact', <www.un.org/partners/business/

otherpages/factsheets/fs1.htm>,
accessed 2 October 2007.
United Nations Environmental
Programme (2000) 'Fuji
Xerox Australia, one of 14
individuals and organizations
to receive the United Nations
Environment Award', UNEP,
1 June, <www.unep.org/
Documents.Multilingual/Default.
asp?DocumentID=135&ArticleID=
2258&l=en>, accessed 8 October
2007.
United States Department of Justice
(2000) 'US DuPont settle environmental lawsuit over sulphuric acid
emergency in Kentucky', 1 August,
<www.usdoj.gov/opa/pr/2000/
August/443enrd.htm>, accessed
10 January 2007.
United States Environmental Protection Agency (2000) 'US, Dupont
settle environmental lawsuit over
sulphuric acid emergency in Kentucky', <www.epa.gov/Region4/
oeapages/00press/000801.htm>,
accessed 21 August 2007.
United States Environmental
Protection Agency and the New
York State Department of Environmental Conservation (2004)
'Reduction of toxic loadings to
the Niagara River from hazardous
waste sites in the United States',
Niagara River Toxics Management
Plan (NRTMP) report, June, <www.
epa.gov/glnpo/lakeont/nrtmp/
hwsreport2004.pdf>, accessed 2
September 2007.
University at Buffalo Regional
Institute (2002) '9.10 residential segregation', December,
<http://regional-institute.
buffalo.edu/sotr/Indicator.
cfm?Indicator=6c1ff8dd-6da1-4-
ce4-aa8c-bfa9f1ab206c>, accessed
2 September 2007.

Utting, P. (ed.) (2002) *The Greening of
Business in Developing Countries:
Rhetoric, Reality and Prospects*,
London: Zed Books.
Verchick, R. R. M. (2004) 'Feminist
theory and environmental justice',
in R. Stein (ed.), *New Perspectives
on Environmental Justice: Gender,
Sexuality, and Activism*, Rutgers,
NJ: Rutgers University Press.
Vogler, J. (2000) *The Global Commons:
Environmental and Technological
Governance*, 2nd edn, New York:
Wiley.
Vogler, J. and M. F. Imber (eds) (1996)
*The Environment and International
Relations*, London: Routledge.
Walker, G., J. Fairburn and K. Bick-
erstaff (2001) 'Ethnicity and risk:
the characteristics of populations
in census wards containing major
accident hazard sites in England
and Wales', Occasional Paper 15,
Department of Geography, Univer-
sity of Staffordshire.
Wanornsornrusri (2007)
'Protest on IRPC electrical
plant still goes on', *Pattaya
Daily News*, 10 September, <www.
pattayadailynews.com/shownews.
php?IDNEWS=0000003808>,
accessed 12 September 2007.
Waterman, P. (1998) *Globalization,
Social Movements and the New
Internationalisms*, London:
Mansell.
WCED (World Commission on
Environment and Development)
(1987) *Our Common Future*,
Oxford: Oxford University Press.
Weale, A., G. Pridham, M. Cini,
D. Konstadakopulos, M. Porter
and B. Flynn (eds) (2000)
*Environmental Governance in
Europe: An Ever Closer Ecological
Union?*, Oxford: Oxford University
Press.

Bibliography

WEF (World Economic Forum) (2003) 'Responding to the leadership challenge', Report developed by the World Economic Forum in partnership with the International Business Leaders Forum, January.

Welch, C. E., Jr (ed.) (2000) *NGOs and Human Rights: Promise and Performance*, Philadelphia: University of Pennsylvania Press.

— (2001) *Protecting Human Rights in Africa: Strategies and Roles of Nongovernmental Organizations*, Pennsylvania Studies in Human Rights, Philadelphia, PA: University of Pennsylvania Press.

Wen, D. (2005) *China Copes with Globalization: A Mixed Review*, San Francisco, CA: International Forum on Globalization.

— (2006) 'China needs an ecologized social democratic system', Interview by Walden Bello, 30 November, Amsterdam: Transnational Institute.

Westergaard, J. and H. Resler (1976) *Class in a Capitalist Society*, New York: Penguin.

Willis, P. and M. Trondman (2002) 'Manifesto for ethnography', *Cultural Studies = Critical Methodologies*, 2: 394–402.

Willmott, M. (2001) *Citizen Brands*, New York: John Wiley & Sons.

World Bank (2005) 'Laos secures $1 billion loans for dam project', *World Bank Press Review*, 4 May.

Xiao, S. (2000) 'TED case studies: face of the body, an insight into the cosmetic giant', Trade and Environment Database, <www.american.edu/TED/bodyshop.htm>, accessed 21 August 2007.

Young, I. M. (1990) *Justice and the Politics of Difference*, Princeton, NJ: Princeton University Press.

— (1995) 'Mother's citizenship and independence: a critique of pure family values', *Ethics*, 105(3): 535–56.

— (2006) 'Responsibility and global justice: a social connection model', *Social Philosophy and Policy*, 23: 102–30.

Young, R. (1980) 'Population policies, coercion and morality', in D. Mannison, M. McRobbie and R. Routley (eds), *Environmental Philosophy*, Canberra: ANU Publications.

Zadek, S. (2001) *The Civil Corporation: The New Economy of Corporate Citizenship*, London: Earthscan.

Index

borders: and environmental
management, 5, 175–208;
contested responsibilities, 205;
delineation of, 176; disputed,
176–7; locked, 177; Mexico-US
border fence, 175; porous, 177,
180 (in South-East Asia, 194–204);
rethinking of, 204–8; species
movement across, 176; symbolic
value of, 176
Boundary Waters Treaty (1909), 181,
185
BP-Amoco company, 164
Brabeck, Peter, 166, 172, 203
Brazil: child labour in, 172;
environmental movements in, 43;
indigenous peoples in, 46
breastfeeding, 166
Brundtland Report, 11, 33, 55
Bucket Brigades, 192–3, 222
Buddhism, 217, 243; Theravada, 211
Burawoy, Michael, 256, 259
Burgerinitiativen, 113
Burma, 160; logging in, 196; migrant
workers, 22–3, 202
businesses, as actors, 139
byssinosis, 122–3

CABWITH citizens, 79
cacao plantations, child labour in,
153–4
Caffe Nero company, 143
Callicott, J. Baird, 253
Calonzo, Manny, 125
Calspan Corporation, 15
Campaign for Alternative Industry
Network (CAIN), 222
Campaign for the Protection of Rural
England (CPRE), 112
Campaign to Save Niagara, 185
Canada, 181–9; environmental
legislation in, 184
Canada-Ontario Agreement
Respecting the Great Lakes Basin
Ecosystem (CAO), 185
Caney, Simon, 72
cap and trade systems, 144
carbon dioxide emissions, 99, 130
carbon sinks, 100

carbon trading, 95
Cargill company, 154
cars: use of, 63–4; rationing of traffic,
in China, 126
Carter, Jimmy, 18
CATNAP acronym, 149
Center for Health, Environment and
Justice (CHEJ) (USA), 19
Chemicals Agency (UK), 153
Chertoff, Michael, 176
Chesterton, G.K., 55
child labor, 153–4, 172, 228
Chilingarov, Artur, 90
Chin, Christine, 40
China, 3, 15, 122, 128, 136, 180, 201;
exemption from Kyoto protocol,
101; pollution in, 126; recycling
(of electronic equipment, 259; of
waste paper and plastics, 248);
timber clearance in, 81
Chulanont, Surayud, 238
China Centre for Legal Assistance to
Pollution Victims, 126
Chipko movement, 43
chlorofluorocarbons (CFCs), 15;
elimination of, 98
chloroform, 17, 222–3
citizen: reinvention of, 157–61; types
of, 73–5
citizen science, 11
citizenization, 4, 27–58
citizenly subject positions, 36
Citizens Clearing House for
Hazardous Waste, 19
citizenship, 71–2, 263; about
negative liberty, 31; active, 241;
and agonistic democracy, 32–6;
and environmental governance,
105–11; and justice, 50; as site of
contestation, 10–11, 50, 57, 62;
corporate, 159, 173–4; cultural,
11, 44; defined in terms of the
city, 47; ecological, 6, 9, 11, 51,
59, 73, 76, 77, 80–1, 86, 127,
136, 158, 213 (and subjectivities,
78–82; new vocabulary of,
239–63); engendering of, 37–44;
environmental, 9–26, 66–7, 76,
239–63; fixation on entitlements,

sweatshops, 35

Ta Viset litter anti-campaign (Thailand), 226
Tai Ban Research Group (Thailand), 232–3
Tantemsapya, Nitasmai, 231
Taylor, Ann, 119–20
Taylor, Jim, 211
Telecommunication Act (Thailand), 236
tetrachlorodibenzodioxin, 181
tetrachloroethylene, 17
Thai Environmental and Community Development Association (TECDA), 226
Thai Rak Thai (TRT) party (Thailand), 196, 219, 235, 236; dissolution of, 238, 196, 235
Thai Sawat company, 201
Thailand, 160, 180, 194, 204; environmental campaigns in, 195, 209–38 *passim*; logging in, 216, 257 (ban on, 219); migrant workers in, 22–3, 176, 202; new political context in, 235–8; occupational health in, 122–3; smuggling of orang-utans, 177–8; North Korean migrants in, 195
Thailand Development Institute (TDI), 225
Thailand Environment and Development Network (TADNET), 228
Thailand Environment Institute (TEI), 224–5, 228, 238
Thailand Exploration and Mining Company (TEMC), 220–1
Thailand Rural Reconstruction Movement, 217
Think Earth project, 227
Thompson, G.F., 165, 166
Thompson, Grahame, 162
Tilly, Charles, 110
toxic cocktails, campaigns against, 222–3
trade unions, 35, 108, 109, 117, 118, 119, 127, 161, 166–7, 188, 193, 204, 215, 237; and environmental

movements, 203; declining influence of, 132, 133
traffic, reduction in, 63
trans-boundary environmental issues, 83, 136, 138, 175, 205, 206–7; in Bay of Gibraltar, 189–94 *see also* pollution, trans-boundary
transdisciplinary research, 68–70
transnational corporations, 160–1, 162, 166, 210–11, 238
transnational networking, 33–5
transportation, just, 240
trees, as legal entities, 252
Turner, B.S., 28–9, 51

Uathavikul, Phaichitr, 225
Union Carbide company, 221
United Church of Christ, 20
United Kingdom (UK): citizenship in, 30; environmental management in, 152–3; environmental responsibility in, 243–9
United Nations (UN), 148, 150, 167–8, 170, 191
UN Centre on Transnational Corporations (UNCTC), 140, 157
UN Children's Fund (UNICEF), 153, 166
UN Conference on Environment and Development (Earth Summit) (1992), 25, 42, 96, 130–1, 140, 149
UN Conference on the Human Environment (1972), 25, 33
UN Development Programme (UNDP), Human Development Report, 156
UN Economic and Social Council (ECOSOC), 96
UN Environment Programme (UNEP), 33, 94, 133, 145
UN Forum on Forests, 94, 103–5
UN Global Compact, 34–5, 152, 148, 164–73
United States of America (USA), 181–9
Universal Declaration of Human Rights (UDHR), 23
Unocal company, 192
urban street scavenging, 80
urbanization, 124–5
utilitarianism, 3, 86